VENUS IN SACKCLOTH

VENUS IN SACKCLOTH

*The Magdalen's Origins
and Metamorphoses*

BY

MARJORIE M. MALVERN

SOUTHERN ILLINOIS UNIVERSITY PRESS

CARBONDALE AND EDWARDSVILLE

Feffer & Simons, Inc. LONDON AND AMSTERDAM

Copyright © 1975 by Southern Illinois University Press

ALL RIGHTS RESERVED

PRINTED IN THE UNITED STATES OF AMERICA

DESIGNED BY PHILIP GRUSHKIN

———

Library of Congress Cataloging in Publication Data

Malvern, Marjorie M
  Venus in sackcloth.

  Bibliography: p.
  Includes index.
  1. Mary Magdalene, Saint—Art. 2. Arts.
3. Mary Magdalene, Saint. I. Title.
NX652.M27M34   704.948′6   75–6197
ISBN 0–8093–0707–3

———

Grateful acknowledgment is made for permission to quote from
"To a White Girl" from *Soul on Ice* by Eldridge Cleaver. Copyright
© 1968 by Eldridge Cleaver. Used with permission of McGraw-Hill
Book Company.

Grateful acknowledgment is also made for permission to quote
from "I Don't Know How to Love Him," "Strange Thing Mystifying,"
and "Everything's Alright," compositions from *Jesus Christ
Superstar*, lyrics by Tim Rice, music by Andrew Lloyd Webber.
Copyright © 1970 by Leeds Music Ltd., London. Used with permission
of Leeds Music Corporation.

TO *Larry Malvern*

CONTENTS

LIST OF ILLUSTRATIONS   *ix*

PREFACE   *xi*

1. Monuments to the Magdalen   *1*
2. The Magdalen's Origins and Early Metamorphoses   *16*
3. The Heroine-Hero of the *Gospel of Mary*   *30*
4. The "Pure Spiritual Mariham" and
   Pistis Sophia Prunikos   *42*
5. The Magdalen's Link with an Ancient Goddess
   of Love   *57*
6. The Rise of the Magdalen in the Middle Ages   *71*
7. The "Biography" of Saint Mary Magdalene   *89*
8. The Magdalen's Impact on Medieval Drama   *100*
9. The Magdalen as a Full-blown Heroine
   in a Late Medieval Play   *114*
10. The Decline of the Mythical Magdalen   *126*
11. The Magdalen in the Spotlight on
    the Twentieth-Century Stage   *141*
12. The Magdalen as WOMAN Born of Man   *151*
13. The Magdalen Monument: A Caveat and
    Some Conclusions   *162*

NOTES   *183*

SELECTED BIBLIOGRAPHY   *207*

INDEX   *213*

List of Illustrations

1. Sculpture of the Magdalen by Carlo Barone Marochetti   6

2. *Eva Prima Pandora* by Jean Cousin le Père   10

3. *The Crucifixion,* Passion scenes from ivory panels   24

4. *The Women at the Tomb,* Passion scenes from
     ivory panels   25

5. *Mary Magdalene* by Quentin Massys   78

6. *Maria Egyptiaca* by Quentin Massys   81

7. Twelfth-century sculpture of the Magdalen   83

8. *The Holy Trinity with Saints John the Baptist and
     Mary Magdalene and Tobias and the Angel*
     by Sandro Botticelli and assistants   86

9. *St. Mary Magdalene,* the *Sforza Book of Hours*   97

10. *Mary Magdalene Preaching* by the Flemish Master of the
     Magdalene Legend   129

11. *The Magdalen* by Correggio   134

12. *School of Love* by Correggio   137

13. *Mary Magdalene* by Moretto da Brescia   138

14. *La Madeleine à la veilleuse* by Georges de la Tour   159

15. *Noli me tangere* by Titian   166

16. *Noli me tangere,* in the style of Orcagna   168

17. *Pietà* by Moretto da Brescia   171

18. *The Magdalen Reading* by Rogier van der Weyden   175

19. *The Magdalen* by Bernardino Luini   176

20. *Venus* by Bernardino Luini   178

PREFACE

A FEMININE FIGURE whose significance reaches beyond specific roles given her in Western literature, the Magdalen excites the curiosity of anyone concerned with the transmission of ideas through a fictionalized figure. The major purposes of *Venus in Sackcloth: The Magdalen's Origins and Metamorphoses* are to sharpen appreciation for the part played by *homo ludens* in the fictionalization of the figure by placing the Magdalen in perspective and to deepen understanding of ideas implanted in the figure almost two thousand years ago and perpetuated through the figure in art and literature right up to the present time. Viewing closely the Mary Magdalene of the New Testament canonical Gospels leads to the discovery of probable reasons for the early metamorphoses of the figure who later becomes a Venus in sackcloth.

I also examine, as does no other scholar to date, the prominent place given the fictionalized Mary Magdalene in second-century Gnostic writings. For only by observing the treatment of the Magdalen in writings from the early Christian period can we begin to grasp the full import of the feminine figure who rises to fame in the West during the Crusades, becomes a saint honored by Jacobus a Voragine in his popular *Golden Legend*, stars as a heroine in medieval drama, survives today in secular literature, and recently costars in a rock opera.

Since my immediate intentions are to point out the significances of concepts embodied in the metamorphosed Magdalen and to illustrate the survival of the transformed figure throughout the Middle Ages and on into the modern era, I do not treat exhaustively the Magdalen pictured in either art or literature.

Instead, I limit the investigation of her roles in Western literature to five plays dating from the twelfth through the sixteenth
century and three works from the twentieth century. To ex-
emplify varied iconographic interpretations of the Magdalen,
I allude specifically to twenty-four of the many works of
art featuring the long-lived figure. Reproductions of twenty
works referred to in the study provide manifestations of the
Magdalen's complexity.

With the hope that readers may experience as directly as
possible roles given the Magdalen in literature, I quote freely
from those works chosen to illustrate both the Magdalen's
longevity and the ideas implicit in the metamorphoses of the
figure. And I use English translations when they are readily
available; otherwise, the translations and paraphrases are my
own. Epigraphs introducing each chapter stand as illumina-
tions for the text and are integrated into the study.

Many people have contributed to my pleasure in studying
the important feminine figure. The bibliography acknowledges
my debts not only to those scholars whose editorial work on
old manuscripts has made possible my particular study of the
Magdalen but also to some of those scholars whose research
into the history of ideas has increased my knowledge and understanding of certain cultural values treated in my study.

For assistance in providing and for permission to reproduce
photographs related to the Magdalen, I acknowledge my gratitude to la Documentation Française and to Caisse Nationale
des Monuments Historiques, Archives Photographiques-Paris;
to the trustees of the British Museum; of the National Gallery,
London; of the National Gallery of Art, Washington; of the
Art Institute of Chicago; of the Courtauld Institute Galleries,
London; of the John G. Johnson Collection, Philadelphia; of
the Louvre. For their courtesy in granting permission to quote
from copyrighted material, I acknowledge my gratitude to
McGraw-Hill Book Company and to Leeds Music Corporation.

I also wish to express here my continuing gratitude for their inspiration, encouragement, and friendly criticism through various stages of my work on the Magdalen to Arnold Williams, Herbert Weisinger, Grant Sampson, Maureen Malvern Sullivan, and especially to Larry Malvern, to whom I dedicate *Venus in Sackcloth: The Magdalen's Origins and Metamorphoses*.

MARJORIE MALVERN

Gainesville, Florida
   8 August 1974

VENUS IN SACKCLOTH

One generation goes, another generation comes, but the earth always remains the same. The sun rises and the sun sets; and returning to its place, it rises there once more.

Whatever has been is what will be, and whatever has been done is what will be done. There is nothing new under the sun. When there is something of which one says, "Look now, that is new!" it has been already in the ages before us.

Ecclesiastes 3:5; 1:9–10

"Everything always is—and the more it changes the more it is the same."

Jubal Harshaw in Robert Heinlein's
Stranger in a Strange Land

Plus ça change, plus c'est la même chose.

I

Monuments to
the Magdalen

I don't know how to love him
What to do how to move him
I've been changed yes really changed
In these past few days when I've seen myself
I seem like someone else
> Mary Magdalene in
> *Jesus Christ Superstar:*
> A Rock Opera
> by Andrew Lloyd Webber
> and Tim Rice

"Let Mariham go out from among us, for women are not worthy
of life."
> Simon Peter in *The Gospel of Thomas*

O, I said to myself, if only man's heart were
omnipotent, powerful enough to wrestle with death!
If only it were like Mary Magdalene—Mary Magdalene
the prostitute—and could resurrect the beloved corpse!
> Nikos Kazantzakis in *Report to Greco*

W<small>HEN</small> today's Magdalen rocks out "I've been changed yes really
changed," she sounds a beat reverberating an ambiguity
perhaps unheard by her audience. The Magdalen who costars in
Jesus Christ Superstar, who appears as Mariham in the *Gospel of
Thomas* and as Mary Magdalene the prostitute in Kazantzakis's
Report to Greco, fascinates anyone concerned not only with the

origins and metamorphoses of long-lived figures but also with the persistence of ideas through time periods tagged as Ages of Faith, of Renaissance, of Enlightenment, of Anxiety, or of Aquarius. Some eighteen centuries separate the Mariham scorned in the *Gospel of Thomas* from the prostitute revered in *Report to Greco* and honored in *Jesus Christ Superstar.*[1] Yet the antiwoman attitude toward the Magdalen, called Mariham by the anonymous second-century writer, does not perish with the passage of time but survives alongside the adoration for the life-restoring prostitute who is hymned by Kazantzakis and the "changed yes really changed" Magdalen given the feminine lead in their rock opera by Webber and Rice. For the Magdalen, long used as a vessel for contradictory ideas, is brimful of paradoxes.

An object of controversy through the centuries of the waxing and waning of Christianity, the Magdalen has inspired theologians to write numerous explications of and panegyrics to the figure whose complexity does not lie exclusively in the Mary Magdalene preserved in the canonical Gospels. Explicated as an archetype of the Christian penitent and sanctified as the supreme example of mystic love of the Christ by Roman Catholic theologians, the Magdalen most recently appears in the work of a Protestant theologian as a quite probable candidate for the flesh-and-blood wife of the man Jesus. This hypothesis Dr. William E. Phipps, an American professor of religion, sets forth in his work *Was Jesus Married?* published in 1970.[2]

The controversial religious figure and the figure who turns up in art and literature for almost two thousand years seem to me inseparable now. The problem of who or what the Magdalen was historically I do not presume to answer. I prefer, rather, to explore as closely as possible the origins and metamorphoses of the long-lived figure who becomes in Western Christendom a "Venus in sackcloth."[3] For observing the transformations of the biblical Mary Magdalene into a mythical figure inevitably deepens our understanding of old ideas and their tenacious grip on the human imagination.

The Magdalen's hold on imaginations stretches back into time and across cultural boundaries. She shows up as a prostitute, derided or praised, seducing men in both the Eastern and the Western worlds, in Jerusalem and in Germany. She appears as a midwife, a preacher, a hermit. She preaches in Ephesus as well as in Marseilles. She brings about the conception of a child for the queen of Marseilles. She restores the dead queen to life and preserves the life of the young prince. She makes gardens grow and vineyards flourish. She lives thirty years without food or clothing in the wilds of Sainte-Baume. The Magdalen's name becomes both a synonym for a whore and the name of a fine Italian wine. Her popular appeal reaches far beyond that of the Mary Magdalene sketched in the Christian canonical Gospels and manifests itself in a multitude of monuments to her memory.

Not only do many churches bear the name of the Magdalen, but colleges, hospitals, benevolent societies for reformed prostitutes, city streets, a river, an island, and women of many countries have been named for her. In the Tyrol, as Louis Réau points out in his valuable and entertaining *Iconographie de l'Art Chrétien*, baby girls born out of wedlock were called "Magdalene." [4] We recall that Chaucer's shipman's "barge ycleped was the Maudelayne." And so ubiquitous is the Magdalen that today one can see now and again anchored at the dock in Tarpon Springs, Florida, U.S.A., a fishing boat sporting the name Magdalene. Today in France one can eat a small cake called a Madeleine. In Germany one can see and smell the *Magdalenrosen*, since white roses were long ago given her name. In England one can eat a peach called Magdalen. "The white Magdalen has a sugar'd winy taste, . . ." a 1706 issue of the *Retir'd Gardn'r* proclaims.[5] Before the end of the twelfth century a vineyard at Lyons was named for the Magdalen, Victor Saxer notes in his well-documented study of the Magdalen cult in the West, *Le Culte de Marie Madeleine en Occident.*[6]

It is during the Middle Ages, a period often referred to as the Age of Faith, that the Magdalen becomes the patron saint of "winegrowers" and gardeners, as well as of pharmacists, glove makers, perfume manufacturers, podiatrists, hairdressers, comb makers, foundrymen, sailors, tawers, barrel makers, and weavers. And she was particularly honored by medieval religious orders for reformed prostitutes, while many prisoners were supposedly freed through her intercession for them.[7]

She is indirectly responsible for the invention in France of a local saint, Saint Rabony, who, good wives believed, had the power to improve ("rabbonir": as to improve wine) "bad husbands." Saint Rabony originated from a phylactery which pictures the Magdalen's recognition of the resurrected Christ and emphasizes it with the word *Rabboni* coming from her mouth.[8] Thus the "good wives" of a French village read the iconographic representation of the event central to Christianity, the risen Christ discovered by the Magdalen in the garden, as told in the Gospel of John.

Iconographic representations of the Magdalen, in company with the Christ or alone, tend to evoke individual interpretations in the artist as well as in the viewer. Often, but not always, identifiable by her long flowing hair and her ointment jar, highly connotative attributes given early to the Magdalen, artists' monuments to the complex figure abound. Three specific works of art illustrate the fictionalized Magdalen's power to bring forth varied interpretations from both artists and viewers. Donatello's fifteenth-century statue in wood, a sixteenth-century relief based on a painting by Jean Cousin, and Marochetti's nineteenth-century marble statue reveal some of the many faces of the Magdalen.

The Marochetti sculpture dominates the master altar in one of the many churches named for the Magdalen, l'Église Sainte-Madeleine in Paris (fig. *1*). The Magdalen, gigantic in size, voluptuous in form, softly draped, her long hair flowing down her back, graceful hands outstretched in a gesture of blessing, looks down on and towers above three angels who touch hands and encircle the Magdalen in what Réau describes as a round dance, "resembling a little too much the ballerinas of the Opera nearby." [9] At least one nineteenth-century Christian, a prefect of the Seine, viewed Marochetti's sculptured Magdalen who reigns over the sanctuary in l'Église Sainte-Madeleine in Paris as a "colossal Juno" who, with her "buxom form," was less suitable to "inspire penitence than sin." [10]

Certainly Marochetti leaves no trace of the popular theological explication of the Magdalen as the archetypal Christian penitent in his representation of Jupiter-Christ's Juno-Magdalen bride. Would the prefect have perhaps found Donatello's fifteenth-century interpretation of the Magdalen more suitable to "inspire penitence" than he felt Marochetti's to be? Or would he have shared one eighteenth-century Christian's reaction to Donatello's statue?

In sharp contrast with Marochetti's playfully hyperbolic statue, Donatello's gaunt figure stands with her bony hands upraised in a frustrated gesture of supplication. Her tense gnarled hands do not quite meet. Anguish fills her wrinkled desert-dried face. Her bare arms, legs, and feet are skeletonlike, and her shriveled body is clothed only in her long, tangled hair. Viewing Donatello's "dried-up, blackened, emaciated, wild-haired" Magdalen so thoroughly nauseated an eighteenth-century Christian that he declared he was forever afterward disgusted with penitence.[11] But the twentieth-century Émile Mâle, in *Les Saints Compagnons du Christ*, expresses admiration for Donatello's sculpted Magdalen as a representation of the body completely annihilated by the soul, for she has, Mâle says, "succeeded in exterminating the flesh which caused her fall." [12]

Donatello's wood-carved, flesh-denying penitent may have held the significance which Mâle finds in it for the ascetic mystics among Donatello's contemporaries, who could contemplate his statue, then located in the Baptistery of Saint John in Florence, as a *memento mori*, a reminder of the inevitability of death. And perhaps the figure, originally painted gold, inspired in penitent prostitutes contemporary with Donatello, hope for a radiant future life in heaven. Donatello's forceful figure strikes me as a tormented victim of a radical split between the spirit and the flesh, for the poignant alienation and unresolved tension in the sexless "soul" connotes no joy in having "exterminated the flesh." Donatello's pathetic mystic, a hermit removed from life, is transformed beyond recognition in Marochetti's marble-sculptured goddess commanding and approving a festive lively dance. Neither Marochetti's monumental Juno-Venus-Magdalen nor

Donatello's desert-dried penitent represents the Mary Magdalene sketched in the Christian Gospels. Yet both works express truths about the mythical figure and about ideas embodied in the fictionalized Magdalen.

In the examination of another iconographic monument to the Magdalen we can sense the magnetic power which the mythical figure holds on the imagination of one who envisions woman as an awesome paradox. The work is a sixteenth-century relief originally in Sens Cathedral but now in Saint Maurice. The relief is a repetition, slightly changed, of Jean Cousin's late fifteenth-century painting *Eva Prima Pandora*, done at the request of Guillaume Sotan, canon of Sens Cathedral, in 1567, Dora and Erwin Panofsky note in their study, *Pandora's Box.*[13]

The painting, now in the Louvre, pictures Eve, the first Pandora, as a neoclassical beauty, nude except for a bit of drapery covering her pelvic area (fig. 2). Half-reclining, she rests her right arm on a skull and loosely holds a leafy branch in her hand, while she nonchalantly rests her left hand on the lid of an ornate jar, Pandora's box containing "Good." A curled snake bracelets her left arm. Her face is in profile, her eyes gazing beyond the picture's frame, her lips slightly parted, her hair neatly coiffed but leaving two strands free to caress her neck. On a pedestal in an archway, which is topped with the inscription *Eva Prima Pandora*, and behind the coyly draped nude, stands a tall open vase with streams of "Evils" rising from its mouth.

At the request of the sixteenth-century canon, Jean Cousin's dangerously seductive Eve-Pandora is transformed into a decorously dressed Magdalen. Eve-Pandora-Magdalen, an Old Testament figure, a Greek mythological figure, a New Testament figure, are superimposed one on the other and united in time. Eve-Pandora's box becomes the Magdalen's ointment jar. And the view of woman as the source of "evil" and of "good," of death and of life, is perpetuated in the metamorphosed Magdalen.

The account of the transformation of Jean Cousin's "Eve the first Pandora" into the Magdalen dramatizes in miniature both the attitudes and the method involved in the fictionalization of Mary Magdalene. The attitudes are dominated not only by an ambivalent attitude toward woman but also by the human desire for continuity. And the method reflects not any historical perspective but an eclectic mingling of the old with the new.

Among other monuments to the Magdalen is the addition to the English language of the word "maudlin," a rather dubious honor, to be sure, but its introduction into print in the seventeenth century underlines the variety of interpretations evoked by the long-lived Magdalen.[14] The name of the Magdalen becomes synonymous with an overly sentimental weeper, particularly with a tearful drunk who is "maudlin-cupped," and who "maudlinly maudlinizes" as he mouths "maudlinisms."

Alongside this evidence of mockery of the tearful penitent there are in the same century prominent English poets who in differing ways celebrate her, poets such as George Herbert, John Donne, Robert Southwell, and Richard Crashaw. It is specifically the maudlin weeper hymned, for example, by Richard Crashaw in his 186-line poem "Saint Mary Magdalene; or The Weeper." And paradoxes aplenty fill the poet's lines to her "wounded heart with bleeding eyes" as he exclaims: "Is she a flaming fountain or a weeping fire?"

> Hail, sister springs!
> Parents of silver-footed rills!
> Ever-bubbling things!
> Thawing crystal! snowy hills,
> Still spending, never spent! I mean
> Thy fair eyes, sweet Magdalene! [15]

Sir Herbert Grierson, in *Cross-Currents in Seventeenth-Century English Literature*, points out in discussing Crashaw's poetry that Mary Magdalene is indeed "the favorite saint of the Counter-Reformation, suggesting images at once voluptuous and pious." [16]

During the sixteenth and seventeenth centuries artists too find the "voluptuous and pious" Magdalen a favorite subject of painting. It is also this Venus in sackcloth who figures prominently in seventeenth-century French literature. Many of the French literary works featuring the Magdalen deal with the reformed prostitute's last thirty years spent as a "contemplative" in the grotto of Sainte-Baume. The Magdalen's appearance as a

2. *Eva Prima Pandora* by Jean Cousin le Père, the Louvre.

hermit results, as we shall see, from fictionalization of the figure early in the Christian period. But the immediate source for the French mystic is the "Life of Saint Mary Magdalene" set down by the thirteenth-century Jacobus a Voragine in his best seller popularly known as the *Golden Legend*. And the "Life" of the Magdalen is, of course, itself a monument to the mythical figure.

Literary works featuring the Magdalen appear as early as the second century of the Christian era and continue to appear intermittently into the twentieth century. The Magdalen stars, for example, in Maurice Maeterlinck's play *Mary Magdalene* and, as we might expect from the tribute paid to her in *Report to Greco*, significantly figures in novels by Nikos Kazantzakis, especially in *The Last Temptation of Christ.*[17]

The Magdalen of the rock opera *Jesus Christ Superstar* is the most recent reincarnation of the figure who held a prominent place in medieval drama. Her role in Resurrection and Passion plays expands from the twelfth through the fifteenth century. She appears on the medieval stage not only as the chief mourner of the Christ, as the penitent anointer of the Christ, as the apostle to the apostles, but also as a worldly lover who, not unlike her modern descendant, is "changed yes really changed" into the Christ's "contemplative" lover. She reaches the stature of heroine in two contrasting plays, the fifteenth-century Digby *Mary Magdalene* and Lewis Wager's sixteenth-century *The Life and Repentance of Marie Magdalene.*[18]

The Magdalen, as well as the handful of other women mentioned by name in the New Testament, shows up in a number of writings designated as apocryphal. But the Magdalen is unique, as far as we know today, in being the only New Testament woman to whom a gospel is attributed. She does, however, share the distinction with her predecessor Eve, to whom a gospel was also attributed. To the same Magdalen as the Mariham scorned by Peter in the *Gospel of Thomas* is attributed the second-century *Gospel of Mary*, even though here also she is disdained by Peter.[19] And in another early work, the *Pistis Sophia*, the Magdalen is the chief questioner and explicator of doctrines attributed to Jesus.[20] The Magdalen's prominent place in both of these works illustrates writers' early efforts to incorporate old mythical figures into Mary Magdalene. The fictionalized figure who emerges from these writings undergoes further metamorphoses but lives on in the complex Magdalen who continues to appeal to artists and writers.

Even in this brief glance at tributes to the Magdalen we can see evidence of a complex figure who could not have held such magnetic appeal for people engaged in such different occupations as those of sailors, vineyard growers, pastry makers, gardeners, reformed prostitutes, weavers, perfume makers, hairdressers, prisoners, and writers and artists through the centuries had she remained in the minds of men simply the Mary Magdalene referred to in the canonical Gospels. Through the centuries of the present era, men have hymned, caricatured, worshipped, mocked the Magdalen in poetry and prose, drama and sermons, prayers and songs, paintings and sculpture, "biography" and novels. And the Magdalen has indeed made the headline of a twentieth-century American newspaper.

Headed *Mary Magadalene [sic] Victim of Libel* and super-scribed in smaller type *Her Gospel Role Important*, the article published anonymously on the religious page of the *State Journal* in Lansing, Michigan, on 28 August 1965, begins: "July 22 each year is dedicated to the memory of the most libeled woman in Christian history." The article states that Mary Magdalene has for centuries been called a "fallen woman" only because of a mistake in identification. A victim of juxtaposition with Luke's story of the "sinner" who washed Jesus' feet with her tears and dried them with her hair, the Magdalen also absorbed "the unsavory reputation of her home town, a notoriously licentious fishing village," the article tells us. And furthermore, we learn that the seven demons which Jesus had cast out of her were "in those days" considered "demons of unchastity" rather than a "serious mental illness."

The article adds that the Magdalen's Gospel role is important enough without "embellishing it with sentimental nonsense about her past" and concludes with a summary of her Gospel role. As one of the women who performed "the kind of humble but essential service which millions of Christian women still perform in the church," she is "patron saint of all women of all ages who have helped finance the mission of the church through bazaars and bake sales." And she was the first Christian to have the privilege of "proclaiming to others the glad tidings which constitute the heart of the gospel."

The same view with identical explanation for the "libel" is expressed by Edith Deen in *All of the Women of the Bible*.[21] But this not uncommon explanation of the complexity of the popular Magdalen skirts the basic questions. I suggest that a close look at the Magdalen's Gospel role, indeed important, will lead toward probable answers to the fundamental questions: What is the nature of the so-called "libel" of the Magdalen? What motives lie behind the "libel" of this particular Gospel figure? And what accounts for the fictionalized Magdalen's smashing popularity victory over the Gospel Mary Magdalene from the early days of Christianity's emergence to today's news?

The "libel" I consider myth. The function of myth may sometimes be, as Theodor Gaster insists it always is, "to translate the real into terms of the ideal, the punctual into terms of the durative and transcendental." [22] The Neoplatonic concept of the Ideal, as we shall see, clearly affects the Magdalen pictured in early writings. But I find a more apt description of both the function and the origins of the fictionalized Magdalen in a statement made by Denis de Rougemont in *Love in the Western World*: "No myth arises so long as it is possible to keep to the obvious openly and directly. On the contrary, a myth arises whenever it becomes dangerous or impossible to speak plainly about certain social or religious matters, or affective relations, and yet there is a desire to preserve them." [23]

I do, however, see in the development of the Magdalen myth an element not mentioned by Denis de Rougemont. That is the play element. Johan Huizinga, in *Homo Ludens: A Study of the Play Element in Culture*, describes this characteristic of myth when he says: "In all the wild imaginings of mythology a fanciful spirit is playing on the borderline between jest and earnest." [24]

Not out of malicious libel but through a desire to preserve ideas and "affective relations" and figures considered dangerous and heretical by early Christian leaders, *homo ludens* works on the "borderline between jest and earnest" in transforming Mary Magdalene into a mythical figure. And the result is the controversial figure whose significance and popular appeal reach far beyond that of the Gospel figure. Only by broadening the perspective in which we view the Gospel figure can we begin to understand either the nature of myths attached to Mary Magdalene or the significance of ideas absorbed by the fictionalized figure.[25]

To increase our understanding of the complexity of the figure who has evoked so many varied monuments to her memory, we closely examine her origins and metamorphoses and survey the fictionalized Magdalen's roles in selected works of literature. The mythical figure, frequently considered a creation of the Middle Ages, clearly takes shape before the setting of the Christian canon in the fourth century. And we may one day discover that some apocryphal writings featuring the Magdalen antedate the canonical Gospels. But assuming for the time being that the Magdalen first makes her public appearance in the Gospels attributed to Matthew, Mark, Luke, and John, we shall review the treatment of Mary Magdalene in these four Gospels and note the other New Testament figures with whom she is early identified before we examine her roles in apocryphal writings. As we note the full import of the Magdalen's role in the New Testament, we begin to discover probable reasons for *homo ludens*'s choice of the Magdalen as a vessel capable of holding controversial ideas.

2

The Magdalen's Origins and Early Metamorphoses

'Anat goes searching for him.
Like the heart of a cow for her calf,
like the heart of a ewe for her lamb,
so is the heart of 'Anat on account of Baal.
    The Canaanite Poem of Baal

The harlot who anointed you with fragrant oil
Laments for you now.
    The Babylonian Epic of Gilgamesh

Then he brought me to the entrance of the north gate of the house
of the Lord, and behold there sat women weeping for Tammuz.
    Ezekiel 8:14

THE canonical Gospels mentioned few women by name, and the majority of those mentioned are called Mary. Mary the mother of Jesus receives nineteen mentions, while Mary Magdalene is named fourteen times. The Magdalen is, however, mentioned in each of the Gospels, five times in the Gospel of John, four times in the Gospel of Mark, twice in the Gospel of Luke, and three times in the Gospel of Matthew.[1]

In the Gospel of Matthew, we first see her with Mary the mother of James and Joseph, and with the mother of the sons of Zebedee at the Crucifixion of Jesus, "looking on from afar," among the "many women" who had followed Jesus from Galilee, "ministering to him." [2] We then see her with the "other Mary" sitting opposite the sepulcher of the Christ.[3] Matthew mentions her again as she goes with "the other Mary" three days later to see the tomb. And an angel appears, tells the women not to be afraid for Jesus has arisen, shows them the empty tomb, and asks them to report the resurrection of the Christ to the disciples. And the women go "quickly from the tomb with fear and great joy," and run to the disciples. They meet Jesus on the way, embrace his feet and worship him, and Jesus tells them not to be afraid but to go tell his "brethren" that they should go to Galilee where they will see him.[4] The women depart and are not again mentioned in the Gospel of Matthew.

The Gospel of Mark, commonly considered the oldest of the canonical Gospels, also first mentions the Magdalen among the "many women" at the Crucifixion. "There were also women looking on from afar, among whom were Mary Magdalene, and Mary the Mother of James the Younger and of Joses, and Salome, who, when he was in Galilee, followed him, and ministered to him; and also many other women who came up with him to Jerusalem." [5] And when Jesus' body was buried, "Mary Magdalene and Mary the mother of Joses saw where it was laid." [6]

We find an event not mentioned by Matthew in the Gospel of Mark, and it is to be of great importance in early medieval art and drama. The three women, when the Sabbath is past, buy spices "so that they might go and anoint him." [7] And "very early on the first day of the week" the women go to the tomb and are "amazed" to see a "young man" clothed in white sitting there. The "young man" tells them not to be afraid, for Jesus has arisen, and asks them to take the message to the disciples "and Peter." [8] "And they went out and fled from the tomb, for trembling and astonishment had come upon them; and they said nothing to anyone, for they were afraid." [9]

Here, modern biblical scholars agree, the extant text of the original Gospel of Mark abruptly ends, for the concluding lines of the original text have been lost. But in Mark 16:9–20, a fragment traditionally added to the extant Gospel, we see attributed to the Magdalen two further characteristics not evident in Matthew's treatment of her.[10] We see the risen Christ appearing first to the Magdalen, and we see a reference to those seven demons that are to cling to the Magdalen through the centuries. "Now when he rose early on the first day of the week, he appeared first to Mary Magdalene, from whom he had cast out seven demons." [11] Mary Magdalene goes to tell "those who had been with" Jesus, as they are mourning and weeping, that Jesus is alive. "But when they heard that he was still alive and had been seen by her, they would not believe it." [12] This is the final reference to the Magdalen in the fragment attached to the Gospel of Mark, but the incredulity of the disciples is further emphasized.

We see that in the fragment linked with the Gospel of Mark the Magdalen is isolated from the other women as the one to whom the risen Christ first appears and as the "apostle" to the doubting apostles. And the parenthetical identification of the Magdalen as a woman from whom Jesus had ejected seven demons is to loom large in the figure who will appear in medieval drama, particularly in the fifteenth-century Digby *Mary Magdalene* where the heroine is hounded by seven flesh-and-blood demons.[13] Also important in the Magdalen of medieval drama is Mark's mention of her among the women who go to buy spices to anoint the body of the Christ, for from this statement emerge her roles, varying from the pathetic to the comic, in the Merchant scenes dramatized in the Passion plays.

Although the Magdalen is mentioned only twice in the Gospel of Luke, she is identified as "Mary, called Magdalene, from whom seven devils had gone out." [14] Luke mentions her among the women who, having been "healed of evil spirits and infirmities," traveled with Jesus and his disciples through "cities and villages" and "provided for them out of their means." [15] And she is mentioned again as merely one of the many women who go to the tomb taking spices to anoint the body of the Christ. The women are greeted by two angels and are sent to report the Christ's having arisen to the disciples, to whom the women's words seem an "idle tale." "Now it was Mary Magdalene and Mary the mother of James and the other women with them who told this to the apostles; but these words seemed to them an idle tale, and they did not believe them." [16] The Magdalen is not, then, in the Gospel of Luke singled out for particular treatment since she is mentioned only twice and then simply in company with the many women who followed Jesus.

John's Gospel reflects, however, a special interest in the Magdalen, and it provides inspiration for the garden recognition scenes of the Magdalen and the risen Christ to become popular in medieval drama and in art. John's Gospel also sets the scene for many artists' representations of the Magdalen's special role in the depictions of the Crucifixion of the Christ and in the moving Pietàs picturing her with Mary the mother of Jesus, sometimes another woman, and John grieving for the dead Christ. The recognition scene, uniquely narrated in the Gospel of John, is not only the basis for the numerous *Noli me tangere* paintings but is also the indirect cause of the invention in France of the Saint Rabony who had the power to "improve" bad husbands.

The Magdalen is first mentioned in the Gospel of John in the scene at the cross where she stands with Jesus' mother and his aunt and with the "disciple whom Jesus loved." [17] The next appearance of the Magdalen in John's Gospel follows the account of Joseph of Arimathea's and Nicodemus's anointing the body of Jesus and placing it in a "new tomb where no one had ever been laid" in a garden near the place where Jesus was crucified.[18] And here we see the Magdalen set apart as she goes alone, while it is still dark, to the Christ's tomb. "Now on the first day of the week Mary Magdalene came to the tomb early, while it was still dark, and saw that the stone had been taken away from the tomb." [19] She runs to Simon Peter and the "other disciple, the one whom Jesus loved," traditionally identified with John, and tells them, "They have taken the Lord out of the tomb, and we do not know where they have laid him." [20] There follows another scene which is to become popular in medieval drama, the race of Peter and John to the tomb. John outruns Peter and finds the tomb empty except for the "linen cloths," and both John and Peter believe that the body has been carried away, "for as yet they did not know the scripture that he must rise from the dead." [21] The disciples therefore return "to their homes." [22]

But the Magdalen remains. Alone, she stands at the tomb, weeping. While she laments, she leans over and sees "two angels in white, sitting where the body of Jesus had lain, one at the head and one at the feet." [23] And when the angels ask her why she weeps, she answers, "Because they have taken my Lord away, and I do not know where they have laid him." [24] As she speaks, she turns and sees Jesus standing nearby, but she does not recognize him. There follows the dramatic recognition scene, unique in the New Testament Gospels.

Jesus asks the Magdalen, "Woman, why are you weeping? Whom do you seek?" The Magdalen, believing that he is the gardener, answers, "Sir, if you have carried him away, tell me where you have laid him, and I will take him away." Jesus calls her by name, "Mary," and she responds, "Rabboni!" She reaches out to touch him or to embrace him, but Jesus says to her, "*Noli me tangere*, for I have not yet ascended to the Father; but go to my brethren and say to them, I am ascending to my Father and your Father, to my God and your God." [25] The Magdalen goes to the disciples and tells them that she has seen Jesus and gives them his message.

The Magdalen is, then, in the Gospel of John pictured in a much more intimate relationship with the Christ than she is in the other canonical Gospels. She stands at the foot of the cross with the mother and aunt of Jesus and with the well-loved disciple. Alone, she goes at dawn to the tomb seeking Jesus. She finds the tomb empty and runs to tell Peter and John that the body has been removed. And after the disciples leave the tomb, the Magdalen stands outside the sepulcher lamenting, until Jesus appears to her in the garden. And Jesus makes sure that she recognizes him by calling her by name. He refuses to let her touch, or embrace, him but sends her to announce to the disciples his coming ascension.

In John's Gospel no mention is made of the Magdalen's having been possessed of seven demons. And the Gospel of John omits the scene shown in that of Mark and of Luke, the scene in which the women go to the tomb to anoint the body of Jesus. Instead, the author of the Gospel of John sets the Magdalen apart from the other women whom he mentions and, in dramatizing her closeness to the Christ, makes her a figure of such importance in the scene central to Christianity that imaginations reach out for more knowledge of the woman to whom the risen Christ appears in flesh still sensitive to touch and to whom the Christ speaks in a human voice.

John's word picture of the Magdalen searching for and lamenting the dead Christ and happily finding him resurrected must have excited in those early Christians to whom it was presented a dramatic shock of recognition. For behind the Christian figures fall shadows of antique figures whose deaths and resurrections were believed to return life to a sterile earth. And these shadows of old fertility deities are still discernible behind the medieval playwrights' augmented versions of John's Magdalen searching for and lamenting the dead Christ and joyously finding him resurrected. Does not an old fertility goddess return to life in the medieval Magdalen who is honored by such people as vineyard growers and gardeners?

That early Christians hearing John's narration of the Christ's resurrection felt a deep sense of similarity between the Magdalen searching for and lamenting the Christ and an Ishtar, an Isis, a Venus, searching for and lamenting a Tammuz, an Osiris, an Adonis, is highly probable. That people during the first centuries of Christianity were quite aware of continued celebrations of ancient gods and goddesses we know from writings of early Christians as well as from those of non-Christians. In the Acts of the Apostles, for example, the citizens of Ephesus are shown still praising the goddess Artemis, despite Paul's mighty efforts to rid all Asia of worship of the "great" goddess.[26] Apuleius, a non-Christian living in the second century of the Christian era, describes in his widely read *Metamorphoses* the worship of Isis, the goddess known to many peoples by differing names.[27] And the fifth-century Saint Augustine in his *City of God* speaks of his own youthful pleasure in the "shameful games which were celebrated in honor of gods and goddesses," including Cybele, "the mother of all gods." [28]

Did the Gospel of John's dramatic emphasis on the Magdalen's role in the resurrection of the Christ recall to early church fathers the words of Ezekiel, the "son of man" to whom the Lord, in the sixth century B.C.E., had shown the "abominations" in the temples of Jerusalem where in one temple Ezekiel saw the women weeping for Tammuz, the old Babylonian vegetation deity? [29] Did the picture of the Magdalen lamenting the dying and reviving Christian deity frighten the Alogi as much as did the opening line of John's Gospel, "In the beginning was the Word," and add fuel to the battle-fire surrounding the Alogi's famous but futile fight to exclude the Gospel of John from the canon? I wonder.

Similarities between the death and resurrection of gods of antiquity and that of the Christ have, of course, been noted by several scholars since the publication of Sir James Frazer's influential *The Golden Bough* in the first decade of the twentieth century.[30] And Mary the mother of Jesus has been linked by Frazer and others with the mother goddesses of antiquity. But I know of no scholar who has pointed out similarities between the Magdalen and the earth goddesses who figured importantly in the resurrections of the ancient heaven gods.

I see similarities between ancient deities and Christian figures as products of cultural cross-fertilization and as traditions transmitted, either orally or through writings, from one place to another, within historical time, rather than as "archetypes" or products of a "collective unconscious" as conceived by Jungians. I do, however, find surprising the neglect of the fictionalized Magdalen by other scholars who are concerned with mythological or mythologized figures. The Magdalen is not mentioned, for example, by E. K. Chambers when he observes, in *The Medieval Stage*, that "side by side with the conception of the heaven-god comes that of his female counterpart, who is also, though less clearly, indicated in all the mythologies." Chambers describes her, in "her earliest aspect," as "the lady of the woods and of the blossoming fruitful earth." [31] Yet Chambers ignores the medieval Magdalen who at once reveals characteristics of the lady "of the blossoming fruitful earth" and plays important roles on the medieval stage.

Although Mary the mother of Jesus participates in the Crucifixion scenes in the New Testament canonical Gospels, she does not play a major role in any of the Gospel accounts of the Resurrection of the Christ. It is, I suggest and wish to emphasize, because the role played by Mary Magdalene in the Gospel of John's drama of the Resurrection of the Christ evokes images of goddesses not unknown to early Christians that the Magdalen in particular excited imaginations and brought about the attribution to her of characteristics beyond those found in the figure sketched in the canonical Gospels.

We have seen her in the four canonical Gospels as a woman from whom, according to Luke and the fragment attached to Mark, seven devils had been ejected. She is one of the many women, according to Matthew, Mark, and Luke, who followed Jesus from Galilee, ministering to him, and who stood "afar off" at the Crucifixion. Or she is, according to John, the one who stands with Jesus' mother and his aunt and his beloved disciple at the foot of the cross.

She goes to the tomb with the "other Mary" (Matthew and Mark), or with the other women (Luke), or alone (John) to see (Matthew and John) or to anoint (Mark and Luke) the Christ. And with the other Mary, Marys, or alone, she is told by one angel (Matthew and Mark) or by two angels (Luke and John) that Jesus has arisen, and is sent and goes (Luke, John, Matthew, and fragment added to Mark) or does not go (extant text of Mark) to tell the apostles who believe (Matthew and John) or who do not believe (Luke and fragment added to Mark). Although the risen Christ appears only to the disciples in the Gospel of Luke, he first appears to the Marys in the Gospel of Matthew. But it is the Magdalen alone who first sees the resurrected Christ, according to the statement added to the Gospel of Mark and according to John's dramatic narration.

The inconsistencies noted in the canonical Gospels' accounts of the resurrection of the Christ bring about inconsistencies of details found in medieval plays and in iconography where we see, for example, now one angel and again two angels at the sepulcher, and sometimes two, sometimes three Marys at the tomb. And the three synoptic gospels, those of Matthew, Mark, and Luke, provide the basis for the extant recorded Resurrection plays, dating from the tenth and eleventh centuries, as well as for the iconographic representations of Jesus' tomb from the fourth into the latter part of the twelfth century, when for the first time the risen Christ is depicted in art.[32]

The tenth-century Benedictional of Saint Ethelwold illustrates the scene which constitutes the first extant recorded Christian drama, the scene showing three Marys at the sepulcher searching for the Christ, who has already arisen. And on two ivory panels from a Christian casket of around A.D. 400 we see carved representations of scenes from the Christ's Passion, the earliest extant representation of the Crucifixion (fig. 3). Matthew's description of Judas hanging himself after his betrayal of Jesus is pictured alongside the Crucifixion of Jesus with the two Marys

3. *The Crucifixion*, Passion scenes from ivory panels (c. A.D. 400).

4. *The Women at the Tomb,*
Passion scenes from ivory panels (c. A.D. 400).

looking on. And on the lower panel are Mary Magdalene and "the other Mary" at the tomb where, according to Matthew, guards, sent by the Pharisees to secure the tomb "lest his disciples go and steal him away and tell the people that he has arisen from the dead," have fallen into a daze at the sight of the angel who appears to the Marys (fig. 4).[33]

The synoptic Gospels' references to the Magdalen therefore provide a model for the undistinguished figure pictured in early representations of scenes from Christ's Passion and in extant plays from the tenth and eleventh centuries. And John's Gospel provides the model for the Magdalen who appears in the recognition scenes of the twelfth-century plays in which the figure of Christ is first represented in drama. Although the characteristics given Mary Magdalene in the four canonical Gospels do form the skeleton for the popular figure, they do not altogether account for the long-lived Magdalen who is pictured in either Donatello's or Marochetti's sculpture or who is immortalized in other Magdalen monuments which we have noted. Eclectic imaginations reach beyond the Gospels' specific references to Mary Magdalene in order, I think, to fulfill a desire not only for a more complex feminine figure closely associated with the Christ but also for retention of old figures scorned by Judeo-Christianity. Even though the fictionalized figure of the Magdalen does not make a strong impact on Western art and literature until the rise of the Crusades, metamorphoses of the Gospel figure begin in the East during Christianity's stormy beginnings.

Very early in the Christian era, the Magdalen was linked with other women mentioned in the canonical gospels. She was, as we have seen in the newspaper article headlining her a *Victim of Libel*, identified with a woman mentioned in Luke 7:37–50. The woman, who was a "sinner," went carrying "an alabaster flask of ointment" to the house of Simon the Pharisee while Jesus was there. "And standing behind him at his feet, weeping, she began to wet his feet with her tears, and wiped them with the hair of her head, and kissed his feet, and anointed them with the ointment." [34] And despite Simon's bitter mutterings against Jesus' allowing the "sinner" to touch him, Jesus forgave the woman her "many sins," for, he said, "she loved much." [35] Jesus tells the woman that her "faith" has saved her and sends her away in peace.[36]

The door is now opened for the entrance of the "holy harlot" onto the Christian scene. With the identification of the Magdalen as Luke's anonymous "sinner," it was possible for imaginations to specify the Magdalen as a prostitute who "loved much" and who visibly expressed her love for the Christ. The sinner who washed Jesus' feet with her tears, wiped them with her long hair, anointed them, and kissed them, clings through the centuries to the composite Magdalen. The stage is already set for the Magdalen's role in drama, from the twelfth-century Easter plays down to *Jesus Christ Superstar*, as the "harlot" who anointed Jesus with "fragrant oil." And when we hear the medieval Magdalen lament the dead Christ, we can also hear in the distance a faintly distorted echo of the lament for the dead Enkidu, the man for whom "the harlot" mourns in the Babylonian *Epic of Gilgamesh*, composed some two thousand years before the advent of Christianity.[37] And behind the Magdalen searching for the dead Christ falls a dim shadow of an ancient 'Anat searching for the dead Baal, the Canaanite god of fertility.[38] For in the metamorphosed Magdalen appear elements of Babylonian and Canaanite traditions against which the prophets, in biblical writings, had long since warned "Israel."

The Magdalen not only becomes the prostitute who anointed the Christ, but she also absorbs the identity of another woman who, having "an alabaster jar of very expensive ointment," anointed Jesus while he, with his disciples, sat at table in the house of "Simon the Leper" in Bethany. The story is told, with minor variations, in the Gospels of Matthew, Mark, and John.[39] In all three accounts, the disciples are shown complaining about the woman's waste of the precious ointment and Jesus is pictured scolding his disciples and telling them that the woman has anointed him against his burial. The Gospels of Matthew and Mark add more prophetic words, words which have long been applied by her devotees to the Magdalen. To his disciples Jesus says of the woman of Bethany: "And truly, I say to you, wherever the gospel is preached in the whole world, what she has done will be told in memory of her." [40]

Since John names the woman "Mary" and links her with Martha who serves the meal at Simon's house, the Magdalen is also identified with Martha's sister Mary who, according to Luke 10:38–42, was praised by Jesus for having chosen "the good portion, which shall not be taken from her," by sitting at Jesus' feet and listening to his teaching while Martha complained about having to do all the serving. From this identification of Mary Magdalene with Martha's sister comes the early church fathers' explanation of the Magdalen as the figure of the "contemplative life" and of Martha as the figure of the "active life." And the attribute of the contemplative is, alongside the attribute of the prostitute, absorbed into the mythical figure who is represented in art and literature.

Through John's account of the raising of Lazarus, another characteristic which survives in the fictionalized figure is added to the Mary Magdalene of the New Testament. John identifies Mary the sister of Martha and Lazarus with the woman of Bethany who had anointed Jesus and dried his feet with her hair. "Now a certain man was ill, Lazarus of Bethany, the village of Mary and her sister Martha. It was Mary who anointed the Lord with ointment and wiped his feet with her hair, and whose brother Lazarus was ill." [41] And the Magdalen becomes that Mary whose weeping for her dead brother moved Jesus to shed the only tears attributed to him by the Gospel writers.[42]

The Magdalen, through the absorption of other canonical Gospel figures, takes on attributes far in excess of those found in the Mary Magdalene specifically mentioned in the Gospels. She absorbs the identity of almost every feminine figure who is pictured in any kind of intimacy with the Christ. She acquires a sister and a brother and so becomes the woman who can move Jesus to weep as well as the figure who is to represent the "contemplative life" so dear to mystics. And she becomes at once a prostitute who has loved much and the one feminine anointer of the Christ, the Anointed.

Homo ludens walks the thin line dividing jest from earnest in simultaneously tightening the bond between the Magdalen and the Christ and transforming Mary Magdalene into a "holy harlot." With her long flowing hair and her ointment jar, the chaste prostitute is to weather the storms of religious controversy and emerge as a highly important feminine figure whose influence goes beyond specific roles given her in Western art and literature.

The metamorphoses of the Magdalen have begun. And they continue during the turbulent centuries of Christianity's beginnings. Writers of works designated as apocryphal increase the complexity of the holy harlot as they augment the importance of her link with the male deity. Second-century Gnostic writers glorify the Magdalene as a heroine. But they attempt to make the heroine "male."

3

The Heroine-Hero of the Gospel of Mary

From a woman sin had its beginning,
and because of her we all die.
>   The Wisdom of Jesus Son of Sirach 25:24–25

The root of wisdom—to whom has it been revealed?
Her clever devices—who knows them?
>   The Wisdom of Jesus Son of Sirach 1:6–7

Proclaiming what pertains to the present world, female prophecy desires to be considered male. On this account she steals the seed of the male, envelops them with her own seed of the flesh and lets them—that is, her words—come forth as her own creations.
>   *The True Prophet*

ATTEMPTS to enlarge the Magdalen who is pictured in the Gospel of John as the woman closest to the Christ by incorporating into her person other women mentioned in the canonical Gospels reveal the efforts of early Christians to create a feminine counterpart for their man-god. And apocryphal writings give further evidence of the desire to link the Magdalen with Jesus. The Magdalen is, for example, specifically referred to in the *Gospel of Philip* as "Magdalene, whom men called Jesus' companion." [1]

The Magdalen figures prominently in several extant apocryphal writings. "We wonder whether Mariamne identifies with Mary the mother of Jesus or with Mary Magdalene," Jean

Doresee remarks when he comments on the frequent appearance of the "mysterious Mariamne" in the Apocrypha.[2] Both internal evidence and knowledge of the mythical Magdalen convince me that Mariamne, sometimes called Mariham, Mary, or Maria the Magdalene, is the Mary Magdalene who undergoes further metamorphoses in the imaginations of the writers of apocryphal works.

The Apocrypha "record the imaginations, hopes, and fears of the men who wrote them; they show what was acceptable to the unlearned Christians of the first ages, what interested them, what they admired, what ideals they cherished for this life, and what they would find in the next," Montague Rhodes James states in the preface to his edition of *The Apocryphal New Testament*. It is, I think, because the Apocrypha record the desires and fears of men, learned or unlearned, that they have, as James says, "indeed exercised an influence (wholly disproportionate to their intrinsic merit) so great and so widespread" on art and literature.[3]

The Magdalen pictured in the Apocrypha reflects, sometimes blatantly and sometimes obliquely, a desire and a fear deep-rooted in human attitudes: a craving for continuity of the familiar and a horror of mortality and the unknown. She is used to fulfill the desire to hang on to the old by uniting it with the new, to keep alive antique goddesses and Eastern dualistic ideas' in the emerging Christianity. She is simultaneously Jesus' "companion" and a vessel for the dualistic view of matter as evil and female, of spirit as good and male. Although again and again damned by Peter as a female and therefore not worthy of life, the Magdalen is, particularly in the *Gospel of Mary* and in the *Pistis Sophia*, the woman privileged to share with Jesus his *gnosis*.

Gnosis is knowledge, but is in Gnostic systems a particular kind of knowledge. It is knowledge revealed to a passive recipient. And receiving *gnosis* is, as Hans Jonas observes in *The Gnostic Religion: The Message of the Alien God and the Beginnings of Christianity*, the goal of all believers in the radically dualistic doctrines called Gnosticism, since it is considered the only possible means of rescuing the "spirit" from the "corrupt" world of "matter." [4] Gnosticism, with its reverence for *gnosis* and its contempt for the world, necessitates a revision of the biblical accounts of the creation and of man's "fall." And the revisions of the biblical cosmogony as well as the doctrines held by the dualistic sects reveal borrowings from old Babylonian, Syrian, Egyptian, and Persian religions, from Neoplatonic and apocalyptic Judeo-Christian ideas.[5] The eclecticism characteristic of the Gnostic systems that grow up within as well as around Judiasm and Christianity illustrates the cultural cross-fertilization which was particularly prevalent during the early centuries of the current era.[6] The cultural cross-fertilization profoundly affects the Magdalen who figures prominently in Gnostic writings as one who is both a receiver and a revealer of *gnosis*.

Although the Gnostic cosmogonies differ in details, they share the idea of the plurality of worlds. There are worlds, or Aeons, varying in number but usually seven or twelve, corresponding to the planets or to the signs of the Zodiac. And the aeons are created by inferior "powers" which, even when they are thought to be descended from the deity, do not know the "true god" and as rulers of the cosmic spheres serve as obstacles in man's attempts to know the deity, who is outside the created universe.[7] Some Gnostic cosmogonies indeed retain the deity of Genesis as the creator of the material world, but the deity is viewed as a "tyrant" who has bound man into the dark world of matter and therefore separated him from the Kingdom of Light. Other Gnostic systems envision the creator of the material world as a feminine figure who may be either a she-devil or the fallen consort of a male deity. In all Gnostic systems, the "true god" rules only in the transmundane "realm of Light," while man on earth is imprisoned in the evil "realm of Darkness." [8]

Man is, like Platonic man, tripartite, composed of body, soul, and spirit. But both the body and the soul, the Gnostics believe, are creations of the "lowly powers" who made the world of matter. And the soul is enclosed in seven "vestments" of appetites and passions, corresponding to the evil powers who rule the spheres. Shrouded in the seven soul-garments is the "spirit," or divine spark, which is a portion of the transmundane deity, a portion that has fallen into the world. The spirit, suffocated by the soul and the flesh, is "ignorant" and can only be freed through acquiring self-knowledge.

Self-knowledge consists of the spirit's coming to know its divine origin, the evil nature of the world in which it is trapped, and its destination. Its destination is union with the deity in the realm of Light. But only through divine revelation can the spirit attain the *gnosis* necessary for its salvation. Revelation is brought to men on earth by a messenger from the realm of Light. The messenger in the Gnostic writings with which we are primarily concerned is Jesus, usually called "The Savior." The messenger's mission is to break through the cosmic spheres, sometimes changing his shape and form to deceive the evil rulers of the spheres through which he must descend, in order to bring *gnosis* to the spirit of man. In some systems, as we shall see, the knowledge imparted by the messenger from the realm of Light comprises "mysteries" such as magic words and specific rituals which may enable the spirit of the initiated to pass through the spheres that block its path to the divine Light. Once the spirit has received *gnosis*, it is ready after the death of the body to shed its soul-garments in its journey through the "wicked" Aeons and at last to go beyond the created universe where it has been exiled and to return "home" to unite with the divine substance from which it originated.[9]

Since spirit is considered male by a number of Gnostic sects, woman must first become man before she can shed her soul-garments and unite with the transmundane deity. We can see efforts to make the heroine a hero in the Gnostic writings starring the Magdalen. And the spirit's shedding its seven soul-garments strikingly parallels the New Testament Mary Magdalene's having had seven demons ejected from her. The soul-garments themselves, representing appetites and passions considered to be evil, are of the very nature of the seven "deadly sins" into which the Magdalen's demons were metamorphosed by early Christians.

The second-century "pure spiritual" Magdalen is pictured in both the *Gospel of Mary* and the *Pistis Sophia* as one of the few people privileged to receive the *gnosis* brought by Jesus from the realm of Light. Only a few are chosen to receive directly from the messenger the *gnosis* which is necessary for the release of the spirit from its "corrupt" soul and body as preparation for its final union with the transmundane deity. And those few, during their term in the "dark prison of the earth," are exempt from obedience to laws, either man-made or made by their "tyrannical" creator.[10]

Both the Old Testament deity and the Mosaic law are scorned by these radically dualistic sects for whom life on earth is worthless. Even though woman-matter is viewed with contempt, the often quoted words of Jesus Son of Sirach, "From a woman sin had its beginning, and because of her we all die," would hold little significance for those Gnostic sects whose goal was death of the body and indeed dissolution of the whole created cosmos.[11] Some Gnostic sects honor both Eve and the serpent for defying the deity of Genesis.

It is the Gnostic reverence for *gnosis* which leads to the adulation of both Eve and the serpent who, according to Genesis, tempted the woman to eat of "the forbidden fruit" of "the tree of knowledge." The serpent, long a symbol of both wisdom and immortality in the Orient, was indeed worshipped by the Ophites and the Naassenes who flourished in the early centuries of Christianity. And to Eve, perhaps because of her resemblance to Wisdom with "her clever devices," was attributed a gospel.[12] The ambivalence toward both life and women stems from incongruities rooted in a radically dualistic view of the multifarious cosmos.

The Gnostics' disdain for the Mosaic law is also a result of a dualistic view of the universe. For a code of ethics becomes irrelevant to the "illumined" man who, feeling only contempt for the body and for the material world, tries to escape the "corruption" of the flesh either through sexual orgy or through asceticism. It is, however, asceticism which is extolled by the writers of both the *Gospel of Mary* and the *Pistis Sophia*.

In the setting of Gnosticism, with its extreme dualism and its exotic eclecticism, the Magdalen plays an impressive role. Famous as the chief questioner in two works referred to by early church fathers, the *Questions of Mary*, the *Great Questions* and the *Little*

Questions, as well as in the extant *Books of the Savior* and *Pistis Sophia*, the Magdalen is credited with her own gospel in the second century of the Christian era.

The *Gosepl of Mary* is written in the form of a dialogue, suggestive of Plato's dialogues in structure but not in style.[13] From the fragment which has come down to us we can see the major role given the Magdalen not only as the woman privileged to possess *gnosis* but even as the teacher of "knowledge" revealed to her by "the Savior." The gospel also reflects an ambivalent attitude toward woman, an old ambivalence that the dualistic view of female as matter and evil in contrast with male as spirit and good not only perpetuates but sanctifies. The gospel is concerned with the nature of matter, of sin, and of salvation, and it includes a portion of the Magdalen's account of the soul's journey through the Aeons to reach the realm of Light.

The first six pages of the Coptic papyrus are lost. The fragment opens with a question concerning matter: "Will, then, matter be saved or not?" Implicit in the answer given by the Savior is the Gnostic three-fold division of man. The Savior answers that all natures, all created things, will be resolved into their own roots "because the nature of matter is dissolved into the roots of its nature alone." Peter, apparently satisfied with the answer, asks what "the sin of the world" is, and the answer reveals the Gnostic contempt for the material world and the procreation which perpetuates it.

"Sin as such does not exist," the Savior says, "but you make sin when you do what is of the nature of fornication, which is called 'sin.' " This man-made "sin" is the cause, Jesus explains, of man's coming into existence and dying, and it is the reason that the "Good" came "to restore the essence of each nature into its roots." [14] He warns the disciples against being led astray, tells them that the "Son of Man" is within them, and asks them to go to preach the "gospel of the kingdom." He reminds them that he has left them no commandment other than his own and has given them "no law, as the lawgiver did, lest you be bound by it." [15] With this typically Gnostic dig at the Mosaic law, the Savior leaves, and the disciples are grieved and afraid.

But Mary cheers her "brethren" as she tells them not to mourn or be irresolute for the Savior's grace will protect them. "Let us," she says, "rather praise his greatness, for he prepared us and made us into men." [16] Peter disregards the Magdalen's statement that she, along with the others, has been made man, and he addresses her as the woman especially chosen to receive *gnosis* from Jesus. "Sister," he says, "we know that the Savior loved you more than other women. Tell us the words of the Savior which you have in mind since you know them, and we do not, nor have we heard them." [17] The Magdalen agrees to "impart" to the men what is "hidden" from them and tells of her having seen Jesus in a vision and of reporting it to him. "Blessed are you," the Savior said, "since you did not waver at the sight of me." She tells her "brethren" that she asked the Savior whether the "mind which sees the vision" sees it through the "soul or through the spirit," and begins to recount the Savior's answer. "Neither," he says. But because of a loss of four pages from the papyrus, we do not know the epistemology set forth by the revealer of *gnosis*.[18]

The remainder of the fragment of the gospel contains a portion of the Magdalen's account of the journey of the soul through the Aeons as it sheds its garments to reach at last "rest in the time of the moment of the Aeon in silence." [19] The Magdalen personifies the garments from which the soul escapes as "forms" of the "fourth power," all of which are "participants in wrath." The seven "forms," so closely akin to the Magdalen's seven "demons" which are transformed into anger, covetousness, lust, gluttony, pride, envy, and sloth, the seven "deadly sins" of Roman Catholicism, the Magdalen names darkness, desire, ignorance, the arousing or jealousy of death, the kingdom of the folly of the flesh, the wisdom of the folly of the flesh, and wrathful wisdom.[20] The seven ask the soul, "Whence do you come, killer of men, or where are you going, conqueror of space?" And the soul answers, "What seizes me is killed; what turns me about is overcome; my desire has come to an end and ignorance is dead. In a world I was saved from a world, and in a 'type,' from a higher 'type' and from the fetter of the impotence of knowledge, the existence of which is temporal." [21]

The Magdalen concludes, and rather like the soul at the end of its journey, is silent, "since the Savior had spoken thus far with her." [22] But Andrew is skeptical and asks the other men what they think about these "teachings" for he does not, he says, believe "that the Savior said this." [23] Peter, agreeing with Andrew, expresses his resentment of the Magdalen by asking if the Savior spoke "secretly with a woman" in preference to them. "Are we," he says, "to turn back and all listen to her? Did he prefer her to us?" And Mary is grieved and asks Peter if he thinks she made it all up or is "lying concerning the Savior." Levi scolds Peter for his perpetual anger and comes to the defense of the Magdalen. "Now I see that you are contending against the woman like the adversaries. But if the Savior made her worthy, who are you to reject her? Surely the Savior knew her well. For this reason he loved her more than us." Levi concludes that they should rather be ashamed and "put on the Perfect Man" and convinces them to go out "to proclaim the gospel." [24]

The Magdalen of the *Gospel of Mary*, pictured as the woman whom Jesus loved more than any other person and the one with whom he shared his secret *gnosis,* is clearly that one whom "men call Jesus' companion." For to her has been revealed "the root of wisdom." As the woman against whom the "adversaries" contend, she is very likely linked with the "sinner" who, in Luke's account, anointed the Christ and was forgiven of her sins because she "loved much." Mingled with the view of the Magdalen as the sharer of Jesus' *gnosis* is the antifeminism which results from the extreme dualism characteristic of, but not peculiar to, Gnosticism itself. For she is also, as we see from her statement that Jesus "has prepared us and made us into men," the woman-matter become male-spirit. She is to Peter at first the privileged woman who can impart the Savior's wisdom to the male disciples, but she becomes an object of doubt and jealousy. An ambivalent attitude toward woman is manifested both in the Magdalen's statement and in Peter's conflicting reactions to her.

We have seen another example of this ambivalence toward the Magdalen in particular and toward woman in general in the *Gospel of Thomas* where Simon Peter says, "Let Mariham go out from among us, because women are not worthy of life." Jesus replies to Peter: "See, I shall lead her, so that I will make her male, that she too may become a living spirit, resembling you males. For every woman who makes herself male will enter the kingdom of heaven." [25] This ambivalence toward women expressed in the *Gospel of Thomas* and in other Apocrypha recurs in the dualistic sects which enter medieval Europe via Provence as early as the twelfth century and continues into the fourteenth century. The statement that women are to be saved by becoming men appears specifically, for example, in writings of the medieval Cathari.[26] The notion of woman-matter being inferior to male-spirit lingers on through the centuries and inevitably colors the paradoxical figure of the Magdalen seen in both literature and the plastic arts of the Western world.

Even Peter's individual resentment of the Magdalen finds its way into Western medieval drama. For example, in a fifteenth-century German Easter play, *Das Erlauer Österspiel III*, Peter says to the Magdalen after she has run to tell him of her having seen the risen Christ, "That rumor I will not believe. Hurry home and mind your spinning. It is a sin and a shame that females run all over the countryside." [27] Peter doubly insults woman by using, instead of the feminine "die Frauen," the pejorative neuter "di weip."

> Der red ich nicht gelauben wil!
> secz dich din haim und spinn vil!
> ez ist eine grosse schant,
> daz di weip lauffent uber lant!
> [Ll. 1386–89]

And Peter threatens to give the Magdalen a clout on the ear, another on the cheek, and a third on the neck, for she is, he says, "ein tor," a fool.

> ich gib dir mit der laffen
> ains an das ar,
> das du wurst ein tor,
> das ander an das wang,
> mag ich dir das ander erlang,
> das dritt an den hals.
> [Ll. 1397–1402]

Even though the medieval German playwright's picture of Peter's resentment of the Magdalen and of womankind in toto is playfully exaggerated, it does perpetuate the old ambivalent view of woman. The persistence of an ambivalent view of woman is, to be sure, no news, but the entrance into medieval drama of the attitude toward the Magdalen specifically attributed to Peter in apocryphal writings demonstrates the transmission of early Eastern traditions into medieval Christendom.

The fact that the *Gospel of Mary* is unique in being the only extant gospel attributed to a New Testament woman gives evidence of the Magdalen's power over human imaginations during the early centuries of Christianity. In order to place her in the role of heroine, the Gnostic writer of the gospel makes a noble effort to transform her into a hero. But the Magdalen, despite her own statement to the contrary, stubbornly remains woman. And the fact that she is shown as *the* woman with whom Jesus has shared his *gnosis* gives further evidence of early attempts to isolate her as the Christ's feminine counterpart.

More efforts to tighten the bond between the Magdalen and the Christ appear in the identification of all the Marys mentioned in the canonical Gospels as one and the same person. Mary the mother of Jesus appears in a vision to the fourth-century Cyril of Jerusalem and announces, according to Cyril: "I am Mary Magdalene because the name of the village wherein I was born was Magdalia. My name is Mary of Cleopa. I am Mary of James son of Joseph the Carpenter." [28] The Magdalen is also identified with the mother of Jesus in two works which were translated into Latin during the Middle Ages, the *Gospel of Bartholomew* and Bartholomew's *Book of the Resurrection*.[29] This "reckless identification of the Virgin Mary with all the other Maries of the gospels is characteristic of these Egyptian rhapsodies," Montague Rhodes James comments.[30]

The blending of all the Marys into one person parallels the identification of the Magdalen with other women mentioned in the canonical Gospels. This "reckless identification" represents, I think, yet another attempt to make the Magdalen the single feminine counterpart for the Christ, whether an Isis for a Christian Osiris or a "companion" for the "true prophet." The mythical Magdalen does seem to fit the description of the "companion" of the "true prophet" described in an apocryphon called *The True Prophet.*[31]

After defining the true prophet as "he who from the beginning of the world, changing his forms and his names, runs through universal time until, anointed for his toils by the mercy of God, he comes to his own time and will rest forever," the document describes the "female being" who has been "created as a companion for the true prophet." [32] "As a female she rules over the present world, which is like to her, and counts as the first prophetess; she proclaims her prophecy with all amongst those born of women." [33] And, not surprisingly, the Gnostic writer goes on to deride "female prophecy." Desiring to be considered male, the female "steals the seed of the male, envelops them with her own seed of flesh and lets them—that is, her words—come forth as her own creations." [34]

The Magdalen of the *Gospel of Mary* is the "prophetess" proclaiming to the disciples revelations secretly given her by the "true prophet." She is considered by Peter to be as inferior to Jesus as is flesh to spirit, as is female to male, and her "female prophecy" seems spurious to both Andrew and Peter. But Levi, by reminding the men that the Magdalen had been "made worthy" by Jesus who knew her well and therefore loved her more than he loved the male disciples, defends the "female being" created as the "companion" for the "true prophet."

The view of the Magdalen as the "female" who rules over the material world survives in the popular figure honored by such people as sailors and vineyard growers in the Middle Ages and lives on, alongside the Magdalen as Christ's companion, particularly in the heroine of the Digby *Mary Magdalene* who is the Christ's "wel-belovyd frynd" sent as an "apostylesse" to Marseilles to proclaim her prophecy amongst all those born of women.

The Magdalen of the *Pistis Sophia* is, as was the heroine of the *Gospel of Mary*, the sharer of Jesus' *gnosis*, the "pure spiritual

Mariham" highly praised by the Savior and resented by Peter. But the Magdalen also absorbs elements of the figure whose story centers *Pistis Sophia*, the Gnostic goddess of wisdom. And the metamorphoses of the paradoxical Magdalen continue.

4

The "Pure Spiritual Mariham" and Pistis Sophia Prunikos

Beside the sea she lives, the woman of the vine,
the maker of wine: Siduri sits in the garden
at the edge of the sea, with the golden bowl
and the golden vats that the gods gave her.
Epic of Gilgamesh

Wisdom exalts her sons and gives help to those who seek her.
Whoever loves her loves life, and those who seek her will be filled
with joy.
Wisdom of Jesus Son of Sirach 4:11–12

When he laid the strong foundations of the earth—
Then I was beside him binding all together;
    I was his daily joy,
      Constantly making merry in his presence,
Rejoicing in the habitable world
And delighting in the human race.
Proverbs 8:29–31

THE *Pistis Sophia* reveals attempts to simultaneously reinstate and dematerialize the goddess of wisdom, Ishtar or Siduri or Athene, long since dethroned by patriarchal monotheism but preserved in the Bible through vivid personifications of wisdom as a woman who is the male deity's "daily joy." The Sophia (Wisdom), sometimes called Pistis (Faith) and sometimes called Prunikos (Whore), is a central figure in Gnostic myths and therefore appears in a number of apocryphal works. Her story is told, for example, in the *Secret Book of John* and in the *Sophia of Jesus Christ* as well as in the *Pistis Sophia*.

The popularity of the Pistis-Sophia-Prunikos type is manifested in the figure of Helen, who was worshipped by the followers of Simon Magus during the very beginnings of Christianity. If Irenaeus, the heresy-battling bishop of Lyons during the latter part of the second century, is correct in believing that Simon Magus was indeed the founder of Gnosticism, the immediate model for both the Sophia of Jesus and the Magdalen "companion" of the Christ may very well have been Helen. Helen deserves, then, a side-glance.

Helen is described by Irenaeus as the woman whom Simon Magus, "who was glorified as a god by many," led about with him "after he had redeemed her from a life of prostitution in Tyre." [1] And Simon Magus said that Helen was the "first thought" of his mind, the Mother of All. But she had been trapped in a human body and held captive by those whom she had created. Helen had transmigrated from one "female vessel" to another through the centuries until she fell into prostitution and was at last redeemed by Simon. The followers of Simon have, Irenaeus writes, "an image of Zeus and one of Helen in the likeness of Athene, and they worship these." [2]

Another account of Helen comes down to us in the *Clementine Homilies* where we see that "Simon goes about in the company of Helen and, even until now, as you see, stirs up the crowds. He says that he has brought down this Helen from the highest heavens to the world; she is the Queen, since she is all-maternal Being and Wisdom (Sophia). For her sake the Greeks and the barbarians fought, imagining an image of the truth, for she who really existed was with the very first God. But by allegorizing certain matters of this sort, fictitiously combined with Greek myths, he deceives many, especially by his performance of many marvelous wonders, so that—if we did not know that he does these things by magic—we ourselves would have been deceived." [3]

The picture of Helen preserved in Irenaeus's writings against heresy and in the *Clementine Homilies* further demonstrates the persistence into the early Christian era of the desire for a feminine deity, a goddess both of wisdom and of generation. Pistis Sophia Prunikos, like Helen, "falls" into the "world of darkness" and is rescued by the male deity. And Pistis Sophia is in Gnostic myth the all-maternal Being, Wisdom, who is in part responsible for the creation of the material world. But in the dialogue called *Pistis Sophia* she is not the only feminine figure favored by the male deity. The mythical Magdalen who, like Helen, had been "redeemed" from a life of prostitution by a deity, and who, like the Pistis Sophia, puts on "sackcloth," stars in the *Pistis Sophia* as the woman whom Jesus will "complete in all the mysteries of the things of the Height." [4] As the heroine of the *Pistis Sophia*, the Magdalen seems to figure, in the language of Neoplatonism, as the "particular" of the "universal" Sophia.

The *Pistis Sophia* opens with a description of Jesus' return to earth, after his ascension to heaven, to complete the teaching of the "mysteries" to his disciples. In the mysteries, elements of Persian, Greek, Babylonian, and Egyptian religions mingle with the new Christianity. And Jesus' warnings against participation in other "mysteries" imply strong competition with the mystery religions which were prevalent during the early centuries of Christianity. In revealing the mystery of the "Treasury of the Light," Jesus narrates the story of Pistis Sophia's fall into darkness and matter, of her putting on sackcloth, of her losing her own name, of her repentances uttered as she travels through the Aeons, twelve in this cosmogony, and of her final redemption into the realm of Light.

We see the disciples, among whom are the Magdalen, called either Mariham or Maria, and Mary the mother of Jesus, gathered at the Mount of Olives when Jesus descends in a dazzling "vesture of light." [5] The disciples are frightened at the sight of Jesus, but he calms them by affirming his divinity. He tells them of his earlier descent, at the command of the "First Mystery," into the world of mankind where he, in the form of Gabriel, found "Maria whom they are wont to call my mother" and cast "powers of Light rulers on her." [6] He announces to the disciples his having just completed the overthrowing of the evil "Powers"

44

which through "fate" and "astrology" had until then ruled the created world. And when he finishes his account of having cleared the path for salvation of the "enlightened," the Magdalen gazes into the air "for the space of an hour." [7] Then, the first to speak, she asks her "Lord" to allow her to "speak with boldness." Jesus answers, "Mariham, Mariham the happy, whom I shall complete in all the mysteries of the things of the Height. Speak in boldness, because thou art she whose heart straineth toward the Kingdom of the heavens more than all thy brothers." [8]

The Magdalen explains at length the previous words of Jesus, and Jesus praises her: "Well done, Maria, because thou art happy beyond every woman who is upon earth, because thou art she who will become the Pleroma of all the Pleromas and the completion of all the completions," in other words, the "fullness" of the divine. The Magdalen, "glad greatly," worships at Jesus' feet and questions him further, and Jesus assures her that he will reveal everything which she seeks.[9] Just as in the *Gospel of Mary,* the Magdalen is set apart as the privileged sharer of Jesus' revealed *gnosis.*

When the Magdalen, "she who is beautiful in her speaking and the happy one," questions Jesus concerning the purification of souls, Jesus praises her for "enquiring aright and giving light upon everything in accuracy and exactness." [10] The Magdalen continues to "enquire aright" and to "give light" as Jesus speaks of the Rulers of the Light and narrates Pistis Sophia's desertion of her "partner" and her "fall" from the realm of Light into the darkness of the Aeons below.

All the rulers of the twelve Aeons below the realm of Light hated Pistis Sophia because she wanted to go above them into the light, Jesus says, and the triple power "Self-willed" caused a "false light of lights" to be made, and he "lusted" for Pistis Sophia and surrounded her with his "material emanations" who "afflicted her" and took away her Light. Pistis Sophia, in her darkness, cried out "greatly" and said a "repentance" to the Light of Lights. "Deliver me, O Light, because evil thoughts came unto me," she cries, and she recounts at length her fall into "the darkness of the Chaos" where she lost her "name." She did "these things" in her innocence, she says, mistaking the triple power Self-willed for the Light of Lights, and she begs to be delivered from the "matter of this darkness." [11]

"I looked out for my partner," she calls to the Light, "that he should come and fight for me, and he came not. And I was looking that he should come and give power to me, and I did not find him. And (I) having sought after the light, they gave to me the darkness, and (I) having sought after my power, they gave to me the matter," and Pistis Sophia begs the Light to wreak vengeance on "them." [12]

Jesus quotes each of Sophia's twelve long repentances, all of which resemble the first one in simultaneously drawing heavily on the biblical Psalms as well as the apocryphal Odes of Solomon and being permeated with contrasts of dark with light, matter with spirit. The first repentance at once paraphrases Psalm 69 (RSV) and anticipates an attribute of the medieval Magdalen.

The Magdalen, when Jesus finishes quoting Sophia's first lament, "comes forward again" to explicate Sophia's words for, she says, "My companion of light hath ear and I hear in my power of light and is wakeful the spirit which is with me." She explains that when David begged the Lord to lift him from "the mire" and save him from those who hated him, the Psalmist "prophesied Sophia." As the Magdalen explicates Sophia's words, also borrowed from the Psalmist, "I put a sackcloth upon me, and I became to them a by-word," she herself seems to "prophesy" the penitent Magdalen, the "Venus in sackcloth" who will later appear in Western art and literature.[13]

At the conclusion of her explication of Sophia's first repentance, the Magdalen is again praised by Jesus: "Well done, Mariham the happy, the all-blessed of the Pleroma, this one whom they will call happy in every generation." [14] Jesus' continued praise of the Magdalen begins to get on Peter's nerves. And at the end of Jesus' recital of Sophia's second repentance, Peter springs up and, with the attitude toward the Magdalen now familiar to us, says: "Lord, we are not able to bear with this woman saying instead of us, and she not letting any of us speak, but she is speaking many times." [15] Peter is then allowed to explain the second repentance, and Jesus, saying "Well done, Peter," tells the third repentance, which Martha, "in humility," explains.[16] The pattern continues throughout the repentances of Pistis Sophia, with "John the Virgin," Philip, Andrew, Thomas, Matthew, James, Salome, Mary the mother of Jesus, and the Magdalen taking turns at the explications.

After Jesus at last reports that he purged all matter from Pistis Sophia, saved her with a crown of light for her head, and united her crown of light with his, he quotes Sophia's hymn to the Light. Maria the mother of Jesus, "according to the world," asks that she be allowed to utter the explanation of Sophia's hymn. She offers her explanation, and Jesus further elucidates the Power of the Light.[17] The Magdalen again springs up to present an elaborate discussion of the "Powers" mentioned in Psalm 85:10 (RSV). The "Powers" which she describes are "Mercy" and "Truth" who met one another and "Peace" and "Righteousness" who kissed one another. When the Magdalen at last finishes her oration, Jesus highly lauds her as "Mariham the happy, this one who will inherit the Kingdom of the Light." [18]

Mary, "whom they are wont to call" Jesus' mother, not to be outdone by the Magdalen, offers a second explication of the four "Powers" by telling an episode in which Jesus, "being yet little," was in the vineyard with Joseph when a "Spirit" came to her seeking Jesus and she, thinking it a "phantasm" come to tempt her, bound the Spirit to the foot of her bed while she ran to the vineyard to tell Joseph of the intruder. But Jesus heard her words, she says, and ran to the Spirit, which was "like to him," and embraced and kissed the Spirit, and they became "only one." Jesus says to Mary, his "mother according to the matter in which" he "sojourned," "Well done." [19] And what seems to anticipate a medieval flyting match, a word-battle, ensues as the Magdalen immediately springs up to offer further meanings of the four "Powers" alluded to in the Psalm. As she finishes her speech, Jesus again praises her as the "inheritor of the Light." Whereupon, Mary the mother of Jesus comes forward again, kisses Jesus' feet, begs him not to be angry with her, and explains the words of the Psalm yet another time.[20]

One might think the "Powers" by now belabored to death. But costumed in medieval "mantelys" and speaking English instead of Coptic or Greek, David's resurrected "Powers" figure in fifteenth-century Western plays. In, for example, *The Castle of Perseverance*, Mercy, Truth, Peace, and Righteousness, so tediously explicated by the Magdalen and Mary the mother of Jesus in the second-century *Pistis Sophia*, walk onto the medieval stage as the "Four Daughters of God" concerned with saving Mankind.[21] So long-lived and so well traveled are personified abstractions!

After Jesus quotes more of Pistis Sophia's hymns to the Light of Lights, with others giving explanations, the Magdalen comes forward and says, "My Lord, my mind intelligent is at every time, for me to come forward at every moment and utter the explanation of the words which she said. But I am fearing Peter, because he is wont to threaten me, and he hateth our sex." [22] Obviously, the Magdalen of the second-century *Pistis Sophia* is referring to the same Peter who will, in the fifteenth-century German Easter play, threaten to give her a clout on the ear, another on the cheek, and a third on the neck; the Peter who will complain about "females" that run all over the countryside when they should be minding their spinning. Just as obviously, ambivalent attitudes toward women do not easily perish.

The Magdalen is allowed to explicate Sophia's words since, Jesus tells her, no one can keep anyone "filled with the spirit" from answering.[23] "Maria the Magdalene" later explains the meaning of seeking everything in an "exactness," and Jesus praises her for seeking "after a manner in which it is worthy to seek." [24] He will, he says, reveal all to her in "great joy with great delight." The Magdalen rejoices and asks further questions concerning the "mysteries of the Height" and Jesus tells her that he will "complete" her with "every Pleroma," with "every power." [25]

When "Maria the Magdalene" again sprang up and explained the ultimate mystery, the "Mystery of the Light," "the Savior wondered greatly at the assertion of the words which she saith, because she had become spirit quite pure." Jesus says to her,

"Well done, O pure spiritual Maria, this is the explanation of the word." [26] And the Magdalen tells Jesus of the need to deliver all men from "Darkness," for, she says, "not only are we compassionate of ourselves but we are compassionate of all the race of mankind." Jesus feels "great mercy" for her, and she, "rejoicing in great joy," questions him concerning the destiny of those who have received the mysteries of the Light and of the "Ineffable." [27]

We may at this point be into a part of the *Books of the Savior*, specifically noted later in the manuscript as the title of the document which follows the *Pistis Sophia*.[28] The style does change, and the eclecticism evident in the whole manuscript runs rampant. But the Magdalen retains her dominant role throughout the remaining documents. The documents, concerned largely with punishments for sins and with salvation through the one acceptable "mystery," give evidence of the incorporation into the Gnostic system of polytheistic concepts and the idea of transmigration of souls.

When Jesus concludes his Zoroastrian-Gnostic explanation of the Ineffable, the Magdalen worships at his feet and, weeping, cries out that her brothers do not understand.[29] Jesus explains further and remarks that he who receives the mystery of the Ineffable "excelleth all the gods and will be exalted over them all" as he announces that he himself is the mystery of the "Ineffable." Jesus adds: "Maria the Magdalene with Johannes the Virgin will become excelling all my disciples" in the Kingdom of the Light.[30] Jesus elaborates on his reign over the Kingdom of Light which will follow the "dissolution of the Universe." Necessary for that dissolution, Jesus says, is continued transmigration of souls until the "number of perfect souls" is completed.[31]

Poor Andrew remains in the dark and begs pity, for he has not understood the complicated mysteries of salvation revealed by Jesus. He therefore receives a stern chiding for his "sin of ignorance" from the Ineffable himself. At the request of the other disciples, Jesus at last forgives Andrew, however, and explaining that he came to purify men of their "matter," he urges the disciples to "renounce all the world with its matter" and seek the "mysteries of purification." [32] After Jesus imparts the mysteries of restoring the dead to life, healing the sick, and casting out demons, he warns the disciples, including the Magdalen, to keep these mysteries "secret" and to use them only to lead unbelievers to faith in him.[33]

We see, in the *Books of the Savior*, that the Magdalen has indeed been well schooled in the fine art of allegorical exegesis. For during her long discussion on types of sinners and punishments inflicted on them by the "dragon of outer darkness," her exegesis with the "four meanings" of the ways of saving the soul from the "Counterfeit Spirit" is applauded by Jesus. "O spiritual one of pure light!" he exclaims to her.[34] The "power of light boils" in Maria the Magdalene as she continues to play the mediator between the "Light of Lights" and his disciples. And it is the Magdalen who expresses extreme happiness for the "greatnesses" revealed to her and the disciples after Jesus has told her that he "despoiled" himself in order to bring the mysteries to "purify men." [35]

The remaining fragments contained in the manuscript bearing the title *Pistis Sophia* were, scholars agree, written later than the *Pistis Sophia* and the *Books of the Savior*, probably in the fourth century. They not only reinforce evidence of the Magdalen's grip on men's imaginations but also further emphasize the tenacity of old religious figures and concepts on human minds during the early centuries of Christianity. Jesus, for example, prays to the "Fatherhood of every fatherhood, the boundless Light," in a mixture of Hebrew, Egyptian, and Persian words.[36] And the Rulers of the Spheres where men continue "working in the intercourse" are metamorphosed Greek gods. Along with Kronos, Ares, Hermes, and Zeus, there is the Aphrodite in whom her creator Ieou has "bound" a "power" taken from the Sophia.[37]

After Jesus lists these Rulers, who have other names known to the "incorruptibles," and praises Iabraoth for forsaking the "mysteries of the intercourse" to "work" in the "mysteries of the Light," the Magdalen, again weeping, begs Jesus to tell her and her brothers how they can save their souls from the "wicked" Rulers. Jesus agrees to reveal more mysteries to his brothers and to his "beloved" Magdalen.[38] He proceeds to describe the Rulers whose "demons" cause men to wage war, to kill, to lie, to forsake the poor, to lust, to fornicate, to commit adultery, and to "do the intercourse continually." Most of these evil Rulers are feminine figures. Besides the Typhon's "Assessor" whose demons cause men to fornicate, commit adultery, and "do the intercourse continually," there is the Paraplex with hair reaching down to her feet and fifteen arch-demons along with many lesser demons under her control. "Ariuth the Ethiopian woman, quite black," and Hecate of the three faces are also in charge of demons whose sole purpose is to cause men to sin.[39]

The picture of the horrors perpetrated on humankind by the wicked Rulers scares the disciples, but Jesus tells them not to fear as he hymns "in the great name," blesses them, breathes into their eyes, shows them a "Great Light," and performs a magic rite with fire and vine wood, a cup of water, two jars of wine, and cakes.[40] He tells them to "hide the mystery" and says that the "Name" in which is "every name" is the great mystery and when it is spoken it will dissolve all evil powers and will "blot out all sins, done knowing or not knowing."[41]

The effort in this fragment to mingle old mysteries and magic with the new religion and to incorporate Greek gods into the Gnostic cosmogony reveals the power held on imaginations by the desire not only for continuity of traditions but also for an easy way out of life's problems. Man, under the power of demons set upon him by wicked Rulers, need not assume responsibility for his own actions. On the contrary, knowing the secret magic trick to perform will "dissolve all evil powers and blot out all sins." The blending of the Sophia with the Aphrodite, along with the emphasis on the necessity to forsake the "mystery of the intercourse," reveals the paradoxical preoccupation with and fear of sexual intercourse, a conflict resulting from the view of matter as female and evil and of spirit as male and good. Reinforcing the view of woman as at once evil and the cause of evil stand the demonic figures of the long-haired Paraplex, the "quite black" Ethiopian woman, and the three-faced Hecate. Yet in this highly eclectic apocryphal work, the Magdalen's closeness to the Christ is again emphasized.

The last fragment deals with punishments for various sins and reveals the nature of a competitive "mystery" which Jesus calls the "greatest of sins." The terrifying punishments administered by "demons" to slanderers, blasphemers, robbers, and "man who sleeps with man" will be multiplied for those who participate in the mystery which is climaxed with the communal eating of a soup containing sperm mingled with menstrual blood.[42]

This particular mystery parallels a celebration of the "love feast," the *agape*, described by the fourth-century Bishop Epiphanius, who in his youth had been "seduced" by some "beautiful women" into a Syrian Gnostic sect.[43] The sect sought its salvation through sexual orgy rather than through asceticism. Epiphanius says that the goal of the sect is not conception. Although they "gratify their lust to the limit," they "appropriate the seed of their impurity to themselves" and eat the "fruit of their shame." [44] The mystery stems from an ancient Oriental reverence for and fear of both the menstrual blood and the semen as the supposed "vehicles of life." The blended menstrual blood and semen is transformed by the Syrian Gnostic sect into "the very Body of the Christ." [45]

Jesus tells the Magdalen and his male disciples that most severe punishments will be administered by "demons" to those who participate in the mystery involving the eating of the sperm-menstrual blood soup. But when the Magdalen asks a final question about the man who discovers no mystery at all, Jesus says that such a "sinner" will receive all punishments at once.[46] The fragment breaks off with the disciples begging Jesus to save them from all these horrible punishments.[47]

The fragments included in the manuscript with the *Pistis Sophia* show, then, man's concern with the problems of evil and mortality and his attempts to resolve the problems through splitting the universe into absolute opposites. Dark, evil, female-matter is in mortal conflict with light, good, male-spirit. To achieve the "good" and immortality, the "enlightened" must, just as in the Eleusinian mysteries, forsake the mystery of sexual intercourse for the mystery of union with the deity.

The Eleusinian mysteries, described by a third-century Christian, Hippolytus, in his *Refutation of All Heresies*, consist of the "lesser" and the "greater" mysteries.[48] The lesser mysteries are the "mysteries of carnal generation." Those "spirituals" initiated into the lesser mysteries will later be initiated into the greater mysteries. In the greater mysteries the chosen few will put on wedding garments and become bridegrooms, "made more masculine by the virginal spirit." The "virginal spirit" is the pregnant one who bears a son who is "the blessed Aeon of the Aeons." [49]

Both the Eleusinian mysteries and the mysteries represented in the *Pistis Sophia* are metamorphosed continuations of ancient fertility rites in which "holy prostitution" devoted to the Mother Goddess restores life to the earth in the spring. But the Eleusinian mysteries and the Gnostic mysteries, directed away from the earth, do not reflect the age-old desire for continuity of life. Instead, they reveal a yearning for radical transcendence of life on this earth. This desire "to break the bonds that keep him tied to earth" is, Mircea Eliade says in his *Rites and Symbols of Initiation*, "one of man's essential nostalgias." [50] Whether or not the desire to escape the body that binds man to earth is in fact universally one of "man's essential nostalgias," Gnosticism, with its radical dualism, does try to banish the earth goddess from her natural setting and place her in the transmundane realm of Light.

But perhaps there is even in Gnostic man also a tenacious desire to retain some tie, however tenuous, with the earth, for the Pistis Sophia is not altogether removed from the life-bearing earth. She is specifically designated as both "the mother of all" and "the consort of the Savior" in two apocryphal works, the *Epistle of Eugnostos* and the *Sophia of Jesus Christ*. "The Son of Man agreed with Sophia, his consort, and revealed himself in a (great light) as bisexual. His male nature is called 'the Savior,' the begetter of all things, but his female 'Sophia, mother of all,' whom some call Pistis." [51]

The Sophia of Jesus, the Gnostic Magdalen, and Simon Magus's Helen all three perpetuate the Greek Athene, born of the head of Zeus. In Sophia's heritage is also the figure of Wisdom who, in the *Wisdom of Jesus Son of Sirach*, is pictured exalting "her sons" and giving "help to those who seek her," for "whoever loves her loves life." [52] It is Sophia's Jewish ancestor, Wisdom, who speaks these words to her sons on earth:

> The Lord possessed me, the first principle of
>   his sovereignty,
>   Before any of his acts,
> Ere then, from of old, I was poured out,
>   From the first, before the beginnings of the world.
>   [Prov. 8:22–23]

Gnosticism does not, however, conceive its Sophia as the Lord's "daily joy,/ Constantly making merry in his presence,/ Rejoicing in the habitable world/ And delighting in the human race." [53]

Nor does Gnosticism conceive its Sophia Prunikos in the likeness of her remote Babylonian ancestor Siduri, the "wise prostitute" and the "maker of the wine," who advises the young Gilgamesh to forsake his frantic search for immortality and enjoy life while he lives:

> You will never find that life for which you are looking. When the gods created man they allotted to him death, but life they retained in their own keeping. As for you, Gilgamesh, fill your belly with good things; day and night, night and day, dance and be merry, feast and rejoice. Let your clothes be fresh, bathe yourself in water, cherish the little child that holds your hand, and make your wife happy in your embrace; for this too is the lot of man.[54]

But Gilgamesh, not unlike the Gnostic myth-makers some two thousand years later, rejects the joys available to man during his days under the sun and continues his "search for wind" in the fatal hope of eluding the dreaded death allotted to every man.

The ambiguous figure of Pistis Sophia Prunikos personifies an attempt to escape inevitable death of human kind by denying life on earth. And in an attempt to preserve a goddess of wisdom in their heaven-oriented cosmos, the Gnostic myth-makers strip the flesh from an Ishtar, a Siduri, a Juno, and so downgrade the attribute of generation explicit in the ancient earth goddesses. A bodyless spirit, Pistis Sophia hovers above the earth. But the earth persists. And *homo ludens*, with his feet on the ground even when his head is in the air, places the spirit of Pistis Sophia Prunikos in the Magdalen. Despite attempts by writers of the Apocrypha to make her male, the Magdalen honored by the Christ as the woman happy beyond all women on earth, "the pure spiritual Mariham," absorbs the feminine attributes of the Sophia, goddess of wisdom and "mother of all."

From the soil that produced the second-century Magdalen springs the mythical figure to be honored in the European Middle Ages by the growers of vines and of fruits, by the makers of wines and of perfumes, by the creators of drama and of art. And both Donatello's fifteenth-century flesh-denying Christian penitent and Marochetti's nineteenth-century voluptuous Christian Juno grow out of the ambiguous Eastern figure.

During the turbulent centuries of Christianity's beginnings, the Magdalen sketched in the canonical Gospels undergoes complex metamorphoses. Bits and pieces of goddesses not quite dead cluster around the Mary Magdalene pictured in the Gospel of John as the woman who, lamenting the dead Christ, seeks him, and finding him resurrected, rejoices. She becomes a prostitute through identification of her with Luke's anonymous "sinner" who anointed the Christ. She absorbs the identity of the woman of Bethany who also, according to the canonical Gospels, anointed Jesus and thus becomes *the* Anointer of the Anointed. Through her acquisition of a sister, Martha, and a brother, Lazarus, she is moved into closer relationship with Jesus. And her closeness to the Christ is further augmented in the Apocrypha where she is shown as the woman whom Jesus loved more than any other, Jesus' companion, "the inheritor of the Light," Christ's feminine counterpart, the Christian goddess of wisdom.

The composite Magdalen becomes a controversial figure among church fathers, and it is not until the end of the sixth century that the Magdalen as a prostitute, the anointer of the Christ, the sister of Martha and Lazarus is accepted, with Pope Gregory's blessing, as the same woman to whom the risen Christ first appears, and then only in the Western Church where in the sixteenth century the composite Magdalen again becomes a subject of open dispute among theologians.[55]

The Magdalen of the Gospel of John and the anointers of the Christ do, however, inspire theologians during the early centuries of Christianity to interpret them symbolically. Since these early interpretations inevitably color the mythical figure who rises to fame during the complex Middle Ages, we shall look at two important treatments of the Gospel figures, that of Hippolytus and that of Origen, both third-century Christians.

5

The Magdalen's Link with an Ancient Goddess of Love

My beloved speaks and says to me:
"Arise, my love, my fair one,
            and come away;
for lo, the winter is past,
            the rain is over and gone."
                              Song of Songs 2:10–11

We all know that Aphrodite is inseparably linked with Love. If there were a single Aphrodite there would be a single Love, but as there are two Aphrodites, it follows that there must be two Loves as well. Now what are the two Aphrodites? One is the elder and is the daughter of Uranus and had no mother; her we call the Heavenly Aphrodite. The other is younger, the child of Zeus and Dione, and is called the Common Aphrodite.

                              Plato's *Symposium*

I learned both what is secret and what is manifest, for wisdom, the fashioner of all things, taught me.

                              Wisdom of Solomon 7:21–22

JUST as writers of apocryphal works tried to incorporate elements of older religions into Christianity, so church fathers set out to demonstrate that the New Testament was a fulfillment of the Old Testament. They saw Old Testament figures as "types" foreshadowing New Testament figures, and they saw the Magdalen, among other "types" of Old Testament figures, as a second Eve. In his *Sainte Marie-Madeleine: Quelle est donc cette femme?* published in 1963, Father Damien Vorreux points out that Hippolytus, along with other early Christians, saw the Magdalen of John's Gospel finding Jesus "the tree of life" in the garden as a fulfillment of Eve separated from the tree of life in the Garden of Eden.[1] The conception of the Magdalen as a second Eve survives, with all its ambiguous implications, to affect the figure of the Magdalen in literature and art. We have seen one example of the conception's survival in the account of the transformation of Jean Cousin's *Eva Prima Pandora* into a representation of the Magdalen.

Another most important influence not only on the figure represented in art and literature but also on the Saint Mary Magdalene honored by the Roman Catholic Church is the identification of the Christ's anointers with the Bride of the Song of Songs. The identification, made by several church fathers, including Hippolytus, is strikingly interpreted by the Neoplatonist Origen in his third-century commentary and homilies on the Song of Songs. Although Origen, in the tradition of the Eastern Church, does not identify as one person the Magdalen, Mary of Bethany and the "sinner" anointer of the Christ, many Western church fathers do attribute to the composite Magdalen Origen's "mystical" interpretations of the anointers of the Christ. The Magdalen's festival day is, as the Roman Catholic missal testifies, celebrated, wherever it is still celebrated, with a part of the Song of Songs.

These are the words spoken by the Bride, or the "maiden," as she longs for her lover in the spring: "Upon my bed by night I sought him whom my soul loves; I sought him, but I found him not; I called him but he gave no answer" (Song of Songs 3:1 [RSV]). And immediately following are the lines devoted to the Magdalen:

> I will rise now and go about the city,
> in the streets and in the squares;
> I will seek him whom my soul loves.
> I sought him, but found him not.
> The watchmen found me, as they went about
> in the city. "Have you seen him whom my
> soul loves?" Scarcely had I passed them,
> when I found him whom my soul loves.

I held him, and would not let him go
until I had brought him to my mother's
house, and into the chamber of her that
conceived me. I adjure you, O daughters
of Jerusalem, by the gazelles or the hinds
of the field, that you stir not up nor
awaken love until it please.
[Song of Songs 3.2–5][2]

Also for the celebration of the Magdalen's day are lines from Song of Songs 8:

Set me as a seal upon your heart,
    as a seal upon your arm;
for love is strong as death;
    jealousy is cruel as the grave.
Its flashes are flashes of fire,
    a most vehement flame.
Many waters cannot quench love,
    neither can floods drown it.
If a man offered for love
    all the wealth of his house,
it would be utterly scorned.
[Song of Songs 8:6–7][3]

The parallel between the Magdalen of John's Gospel, shown seeking the Christ and finding him, and the Bride of the Song of Songs, searching for her "Beloved" and finding him, is obvious. But the total impact on the mythical Magdalen of the linking of her with the Bride celebrated in the old Song is less readily perceived and, I think, more profound. However interpreted, the Song of Songs connotes, as it denotes, eroticism, an unashamed eroticism. Even though the frank eroticism permeating the Song flashed danger signals to Judeo-Christianity, the hymn to sexual love retained a powerful hold on both Jewish and Christian imaginations. And the Magdalen's long-lived grip on imaginations stems, at least in part, from a power similar to that of the Song of Songs.

To guard against the power of the Song's sensual imagery, first Rabbinical and then Christian Neoplatonists devised symbolical interpretations of the dramatic poem. The method of interpretation, commonly referred to as allegorical, is based on the idea that layers of meaning are hidden beneath the surface of words or figures or events. It is the very method used by the "pure spiritual" Magdalen in her fourfold explication of the ways of saving the soul from the "Counterfeit Spirit," the explication for which Jesus, in the *Pistis Sophia*, so highly praised the "inheritor of the Light." Origen applies to the Song of Songs, however, the threefold rather than the usual fourfold method of exegesis.[4] The threefold method reflects application of the Platonic idea of the tripartite man, body-soul-spirit, to the interpretation of the written word.[5] And Origen uses the Platonic belief in "the correspondence between all things on earth and their celestial prototypes" to defend the validity of his ability to make "manifest what is hid" under the words of the Song of Songs.[6] To support the Platonic doctrine of correspondences, Origen explicates at length words from the book of Wisdom which is, like the Song of Songs, anachronistically attributed to Solomon: "I learned both what is secret and what is manifest, for Wisdom, the fashioner of all things, taught me." [7]

Origen's use of the tripartite man and his attempt to separate the soul from the body reflect an affinity with Gnosticism. And like the Gnostics, Origen also borrows the famous Greek dictum "Know thyself" and transforms the Greek concept into the necessity for the Soul to come to know herself, her origin and destination, "while she is set among the mysteries." [8] The Soul must, Origen adds, "give heed to the recognition of herself through the study of doctrine and sacred pursuits." [9]

Origen interprets the Bride of the Song of Songs as the Soul, Psyche, and the Bridegroom as Love, Eros-Christ.[10] The Bride is also the "Mary who anoints the feet of Jesus and wipes them with her hair." [11] And she is at the same time the Church or Jerusalem, "the mother of all of us," present from the beginning of time.[12] The Bride-Church must be purified of "false teachings" which she learned living among the "heathen." [13] Purified, she then unites with her Bridegroom-Word-Christ, who provides the "living water that is to turn her arid lands into the fruitful paradise of the second Adam and Eve." [14]

Origen recognizes the Song of Songs as an epithalamium. It is not, however, a "carnal" wedding song but is, he says, "a drama of mystical meaning." [15] He strongly urges that no one read the Song unless he is free of "passion." [16] For it will, he says, lead any man who "lives only after the flesh" to "fleshly lust." Origen praises the Greek sages for producing similar works intended to lead man to the "truth" through "heavenly love." [17] But, Origen adds, clearly alluding to Plato's *Symposium*, those "banquets of words" have too often been "perverted" by "carnal men" to "foster vicious longings and the secrets of sinful love." [18] He admonishes his audience: "Mortify your carnal senses." [19] And again, "If these words are not to be spiritually understood, are they not mere tales? If they conceal no hidden mystery, are they not unworthy of God? He, therefore, who can discern the spiritual sense of Scripture or, if he cannot, yet desires to do so, must strive his utmost to live not after flesh and blood, so that he may become worthy of spiritual mysteries and—if I may speak more boldly—of spiritual desire and love, if such indeed there be." [20]

The scripture, Origen says, uses names applicable to the "outer man" for the "inner man," and just as "illicit love" may happen to the outer man so that he loves a "harlot" or an "adulteress" so it may happen to the inner man.[21] Origen distinguishes Eros, "carnal love," from Christ-Eros, "spiritual love," but says that both Christ and Eros "throw the dart" which gives the "wound of love." [22] Darts from unseen demons bring men to fornication and other sins, but the "sweet dart of Christ's knowledge" makes the "smitten one" burn with love for the Word, gives "health-bestowing wounds." [23]

Origen not only echoes the Gnostics but also recalls the distinction between the "Common" and the "Heavenly" Love drawn by Pausanius in Plato's *Symposium*. Origen does not, however, contend, as does Pausanius, that homosexual love, inspired by the Heavenly Aphrodite "who has no female strain in her" ranks above heterosexual love produced by the Common Aphrodite "who owes her birth to the conjunction of male with female." [24] Origen says, "We use love well if its objects are wisdom and truth," but when "love descends to baser levels, then we love flesh and blood." [25] The self-emasculated Origen exclaims: "How beautiful, how fitting it is to receive a wound from Love! One person receives the dart of fleshly love, another is wounded by earthly desire; but do you lay bare your members and offer yourself to the chosen dart, the lovely dart; for God is the archer indeed." [26]

Origen's rhapsody on the "wound of Love" echoes down the centuries to resound in a sixteenth-century liturgical hymn to be sung on 22 July in honor of the Magdalen. In a hymn attributed to Roberto Francesco Bellarmino, the Magdalen is pictured as "wounded by love" of the Christ, "Father of heavenly light." "With a glance" he "lit a fire of love in Magdalen and thawed the icy coldness of her heart" so that she ran to anoint the Christ's "sacred feet, wash them with her tears, wipe them with her hair, and kiss them with her lips." [27]

Although one may speak of having a "passion" for God, Origen says, the love that exists in one who loves God is "charity, which is God," and charity, "in whomsoever it exists loves nothing earthly, nothing material, nothing corruptible." [28] Origen's rejection of the material and the "corruptible" leads to his belief that the soul has "inner senses" which Christ satisfies.[29] And this belief is implicit in his exegesis of the opening words of the Song of Songs: "O that you would kiss me with the kisses of your mouth!" The Bride is not, Origen insists, longing for her lover's kisses, but she is the Church-Mary-Soul longing for the "holy mysteries" of the Church, "the Word of God." [30] The Christ, Origen continues, delights all the senses of the "perfected Soul," for she can taste, smell, see, hear, and touch him.[31] And when the Bride exclaims to her Beloved, "Your anointing oils are fragrant," she is, Origen says, speaking of the "cosmetics" of the Soul. The "cosmetics" lead the Bride to the discovery of the "vanity of the world" and the "deceitful marvels of perishable things" and finally to the knowledge of the "mysteries" and of the "divine judgments." [32]

The ointment used by the Bride to anoint her lover is that used by Mary of Bethany to anoint the Christ, Origen explains.[33]

Furthermore, the ointment is Christ "which makes those who are anointed to be Christs themselves." When the Bride-Soul-Mary anoints the feet of the Bridegroom-Christ-Word and wipes them with her hair, the whole Church is filled with the fragrance of the "Holy Spirit." [34]

The fragrance of the Bride's ointment drifts onto the Magdalen and adheres to her until her dying day and lingers on "for seven days" after her death in the Provençal oratory where she dies. Jacobus a Voragine informs us that the "perfume of her sanctity" filled the oratory of Bishop Maximinus at Aix en Provence for seven days after her soul had flown to heaven and before her body was buried with great ceremony. [35]

Origen finds himself in great difficulty when he sets out to allegorize the lines:

> My beloved speaks and says to me:
> "Arise, my love, my fair one,
>   and come away;
> for lo, the winter is past,
> the rain is over and gone.
> The flowers appear on the earth,
> the time of singing has come,
> and the voice of the turtledove
>   is heard in our land.
> The fig tree puts forth its figs,
>   and the vines are in blossom;
>   they give forth fragrance.
> Arise, my love, my fair one,
>   and come away."
>   [Song of Songs 2:10–13] [36]

Origen confesses that he is like "a hunter, following a hot trail," and thinking he is close to the "hidden lair, he is all of a sudden forsaken by the track-marks" as he tries to chase down the "meaning of the words of the Scripture." [37] But he does manage to find "hidden meanings" to make the passage "spiritually" acceptable.

The Word-Bridegroom, Origen decides, is in these words of the Song exhorting the Soul-Bride "to forsake things bodily and visible and to hasten to those things that are not of the body and are spiritual." [38] And when the Bridegroom says, "Lo, the winter is past, the rain is gone," he "both indicates the actual time of the Passover," when he "suffered," and the fulfillment of the "prophetical showers." [39] Origen hastens to add, "fearing lest perhaps the meaning, which was obvious to us at the moment, should escape our memory," that with the "coming of the Lord the flowers appear on the land, the fig tree bears, and the vineyards yield their sweet smell." [40] The Song's lines hymning the resurrection of life on earth test Origen's ingenuity, but he cannot resist their power and indulges in a second long spiritual exegesis, applying to the Church these lines celebrating the annual death of winter and rebirth of spring.[41]

In one of his sermons on the Song of Songs, Origen elaborates on the absolute distinction between "carnal" and "spiritual" love. "And as one sort of food is carnal and another spiritual, and as there is one drink for flesh and another for spirit, so there is love of the flesh which comes from Satan, and there is another love, belonging to the spirit, which has its origin in God; and nobody can be possessed by the two loves." [42] It is just such a radical dualism which is embodied in the Magdalen as the ambiguous Venus in sackcloth.

Origen's dualism leads to his drawing another unfortunately long-lived distinction between seeming opposites. In attempting to interpret the Bride's words, "I am dark but comely, O daughters of Jerusalem" (Song 1:5), he sets forth the idea that "black" is "evil" while "white" is "good." Here the Bride-Anointer is the "sinner" who anointed the Christ. She is "black" as a sinner but is becoming beautiful and therefore "white and good" through penitence.[43] "She has repented of her sins," Origen says, and "beauty is the gift conversion has bestowed; that is the reason she is hymned as beautiful. She is called black, however, because she has not yet been purged of every stain of sin, she has not yet been washed unto salvation, nevertheless she does not stay dark-hued, she is becoming white." [44] He warns his congregation to "take heed lest your soul be described as black and ugly" and exhorts them to repent so that they may acquire not altogether white souls but a sort of "Ethiopian beauty." [45]

In less than "spiritual" language, Origen describes the breasts of those who are to be the "Brides of Christ." "The breasts of the chaste are not bruised," he says, "but the paps of harlots are wrinkled with folds of loose skin. The breasts of the chaste are firm and round and rosy with virginity. Such receive the Bridegroom-Word." [46]

Through Origen's identification of the Christ's anointers with the Bride of the Song of Songs, the Magdalen becomes the Christ's sister-bride, "soror mea sponsa." Despite the fact that Origen was anathematized by the Roman Catholic Church, his mystical interpretation of the Song survived. And although Origen does not view the anointers of the Christ as the Magdalen, the Western Church, accepting the popular identification of the Magdalen with both the prostitute and the woman of Bethany pictured in the canonical Gospels as anointers of Jesus, celebrates the Magdalen as the Bride of the Song of Songs.

The Magdalen as the Christ's sister-bride lives on both in the literary figure and in the Mary Magdalene honored by the Roman Catholic Church. Raymond-Léopold Bruckberger, for example, subscribes his twentieth-century Neoplatonic "biography" of the Magdalen "soror mea sponsa." [47] And just as Origen could not quite escape the use of erotic language in his allegorical exegesis of the old love Song, so Bruckberger could not avoid the use of erotic language in his life of the beautiful "courtesan" who becomes the Christ's mystic sister-bride.

"In all allegory there is mystery," Henry Osborn Taylor observes in *The Classical Heritage of the Middle Ages*, "and in all allegory mysticism, with its inherent spirit of contradiction and paradox, is implicit." [48] The spirit of contradiction and paradox implicit in Origen's interpretation of the Song of Songs shows up explicitly in Origen's failure to escape the power of erotic language and images in his attempt to "spiritualize" the sensuous love of the Bride and her Beloved into the love of the Church-Mary-Soul and the Word-Christ. The paradox, an erotic asceticism inherent in mysticism, lives on in the mythical Magdalen who takes on the appellative "Venus in sackcloth."

The sensuality, the frank eroticism expressed, and indeed

celebrated in the Song of Songs, no mystical, symbolic, Neoplatonic interpretation can hide. Nor can Rabbinical and Christian
use of allegorical exegesis as a means of incorporating the old love
song into Judeo-Christianity hide the reality of the ancient song's
appeal to desires deep in humanity. The spell cast by the Song of
Songs on the human imagination springs not from mystical
interpretations of the "hidden meanings" of the Song but rather, I
think, from the Song's own religious and universal power. Its
universal as well as its religious power is evident in the fact that
there exist Egyptian, Babylonian, Hindu, and Greek parallels to
the Song of Songs.[49] The religious power of the Song grows out
of its transcendence of the fear of death through the celebration of
the "mystery" of sexual love and of life on earth.

"In pre-modern societies," Mircea Eliade states in *Rites and
Symbols of Initiation*, "sexuality, like all the other functions of life,
is fraught with sacredness. It is a way of participating in the
fundamental mystery of life and fertility." [50] The continuity of
life on earth is evoked by the dramatized sexual union of woman
with man. And Theophile James Meek argues convincingly that
the Song of Songs originally represented the ritual wooing and
marriage of a goddess and a god for the revival of life in the
world. The goddess, Mother Earth, whatever her name, lan-
guishes for the heaven god, searches for him, finds him, and unites
with him, and so revives the fertility of the vineyards, of the
fields, of the flocks, and of humanity.[51] The ancient concept of
nature's seasonal death followed by joyous rebirth is transformed
by Judeo-Christian thought to become a part of the liturgies
during Passover and Easter, as Meek points out.[52]

In the heart of the old fertility song, the Sister-Bride searching
for and finding her Bridegroom, sounds a beat akin to that of the
lament of Isis as she searches for her brother-husband Osiris. Isis
laments:

> O Beautiful Boy, come to thy house,
> immediately, immediately, I do not see thee,
> my heart weepeth for thee, my two eyes follow
> thee about. I am following thee so that I may
> see thee, I wait to see thee, Beautiful Prince,
> lo, I wait to see thee.

And finding Osiris, her "Lord," she rejoices:

> O An, it is good to see thee. Come to thy
> beloved one, Beautiful Being triumphant!
> Come to thy sister! Come to thy wife! [53]

It is the heart of the Song of Songs which centers the Magdalen's festival day.

"It may be a far cry," Wilfred Schoff says in "The Offering Lists in the Song of Songs and Their Political Significance," "from an Oriental Goddess of Love with her many names, Ishtar, Shulmanitu, Aphrodite, Venus, to the Daughter of Jerusalem, the Bride of Yahweh, the Holy Catholic Church," and Schoff adds that it is also a far cry from Tammuz or Adonis to Yahweh or the Christ, "but the connection of both with the original types is unbroken and unmistakable." [54] The connection of the Magdalen with a goddess of love is also, I think, unbroken and unmistakable. For when Origen linked the Christ's anointers with the Bride of the Song of Songs he, though quite unintentionally, not only secured the link between the composite Magdalen and an ancient fertility goddess but also assured the Magdalen's long-lived grip on human imaginations.

The great goddess of antiquity was, Erich Neumann observes in *The Great Mother*, "in the patriarchal development of the Judeo-Christian West, with its masculine, monotheistic trend toward abstraction, disenthroned." Neumann adds that the goddess did, however, survive in Christianity through underground doctrines, and Neumann sees her survival, as did Frazer and other earlier scholars, in Mary the mother of Jesus.[55] The medieval cult of the Virgin Mary lends support to Neumann's observation. But the "great goddess," with all her ambiguity, visibly survives in the mythical Magdalen shaped around the Mary Magdalene of the New Testament canonical Gospels. For it is the Magdalen who was primarily used as a vessel to hold "underground doctrines" in such apocryphal writings as the *Gospel of Mary*, the *Pistis Sophia*, and the *Books of the Savior* and to whom attributes of a seductive goddess of love, of a goddess of wisdom and of generation, were attached. And it is, as we shall see, the Magdalen whose rise to fame in the West during the surfacing of "underground doctrines" in the complex Middle Ages rivals the cult of the Virgin Mary.

The survival into the Middle Ages of the Magdalen to whom early Christian imaginations gave characteristics of ancient goddesses may be accounted for by the continuing life of the composite Magdalen in sermons preached by Western priests who, through the centuries, use her as an example of the Christ's sister-bride, the Christian penitent, the recipient of the Christ's love and mercy, the first to whom the risen Christ appeared, a second Eve, the apostle to the apostles, the contemplative soul, the Church itself. And coinciding in time with the survival of the Magdalen in sermons is the continuing vitality in medieval traditions of ancient gods and goddesses themselves.

One of the ways in which ancient deities survived throughout the Middle Ages has been treated by Jean Seznec in *The Survival of the Pagan Gods.*[56] The gods survived, Jean Seznec points out, through the use of Euhemerism from the early Christian period into the Middle Ages.[57] Euhemerus, in the third century before the advent of Christianity, set forth the idea that gods were "recruited" from mortal men, and the idea was used by early Christian writers as a weapon against "paganism."[58] Saint Augustine, for example, defends the idea set forth by the "historian Euhemerus."[59] Although Augustine argues against the "shameful" worship of the "Great Goddess," he does accept the words of "those grave historians" who consider deified "mortals" as deserving "divine honors from mortals because they conferred on them many benefits to make this life more pleasant for them."[60] Augustine also preserves many of the gods and goddesses of antiquity by incorporating them into Judeo-Christian "history," and he draws a scholastically "nice distinction" between "history" and "fable." Mercury and Hercules, for instance, Augustine places in the time of the Exodus from Egypt. And "far more ancient than these," Augustine adds, was Minerva (Athene), "the inventress of truly many works, and more readily believed to be a goddess because her origin was so little known. For what is sung about her having sprung from the head of

Jupiter (Zeus) belongs to the region of poetry and fable, and not to that of history and real fact." [61]

It is as "benefactors of mankind," Jean Seznec notes, that the deities of antiquity figure in Peter Comestor's popular twelfth-century *Historia scholastica*, where Isis assumes the role of teacher of the alphabet and writing to the Egyptians; Minerva the role of teacher of the arts, including the art of weaving; Venus the role of teacher of the courtesan's art.[62]

While the ancient gods and goddesses survive in medieval "historical" traditions, beatified Christian figures assume the roles of the old deities as "benefactors" of medieval "mankind." The Magdalen, as patron saint of many craftsmen, including the weavers, assumes the role of Athene-Minerva. And in a medieval Easter play, we shall see her mocked when she takes over Venus's role as the teacher of the courtesan's art.

"The pagan divinities," Jean Seznec observes, "served as a vehicle for ideas so profound and so tenacious that it would have been impossible for them to perish." [63] The Magdalen also becomes, through eclectic imaginations of writers of apocryphal works and through Origen's mystical interpretation of the Song of Songs, a vehicle carrying ideas apparently so deeply planted in cultural traditions that they cannot be uprooted. The Magdalen embodies the paradoxical ideas of the feminine as the source and destroyer of life, as the dangerous but fascinating seducer of men, as the pure spirit Sophia-Wisdom.

To the mythologized Magdalen we may apply Joseph Campbell's observation: "The Sumero-Babylonian astral mythology identified the aspects of the cosmic female with the phases of the planet Venus. As morning star she was the virgin, as evening star the harlot, as lady of the night sky the consort of the moon, and when extinguished under the blaze of the sun she was the hag of hell. Wherever the Mesopotamian influence extended, the traits of the goddess were touched by the light of this fluctuating star." [64] And a Tammuz calls for an Ishtar or a Siduri, an Adonis for an Aphrodite or a Venus, even if she must put on sackcloth to enter the holy circle.

By shaping myths around the Mary Magdalene sketched in the

canonical Gospels, writers during Christianity's stormy beginnings gave to the composite Magdalen conflicting attributes of
the great goddesses of antiquity and so not only fulfilled a desire
for continuity of old concepts and figures but also bequeathed to
the Western world the prototype for the long-lived Magdalen.
More myths are, however, attached to the Magdalen before the
prototype is fulfilled in the highly popular figure who is both
worshipped and caricatured during the complex Middle Ages.
We turn now to the later metamorphoses of the figure and to her
rise to fame in medieval Europe as Saint Mary Magdalene.

6

The Rise of the Magdalen in the Middle Ages

Earth, Earth, O Earth, our mother!
May the All-Wielder, Ever-Lord grant thee
Acres a-waxing, upwards a-growing,
Pregnant with corn and plenteous in strength.
                          Anglo-Saxon Charm

Terrified by the thought of hell, I had condemned myself to this
prison, my sole companions being wild beasts and scorpions.
Often, however, a chorus of dancing girls cavorted around me.
Emaciated, pale, my limbs cold as ice, still my mind boiled with
desire. Lust's fires bubbled about me even when my flesh was as
good as dead. Completely helpless, I would fling myself at the feet
of Jesus, water them with my tears, wiping them with my hair.
                          Saint Jerome, Letter to Eustochium

I call Abelard to witness. In the name of wife there may be
something more holy, more imposing, but the name mistress was
ever to me a more charming sound.
                          Heloise to Abelard

ALTHOUGH the prototype for the popular figure of the
Magdalen was created during the early centuries of Christianity,
the Magdalen does not emerge as a highly popular figure in the
Western world until the twelfth century. It is in the century
which Charles Homer Haskins characterizes as a period of
"intensification of intellectual life," and which Steven Runciman
designates as "a great age of heresy" that the fictionalized
Magdalen is resurrected in Western Christendom.[1] It is not, I

think, mere chance that the Magdalen again captivates imaginations in the century of the Cathari, of the Waldensian men and
women "preachers," of the wandering scholars, of Eleanor of
Aquitaine and her "courts of love," of the Crusades, of the
ill-fated lovers Heloise and Abelard.

The Magdalen's rise to fame in the West coincides with the
emergence of dualistic ideas similar to those we have seen
prevalent during the early centuries of Christianity when the
Magdalen myth was taking shape in the East. The Crusades, as
Steven Runciman observes in *The Medieval Manichee*, carried old
Eastern dualism into the West, particularly into France and
Germany.[2] And the Magdalen was, as we shall see, one of the
vessels in which the old radical dualism was carried.

In the very places where the Magdalen attracts especial
attention, the old dualistic split between the "material" and the
"spiritual" surfaces above ground. The Gnostic contempt for the
material world, with its concomitant ambivalence toward woman,
parallels, for example, views held by the Waldensians founded
about A.D. 1170 at Lyons, where in the same century a vineyard
was named for the Magdalen. Both men and women, Bernard
Gui writes in the fourteenth century of the Waldensian "heretics," "ran about through the towns" preaching in public and in
churches. They had certain gospels and books of sayings by such
people as Saint Augustine and Saint Jerome translated into
French, and these they used as texts.[3] "Also," Bernard Gui
records, "the Waldensians recommend continence to their
believers. They concede, however, that burning passion ought to
be satisfied, in whatever shameful way." [4]

In the same century in Provence the wandering preacher
Henry the Monk urged his male followers to marry prostitutes, to
burn their cosmetics, and then to lead "chaste" lives with them.[5]
Meanwhile, the Cathari were insisting that only women who
became men could be elected for "salvation" and that marriage
was "fornication." [6] And in twelfth-century Paris the upsurge of
radical dualism led the famous love of a guilt-ridden Abelard and
his "sister"-bride Heloise to its tragic conclusion.

Parallel with the spread of dualism and the rise of the

Magdalen cult came an increase both in asceticism and conflicting views of Eros and of woman. We perceive something of the persistence of the old ambivalence toward woman in the distinctions drawn by Ernst Robert Curtius between the four views of Eros dominating the twelfth century.[7] Curtius, in *European Literature and the Latin Middle Ages*, categorizes the major views as asceticism, mysticism, humanism, and profligacy. The ascetic ideal, represented by Bernard of Morlaix in his *De contemptu mundi*, curses Eros and womankind.[8] We can readily see that Bernard of Morlaix perpetuates the attitude evident in the second-century Apocrypha whose writers also held the world and woman-matter in contempt.

Mysticism, represented by Bernard of Clairvaux, who wrote no less than eighty-six sermons on the Song of Songs, spiritualizes Eros, as we have seen Origen attempt to do in his commentary and homilies on the Song of Songs. Humanism, exemplified by Bernard Silvestris of Tours, consecrates Eros. Since Bernard Silvestris, in his *De universitate mundi*, turns back to ancient Eastern sources, he blends religion with sexuality and views woman as a generative force. On the contrary, profligacy, which Curtius illustrates with the Latin poem "The Council of Love at Remiremont," debases Eros and mocks woman.[9] But "The Council of Love at Remiremont" is actually a parody on the "religion of love" which suddenly appears in Provence shortly before the Magdalen's rise to fame. Eleanor of Aquitaine and her daughter Marie hold "courts of love" to teach the "art of love" and to encourage devotion to the religion of love. Courtly love is, at least in part, a by-product of a society in which woman is viewed more as an object, a piece of property, than as an intelligent human being. And the religion of love is also a reaction against a doctrinaire view of sexual love as "sin." The religion of love therefore deifies the "carnal Eros" which Origen had tried to banish from the minds of his third-century congregation. And courtly love places woman on a pedestal and idolizes her, particularly if she is an adulterous "lady." The medieval figure of the Magdalen takes on characteristics revealing all of these conflicting views of Eros and of woman. The contradictory attitudes toward woman color especially the figure represented in the Christian drama.

By the time the playwrights isolate the Magdalen for special attention, however, Mary Magdalene has become an important religious figure in the Western Catholic Church. Around the religious figure cluster more myths which bring about further metamorphoses of the Magdalen. Victor Saxer has thoroughly treated the Western cult of the Magdalen in *Le Culte de Marie Madeleine en Occident,* and he has touched on the Eastern origins of the cult in an article, "Les Saintes Marie Madeleine et Marie de Béthanie dans le Tradition Liturgique et Homilétique Orientale." [10]

That the cult of the Magdalen actually originates in the East should not surprise us since we have seen the prominent place given her in early Eastern writings. First honored as simply one of the "myrophores," myrrh-bearers, who go to anoint the body of the Christ, she soon gains glory as a "preacher." [11] The Magdalen is, by the seventh century, individually honored at Ephesus on 22 July. There had grown up sometime in the sixth century a belief that her tomb was next to the Seven Sleepers' Cave at Ephesus.[12] The "great and admirable" Magdalen, one liturgical notice reports, "despite the weakness of her sex," had, after Christ's ascension, gone with John the Evangelist to "preach" at Ephesus where she, "being mortal," died on 22 July and was buried "near the Seven Sleepers' Grotto." [13] But her body was supposedly moved to Constantinople in the late ninth or early tenth century, and there too she was honored on 22 July.[14] An eleventh-century notice from a Coptic church indicates that she was also honored in Egypt as one who had preached there.[15]

The linking of the Magdalen with John at Ephesus may derive from the much-copied but highly controversial *Acts of John.*[16] Clearly a popular work, the *Acts of John* combines an adventure tale with blatantly dualistic ideas, and it includes a pastoral scene in which Jesus and the disciples join in a round dance. John, in the *Acts,* is shown destroying the temple of Artemis (Diana) at Ephesus and converting the people who are still, John says, echoing Paul's words in the Acts of the Apostles, "being corrupted" by their "ancient mysteries." [17] John is also pictured at his approaching death praying to Jesus as "thou who hast kept me pure for thyself and untouched by union with woman; who when I wished to marry in my youth didst appear to me and say to me, 'John, I need thee.' " John thanks Jesus for having rid him of the "foul madness that is in the flesh." [18]

From the *Acts of John*, or a similar source, must come not only the linking of the Magdalen with John as a "preacher" at Ephesus but also the medieval explanation for the Magdalen's having become a prostitute. John Mirk says in his *Festial* that, "as many bokys tellyth," when John the Evangelist should have married the Magdalen, Christ bade John to follow him, "and soo he dyd," and the Magdalen was "wrath" and therefore gave herself "all to lechery." [19]

Just as the Gospel of John sharpens the Magdalen's closeness to the Christ, so popular legend closely links the Magdalen with John. "John the Virgin" was, as we have seen, one of the disciples pictured in the second-century *Pistis Sophia* where Jesus announced that "Maria the Magdalene and John the Virgin" would excel all his disciples in the "Kingdom of the Light." And the Magdalen of the *Gospel of Mary* is the one who "preaches" to the male disciples and who goes with them to "proclaim the gospel."

The old Eastern tradition of the Magdalen as a preacher was taken over by Aix-en-Provence in the early twelfth century when Aix claimed to have been evangelized by the Magdalen in the first century of the Christian era and to have her tomb.[20] Traditions do not easily perish. They travel, sometimes disguised, sometimes as stowaways. Behind the Western medieval Magdalen is the Magdalen of the Apocrypha.

Aix was only one of many French cities which honored the Magdalen. Marseilles, believing that the Magdalen had come from Aix to convert Marseilles from the worship of antique deities, rebuilt in the thirteenth century a temple, later believed to be the temple of Diana, and dedicated in the rebuilt chapel an altar to the Magdalen.[21] On the altar was a bas-relief in marble representing the Magdalen preaching in Marseilles. At this altar during Easter services, from the thirteenth into the eighteenth century, a procession chanted in Provençal a song which recalled the Magdalen's conversion of the king and queen of Marseilles. The tradition continued through the centuries until the Provençal song was suppressed, and finally mass was forbidden to be held in the building, and in 1781 the Magdalen-Diana chapel was demolished.[22]

In the tradition of the Magdalen's succession to Diana at Marseilles, we see again the association in the human imagination of the Magdalen with the great goddesses of antiquity. The linking of the composite Magdalen with the goddess Diana, a protector of woman and of life, directly affects the Magdalen whose "life" is recorded by Jacobus a Voragine. For it is the Saint Mary Magdalene of *The Golden Legend* who brings about the conception of a child for the queen of Marseilles, restores to life the queen who dies in childbirth, and preserves the lives of the baby and the mother. The attributes of a fertility goddess implicit in the Magdalen of the apocrypha begin to bear fruit with the rising popularity of the saint during the period frequently designated as the Age of Faith. As the patron saint of gardeners and vineyard growers she, like the "Earth, our mother" addressed by the Anglo-Saxon tiller of the soil in his charm, provides for medieval man "pregnant acres a-waxing." [23] She reflects the humanistic view of woman as a generative force, the view expressed by Bernard Silvestris in his *De universitate mundi*.

Yet, like the fourth-century Saint Jerome, the medieval Magdalen is also "condemned" to the "prison" of an ascetic hermit, detached from the blossoming earth.[24] For attached to the Magdalen during the Middle Ages is the legend of Mary of Egypt, a beautiful prostitute who, according to legend, in the third century was suddenly converted to Christianity and, deciding to deny forever after the pleasures of the flesh, became a hermit. Fed only by loaves she took with her and clothed only in her long hair, she spent the remaining forty-seven years of her life as a penitent in the desert. Like the fourth-century Jerome, Mary of Egypt too was tormented by the "cravings of the flesh" for the first seventeen years of her life away from men, but she finally conquered the "fires of lust" that "bubbled about" her.[25]

The legend of the converted prostitute living the life of a hermit, being fed by angels, and clothed only in her long hair was absorbed by the Magdalen. And during the sixteenth century, Quentin Massys, in a pair of easel paintings, links the Magdalen with Mary of Egypt (figs. 5 and 6). Each of the nude hermits kneels on the earth in prayerful attitude, the Magdalen with her ointment jar and its lid beside her, and Mary of Egypt with her three loaves of bread near her. Eroticism mingles with asceticism in the two chaste prostitutes whose torsos are lightly veiled with long flowing hair.

Although Mary of Egypt continued to be honored throughout the Middle Ages, the Magdalen, considered to be the first hermit, was the patron saint of the many Christian mystics who became hermits during the rise of radical dualism in the West.[26] Embalmed in the patron saint of the medieval ascetics is the "pure spiritual Mariham" of the *Pistis Sophia*. And this flesh-denying Magdalen is the subject of Donatello's provocative sculpture which we noted among the many monuments to the Magdalen.

An *Old English Martyrology*, written about A.D. 850, tells of the Magdalen's having had such a "great longing" for the Christ after his ascension that "she could no longer bear to look on any man" and therefore went "into the desert and lived there thirty years unknown to all men." She ate no human food, the legend tells us, but was daily taken to heaven by angels where "she heard something of the heavenly joys" and so "she never hungered nor thirsted." A "mass priest" found her as she was dying and buried her, "and many miracles happened at her grave." [27]

The legend of the Magdalen as a hermit is also found in a *Vita eremitica beatae Mariae Magdalenae*, which Victor Saxer believes probably came from Italy in the ninth or tenth century.[28] To the title was added in the twelfth century the designation of the Magdalen's place of hermitage as the grotto Sainte-Baume in the diocese of Marseilles.[29] From the legend, incorporated into Jacobus's life of the saint in the thirteenth century come the many and varied iconographic representations of the Magdalen as a

hermit. And Victor Saxer considers the *Vita eremitica* of the Magdalen, which appeared in many versions and was widely read during the twelfth century, the "literary" cause of the increase of hermit life in the medieval West.[30]

The medieval cult of the Magdalen was, however, by no means confined to ascetics. Throughout England, France, and Germany, with rapid multiplication of Magdalen relics and sanctuaries during the eleventh century, Mary Magdalene soon replaced the apostles and even Mary the mother of Jesus as a venerated saint.[31] Exeter, claiming to have a finger of the Magdalen, built in the tenth century the first Western sanctuary dedicated to Saint Mary Magdalene.[32] An eleventh-century rumor that a certain monk had carried the Magdalen's body from Jerusalem to Vézelay spread throughout France and drew so many pilgrims to view her "relics" that Vézelay became the center of the Magdalen cult. And Vézelay remained the pilgrimage center until the end of the thirteenth century when disputes arose among other churches who also claimed to possess the Magdalen's body.

The Church of the Magdalen, built in the twelfth century on Vézelay's "eternal hill" overlooking fertile valleys, which were during the Middle Ages filled with vineyards, rose to fame during the second Crusade. The old crypt in the well-restored Basilique de la Madeleine remains a shrine supposedly holding the Magdalen's relics. And in the crypt one can see today, among many tourists, some few "pilgrims" lighting votive candles to the once widely revered patron saint of winegrowers.

A twelfth-century statue of Sainte Marie-Madeleine, originally on the west façade of the Romanesque church now stands on a tall column in the nave. Although damaged, the figure's smiling,

5. *Mary Magdalene* by Quentin Massys.
COURTESY, JOHN G. JOHNSON COLLECTION, PHILADELPHIA

individualized face reveals the artist responsible for the work as a skilled craftsman and suggests that he was a man who did not view the Magdalen as simply one of the myrrh-bearers (fig. 7). The figure of the reformed prostitute who carries a torch in her right hand testifies to the safe journey of the old Eastern "Mariham the happy" to the West. "Maria the Magdalene" who shared Jesus' *gnosis*, who gave "light on everything," along with the "holy harlot" who anointed the Christ, appears in Vézelay as *La Madeleine*, a goddess of fertility, "the keeper of the vats," the mystic Bride of the Christ, a miracle worker.

Words broadcasting a particular miracle attributed to the Magdalen increased her fame throughout medieval Christendom. At Vézelay during Easter of 1146, Eleanor of Aquitaine and King Louis VII were present to hear the venerable Bernard of Clairvaux preach on behalf of the second Crusade. Eleanor and King Louis, as well as the famous Bernard, drew such a large crowd for the outdoor ceremony that the platform set up on the church grounds collapsed. Yet no one was injured. For the Magdalen had saved everyone present on that Easter Day.[33]

Reports of Magdalen miracles multiplied, liturgical celebrations of Saint Mary Magdalene increased, and the popular appeal of the complex Magdalen manifested its growth in numerous monuments dedicated to her. Many of those monuments, which we have viewed earlier, give ample evidence of *homo ludens*'s linking the Magdalen with goddesses of antiquity. As patron saint of the winegrowers and of gardeners, the Magdalen is consecrated by *homo ludens* as a "generative force." And like the Egyptian Isis, the Magdalen becomes a protector of ships at sea. As patron of the weavers, she reincarnates Athene-Minerva. Revered by medieval mystics, she is a "spiritualized" Venus. Transformed into a goddess, the medieval Magdalen herself takes on the power

of metamorphosis. She restores the dead to life, brings food for man from the earth, makes wine of the grape. And between the antique goddesses of love, of wisdom, of fertility and the patron saint of medieval people are the intermediary figures of the Magdalen-Sophia-Prunikos and the Bride of the Song of Songs.

Through Bernard of Clarvaux's sermons on the Song of Songs, the medieval Magdalen becomes, as the anointers of the Christ were in Origen's third-century allegorical exegeses of the Song, the sister-bride of the Christ. Bernard, like Origen, equates the Mary-Church-Bride with the contemplative soul and lauds the divine love which leads to "contemplation." [34] In his explication of the Bride's description of herself as "dark but comely," Bernard also perpetuates the old dualistic idea of dark as "evil" and white as "good," but he specifies "good" as "humility." [35] Thus the *Dames Blanches* in France and *Weissfrauen* in Germany, religious orders of reformed prostitutes devoted to the Magdalen, wore white vestments and were called "White Ladies." More importantly, however, Bernard's ecstatic rhapsody on the love and desire of the Bride-Magdalen-Church-Soul for the Bridegroom-Christ revives Origen's erotic asceticism just as it opens the door for the Magdalen's entrance into the Middle Ages as the Christ's sister-bride.[36] And on 22 July the medieval Magdalen is honored in liturgical celebrations with those lines spoken by the Bride of the ancient Song as she searches for her Beloved and finds him, when "Lo, the winter is past."

Although Bernard's mystic devotion to Mary the mother of Jesus permeates many of his sermons on the Song, his identification of the Magdalen with the Bride searching for and finding her Bridegroom contributes not only to augmented liturgical celebra-

7. A twelfth-century sculpture of the Magdalen, Basilique de la Madeleine, Vézelay.
PHOTOGRAPH COURTESY OF CAISSE
NATIONALE DES MONUMENTS HISTORIQUES,
ARCHIVES PHOTOGRAPHIQUES-PARIS

tions of the Magdalen but also to a renewed interest in the figure among writers and artists.

Three centuries after Bernard's death, Botticelli, perhaps best known for his *Birth of Venus*, pictures the Magdalen with Bernard of Clairvaux in adoration of Mary and the child Jesus. Botticelli's late fifteenth-century painting *Vierge Glorieuse*, now in the Louvre, makes visible the ambiguity in the Magdalen who was used as a vessel to carry into medieval Christendom the paradox of erotic asceticism placed in the fictionalized figure during the early centuries of Christianity. Botticelli's "contemplative" mystic, despite her thirty years alone in the desert, does not display the tangled cloak of hair with which Donatello clothes the hermit. On the contrary, Botticelli's Venus in sackcloth displays a gown of carefully groomed long brown hair, for she is at once the patron saint of hairdressers and the "heavenly Venus" who joins the twelfth-century Bernard to honor the virgin and child.

The same figure of the Magdalen who is shown in company with Bernard of Clairvaux in Botticelli's *Vierge Glorieuse* appears in a work painted by Botticelli and his assistants for a superaltar in a convent for reformed courtesans (fig. *8*). One of the large panels depicting scenes from the life of the Magdalen pictures *The Holy Trinity with Saints John the Baptist and Mary Magdalene and Tobias and the Angel*. The story of young Tobias protected by an angel is derived from an Old Testament Apocryphon, and the miniature figures of Tobias and the angel placed near the Magdalen's feet probably allude to the orphaned children of the penitent courtesans. The Magdalen is, of course, here represented as not only the mystic hermit but also the patron saint of reformed prostitutes. Centering the painting is the crucified Christ. A dove, representing the "Holy Ghost," with wings outspread rests on the Christ's shoulders while God the Father, surrounded with human-faced angels, lifts the cross and looks with compassion outside the picture at the viewer. The Magdalen shares the foreground with John the Baptist who, according to the Gospel of Matthew, lived as a hermit in the wilderness before he announced the coming of the Messiah. John the Baptist, whose tilted head mirrors that of the Christ, lifts the drapery away from the crucified Christ and, like God the Father, looks out at the viewer. But the Magdalen, with her gaunt face in profile against a halo, looks intently on the Christ and with her hands uplifted reaches out as if to embrace the dead Christ whose divinity is also marked with a halo.

Botticelli's uneasy synthesis of the "Common" and the "Heavenly" Aphrodite in the figure of the Magdalen suggests an incongruity perhaps sensed but unresolved by the Italian Renaissance artist. The incongruity implicit in Botticelli's Magdalen is to be made explicit by the sixteenth-century Lewis Wager. We shall in fact see the English playwright setting out with a will to resolve the paradox inherent in the fictionalized Venus in sackcloth.

The medieval upsurge of interest in the fictionalized Magdalen results, then, in further metamorphoses of the figure which grew out of cultural cross-fertilization during Christianity's emergence. Reasons are sought for her life of prostitution, and blame for it is placed on Jesus' having taken her betrothed John from her. She is linked with John as an evangelist at Ephesus, and her role as a preacher in the East is transported, along with her "relics," to France, where she takes over the temple of Diana and the "mysteries" of the goddess. She becomes, like the reformed prostitute Mary of Egypt, a penitent hermit but with her hermitage localized in the wilds of Sainte-Baume. She becomes a miracle worker, capable of preventing death and of bringing forth life. The potential of the complex Magdalen created in the East during early Christianity's struggles with competing religions is essentially realized during the time of the Crusades.

It is during this period of renewed cultural cross-fertilization, accompanied by encounters with other religions, that the Magdalen captures the imaginations of Western artists. Medieval playwrights are especially drawn to the complex Magdalen, whom they use, as did second-century writers, to embody conflicting views of woman and of Eros. In order to see Medieval *homo ludens* at work in his treatments of the long-lived figure, we review the "life" codified by Jacobus a Voragine and then survey

8. *The Holy Trinity with Saints John the Baptist and Mary Magdalene and Tobias and the Angel* by Sandro Botticelli and assistants.

PHOTOGRAPH COURTESY OF COURTAULD INSTITUTE GALLERIES, LEE COLLECTION, LONDON

the Magdalen's role as it expands and undergoes metamorphoses in Christian plays from the twelfth into the fifteenth century when the Digby playwright restores to the fictionalized Magdalen her role as heroine in his spectacular *Mary Magdalene.*

7

The "Biography" of Saint Mary Magdalene

> Vergil testifies,
> And well he knew the female character,
> That never any woman was so stanch
> As not to be capricious and unfixed—
> An easily offended animal.
> *The Romance of the Rose*

> For trusteth wel, it is an impossible
> That any clerk wol speak good of wyves,
> But if it be of hooly seintes lyves,
> Ne of noon oother womman never the mo.
> Who peyntede the leon, tel me who?
> By God! if wommen hadde writen stories,
> As clerkes han withinne hire oratories,
> They wolde han writen of men more wikkednesse
> Than al the mark of Adam may redresse.
> *The Wife of Bath's Prologue*

> In the popular imagination the saints were living and were as gods.
> Johan Huizinga, *The Waning of the Middle Ages*

CHAUCER'S Wife of Bath makes her bold pitch for Women's Liberation a century after the "clerk" Jean de Meun was mocking woman in his conclusion to the much-read *Romance of the Rose* begun by Guillaume de Lorris while the "clerk" Jacobus a Voragine was speaking "good" of woman in his "hooly seintes lyves." [1] At the peak of the Magdalen cult, in the thirteenth century, the Magdalen's "life" appears in Jacobus's *Legenda Sanctorum*, the legends of the saints, a work so popular and so widely translated that it came to be known as the *Golden Legend*.[2] Like many of the Apocrypha from the very first centuries of Christianity, the *Golden Legend* provided at once religious teachings and stories of adventure and romance starring Christian figures. Jacobus's *Legend* also served as a source book both of "exempla" for medieval preachers and of stories and figures for writers and artists during the closing of the Middle Ages and on into the modern period.

It is the composite Magdalen whose life Jacobus narrates, and not surprisingly he concentrates on her mission to Marseilles and the wondrous miracles she performed there, before and after her death. He does, however, open his story with the narration of her repentance. And as is his custom, he prefaces the story with an etymological explanation of the saint's name, for to the medieval Jacobus the meanings of a person's name reveal the individual's character. If the name does not reveal the expected character, etymology is distorted to bring out the traits Jacobus wishes to emphasize. Two of the meanings applied to "Mary" by Jacobus have a familiar ring. They remind us not only of the Magdalen in the *Gospel of Mary* enlightening the male disciples with knowledge secretly given her by the Christ but also of the "pure spiritual Mariham" who is, in the *Pistis Sophia*, chosen to share the divine "light" with the Light of Lights.

"Mary" is interpreted, Jacobus begins, "bitter sea, or illuminatrix, or illuminata," which symbolize penance, inward contemplation, and heavenly glory. These are, Jacobus says, the three things for which Jesus praised Mary when he told Martha that her sister Mary had chosen the "best part." As the "illuminata," the enlightened, the Magdalen is now illumined with the light of perfect knowledge in her mind, and she will be illumined with the light of glory in her body.[3] She is called "illuminatrix," the giver of light, Jacobus explains, because she "drank avidly" of the light which afterward she poured out in abundance, and through "inward contemplation" she received the light with which she later enlightened others.[4] Within the medieval figure of the

Magdalen as "the enlightened" and "the giver of the light" glows the still perceptible "Inheritor of the Light" who starred in second-century Gnostic writings. And Jacobus, like the earlier writers, also emphasizes the close bond between the Magdalen and the Christ.

Holding to the old tradition of identifying the Magdalen with the "sinner" who, according to the Gospel of Luke, anointed the Christ, Jacobus explains "bitter sea" as the sea of bitter tears shed by the Magdalen to wash the feet of Jesus. "Magdalene" is the same as "remaining in bondage," Jacobus explains, or it means "armed, or unconquerable, or magnificent," and these words describe what the Magdalen was before, in, and after her conversion. Before her conversion she remained a prisoner bound to eternal punishment for her many sins, but she put on the "armor of penitence," and thus, unconquerable, became magnificent through the "superabundance of grace" that followed her conversion.[5]

The Magdalen, like many a mythical figure, has no childhood but springs into life a full-blown woman. She is, however, given parents by Jacobus. Her father is called Syrus and her mother Eucharia, and Mary Magdalene came of royal lineage.[6] She was, Jacobus tells us, as beautiful as she was rich. She owned the castle Magdala, while her brother owned a large part of Jerusalem, and Martha held Bethany. Martha was, however, entrusted with protection of her brother's and sister's properties since Lazarus was in the army, and the Magdalen so completely abandoned her body to "voluptuous pleasure" that she lost her own name and was called only "the sinner." [7] Jacobus's explanation for the identification of the Magdalen with Luke's anonymous "sinner" recalls the second-century Sophia Prunikos. Just as the Pistis Sophia lost her name when she fell into the "darkness of the matter," so the medieval Magdalen loses her name when she falls into prostitution.

Details of the Magdalen's life of "sin," ignored by Jacobus, are, as we shall see, filled in by some playwrights contemporary with him. And in the Digby play *Mary Magdalene*, the heroine's castle appears on stage to be besieged by the seven "deadly sins."

Jacobus promptly tells the story of the Magdalen's journey to the house of Simon the Leper to wash Jesus' feet with her "bitter sea" of tears, wipe them with her hair, and anoint them with precious ointment. Jacobus explains her going to the house of Simon to find Jesus as "divine inspiration." But the anointing scene holds for Jacobus none of the symbolic significance which it held for Origen or for Bernard of Clairvaux. Jacobus explains it simply as a custom of the people living in "that hot climate" to use ointment frequently. Following Luke's account, Jacobus concludes the anointing scene with Jesus reproaching Simon for his insult to the Magdalen and forgiving the woman "because she loved much."

But Jacobus goes beyond Luke to point out the close bond of love established between the Magdalen and the Christ. From this time onward, Jacobus says, the Lord held her in great favor and demonstrated publicly many signs of his love for her, and he enumerates the favors bestowed upon the Magdalen by Jesus.[8] Jesus expelled seven demons from her, admitted her completely into his love, welcomed her into his friendship, accepted her hospitality, and was always delighted to defend her against those who criticized her. He could not keep from weeping when he saw her in tears.[9] And it was for love of her that the Christ resurrected her dead brother Lazarus and cured her sister Martha of a flow of blood which had plagued her for seven years. It was the Magdalen who had the honor to stand at the foot of the cross when Jesus died, to anoint his body after his death, to stay at the tomb when the disciples went away, to be the first to whom the risen Christ appeared, and to be chosen by him as an "apostle to the apostles." [10] With the summary of the favors bestowed upon the composite Magdalen by the Christ concluded, Jacobus plunges enthusiastically into the medieval story of the Magdalen's journey to Marseilles.

Fourteen years after the Christ's ascension, the story goes, Mary Magdalene was entrusted to Saint Maximinus, one of the "seventy-two disciples of the Lord," by Saint Peter to go out to "sow the word of God." The Magdalen, along with Martha and Lazarus and a number of other Christian missionaries, was thrown by the "infidels" into a ship without a rudder and launched into the deep. But the ruse to drown the Christians failed, of course, for the ship was "guided by the power of God" safely to the port of Marseilles. Since no one there would give the strangers shelter, the Christians had to take refuge beneath the porch of a "pagan" temple. It was Mary Magdalene who, when she saw the "pagans" going to worship their "idols," arose "with calm mien and prudent tongue" to convert the people of Marseilles to Christianity. And everyone there marveled not only at her beauty but also at her "sweet eloquence." No wonder, Jacobus exclaims, to hear such eloquence on lips that had kissed the feet of the Savior.

The Magdalen, despite her sweet eloquence, has a difficult time in her attempt to convert the king and queen of Marseilles to her religion. Three times she has to appear in a vision to the king and queen with threats of God's wrath on the "heathen" before she can even convince them to give her and her fellow Christians shelter and food.[11] Finally the king asks her, one day when she is preaching to his people, to give proof of her religion by bringing about the long desired but never realized birth of a son for him and his wife. The Magdalen prays for the queen's conception, and right away the queen is pregnant. The king then decides to find out if all the Magdalen says about her God is true by going to question Peter in Rome. The queen complicates matters by insisting that she must go along with him. He argues against the queen's going since she is pregnant. But the queen, weeping at his feet, pleads, "as is the custom of women," until the king gives in to her wishes.[12] After the Magdalen puts the "sign of the cross on their mantles" to protect them from the "ancient enemy," they set sail, leaving the Magdalen in custody of their property in Marseilles.[13]

As we might expect, a storm descends on the ship at sea. The prince is born "before the natural term," the queen dies, and the infant seeks his dead mother's breast and weeps "piteously."[14] The father mourns, the seamen scream, start to throw the bad-luck corpse into the sea to stop the tempest, and the poor royal "pilgrim" is distraught. But suddenly the king sights a hill not far away from the ship and, by "pleas and bribes," persuades the seamen to let him go ashore to place his dead wife with his living infant son on her breast in a protected spot on the stony hill.

Weeping, the king cries out to the Magdalen: "O Mary Magdalene, it was to my ruin that thou didst land upon the shore of Marseilles! Why did I, unhappy man, set sail on this journey at thy admonition? Was it so that my wife should perish this way that thou didst petition God?" After further lamentation, the king begs the Magdalen, if she is "powerful," to protect his wife's soul and to keep his son from perishing. He wraps his dead wife and his crying son in his cloak and returns to the ship and soon lands in Rome.[15]

The king is taken by Peter to Jerusalem to be instructed in the Roman Catholic faith. And as he sails homeward, he returns to the hill to discover that the Magdalen has restored the queen to life, preserved the child, and taken the queen and the young prince on a tour of Jerusalem. The king and the queen hymn praises to the "blessed and glorious Mary Magdalene" who has served the queen as a midwife and watched over the child.[16] The royal family sails back to Marseilles to find the Magdalen preaching to the people.[17] Weeping, they fall at her feet and tell the "holy woman" all that has happened to them. The queen and the king are "baptized" by Saint Maximinus; the people of Marseilles destroy their temples and build Christian churches and choose Lazarus as bishop. The remaining missionaries then go to Aix to convert the people there to Christianity, and Maximinus is made bishop of Aix.[18]

Meantime, the Magdalen, avid for "heavenly contemplation," hastens to a cave "made ready for her by the hands of angels" where she remains for thirty years unknown to anyone.[19] Since the cave has no water, no herbs, no trees, the Magdalen has no "earthly food" to sustain her. But seven times daily she is taken by angels to heaven where she hears with her "bodily ears" the glorious chants of heaven and is returned "satisfied" to her grotto.[20]

One day a priest, living in a "cell" not far from the Magdalen's grotto, sees the angels lifting the saint into the air and, after the space of an hour, returning her to her cave. He runs to see if the vision is real, but as he draws near the grotto, his legs become paralyzed so that he cannot move them forward. When he cries out, the Magdalen asks him to come nearer to find out the "mystery." She explains "in a voice of angelic sweetness" that she is the notorious sinner who washed the Savior's feet, wiped them with the hairs of her head, and obtained pardon for her sins. She tells the priest that she has lived in the grotto for thirty years, but the time has come for her to leave the earth forever. She requests the priest to tell Bishop Maximinus that on "Resurrection day" she will be led by angels to his oratory. Of course the priest obeys her request.[21]

An illumination from the late fifteenth-century *Sforza Book of Hours* pictures simultaneously Jacobus's narration of the Magdalen's role as a goddess of life and as a hermit lifted to heaven by angels (fig. *9*). While the startled priest, kneeling behind the Magdalen's grotto, gazes in awe at the heaven-bound Magdalen clothed in her luxuriant gold brown hair, the king of Marseilles, aboard his ship, sights on earth his resurrected wife nursing the young prince. The illumination, brilliant in its representation of the roles played by the "blessed and glorious Mary Magdalene" during her mission to Marseilles and during her stay in the grotto of Sainte-Baume, does not, however, picture the Magdalen's death, which is carefully narrated by Jacobus.

On "Resurrection morning," Jacobus reports, Maximinus sees the Magdalen at his oratory surrounded by angels and "raised two cubits above the earth" with her arms extended. The bishop is afraid to go near her, but she bids him stay. "And Maximinus himself," Jacobus says, "tells in his book" that the Magdalen's face was more radiant than the sun. The Magdalen dies as soon as the bishop has given her "the body and blood of the Lord," and her soul flies to heaven. But the perfume of her sanctity fills the oratory for seven days. Her body is buried with great pomp.[22]

The Magdalen's body was, though, "in the year 769," Jacobus continues, moved from Aix, a city which had been "utterly destroyed" by the "pagans." [23] The Magdalen appeared in person to the monk who had been sent to remove her bones from the marble tomb engraved with her "history" to give her approval. And the Magdalen's new tomb at Vézelay became a place of pilgrimage.

Jacobus denies the reports by "certain authors" that the Magdalen became a prostitute because, when she was about to be married to John the Evangelist, the Christ interrupted the wedding ceremony to call John to him. That is, Jacobus says, "a false and frivolous tale," for the espoused wife of John remained a virgin all her life and was often in company with the mother of Jesus.[24]

The miracles of the Magdalen reported by Jacobus include her restoring to life a soldier who had been slain in battle so that he could "receive the last unction" and thus go to heaven; her saving a pregnant woman on a storm-tossed ship in exchange for the woman's vow to give her child to the Magdalen's abbey at Vézelay; her restoring sight to a blind man who longed to see her church at Vézelay; her freeing a man from prison. And she convinced a "depraved clerk of Flanders," who was nevertheless, Jacobus says, devoted to her, to renounce the world and enter her monastery. And at his death, the Magdalen was seen standing at the bier and taking his soul, in the form "of a white dove," to heaven amidst chants of praise.[25]

Jacobus, despite his didactic intent, like the second-century writers of Apocrypha, pictures the Magdalen both as a goddess of life and as the Christ's feminine counterpart. The medieval Magdalen must have learned well the "mysteries" of healing the blind and restoring the dead to life, miracles which were, according to the fragments attached to the *Pistis Sophia*, taught her and the male disciples in secret by the Savior. The Magdalen pictured in the *Golden Legend* also retains radically dualistic

9. St. Mary Magdalene, illumination from the *Sforza Book of Hours*.

BEAT

concepts placed in the figure by writers of the *Gospel of Mary* and the *Pistis Sophia*. And again the medieval Magdalen is used as a vessel for the paradox of erotic asceticism. Despite the contemplative soul's rejection of material food, the Magdalen's material body becomes to her devotees in the Middle Ages a prized possession, supposedly transported from one spot of "holy ground" to another through the centuries.

From the controversial religious figure emerges a feminine figure whose influence on Western literature is profound. Just as the thirteenth-century Magdalen fulfills the prototype of the paradoxical figure shaped during the early Christian era, so the medieval Magdalen serves as a model for the many "chaste prostitutes" who during later centuries figure in romances, in plays, in novels, in films. The holy harlot, the Christ's sister-bride, the "pure spiritual Mariham" unite in the Magdalen of the *Golden Legend*, in the saint who brings about the conception of children, preserves and restores life, "enlightens" the "unenlightened," and finally takes on the radiance of the sun itself during her thirty years as a "contemplative" in the desert.

Jacobus's picture of the Magdalen as a hermit is the immediate source of the Venus in sackcloth celebrated by seventeenth-century poets in both England and France. And it is the inspiration for many artists' representations of the Magdalen. We have noted the fifteenth-century Donatello's compelling interpretation of the legendary figure. Donatello transforms the figure so that the Magdalen seems to suffer from unsatisfied hunger, physical and spiritual, rather than to joy in the heavenly food provided by the angels. And we have seen Marochetti's nineteenth-century sculpture derived from Jacobus's description of the Magdalen's being lifted from the earth by angels. But the Magdalen who centers the ring of angels in the sanctuary of l'Église Sainte-Madeleine decidedly bears no resemblance to a hermit who has lived thirty years without "earthly food." She suggests rather the view of the saint as a living goddess who has long enjoyed the fruits of her earth.

Although Jacobus's "life" of Saint Mary Magdalene serves as a handbook for artists and writers, it does not prevent *homo ludens* from exercising his own imagination in his treatment of the fictionalized figure. It is the fictionalized figure who appeals most strongly to playwrights from the first visible expansions of her role in the twelfth-century Christian plays to the fifteenth-century Digby *Mary Magdalene* and on into literature of the twentieth century.

In a twelfth-century Easter play, the Magdalen is for the first time, so far as we know, isolated by a playwright for special attention. To begin to appreciate the significance of the literary figure, we look at her roles in three medieval plays that clearly illustrate the nature of the Magdalen's expanded dramatic role. We can see the Magdalen's impact on drama by viewing her role in a twelfth-century Easter play from Tours, in a thirteenth-century Passion play from Benediktbeuern, and in a fifteenth-century French play by Jean Michel. We then observe the Digby playwright's full treatment of the fictionalized Magdalen as a heroine.

8

The Magdalen's Impact on Medieval Drama

Hail to thee, most beautiful,
  most precious gem,
hail, pride of virgins,
  most glorious virgin.
Hail, light of the world,
  hail, rose of the world.
Blanziflor and Helena,
  Venus generosa!

The God of love flies everywhere
  and is seized by desire.
Young men and young women
  are rightly joined together.

Hail, o world
  so rich in joys.
I will obey you always.
      Songs from *Carmina Burana*

So popular and so many-sided a figure as the Magdalen inevitably captured the imaginations of playwrights during the time of the wandering scholars, of the Crusades, of the rise of "Humanism," of the spread of conflicting views of Eros and of women. From the twelfth-century Easter play of Tours to the Benediktbeuern Passion play and on into Jean Michel's *Mystère de la Passion* of the fifteenth century, the Magdalen's role in the drama expands. The enlargement of the Magdalen's role in

Resurrection and Passion plays so closely parallels the growth of the plays themselves that the renewed interest in the Magdalen seems indeed responsible for the continued expansion into the fifteenth century of those plays performed during the Easter season.

In the first expansions of the literary figure, we see an attempt to isolate the Magdalen as the woman closest to the Christ, an attempt parallel with that we observed in the apocryphal writings of the early Christian period. We see also, as we saw in the transference of the Magdalen's role as an evangelist from the East to the medieval West, an attempt to localize the figure. The playwright begins to clothe the Magdalen in the fashions of his own contemporaries and to give her the language of his own people. The medieval playwright tries to humanize the Magdalen, and it is not surprising that he also attempts to humanize the Christ.

During the twelfth-century Renaissance, the simple *Quem quaeritis* play dramatizing the synoptic Gospels' accounts of the visit to the tomb by the Marys to discover that the Christ has arisen is expanded to include the recognition scene between the Magdalen and the Christ, the scene pictured only in the Gospel of John. The Magdalen is given by playwrights extended songs of lamentation for the Christ. It is during the complex twelfth century that playwrights simultaneously restore to the Magdalen the attribute of the ancient earth goddess lamenting the death of the heaven god and emphasize the manness of the Christ.

A long poetic lament for the Christ, "Deus et homo," is given the Magdalen by a Tours playwright.[1] The lament given the Magdalen in the Easter play from Tours links her at once with the Bride of the Song of Songs and with the twelfth-century audience. The Magdalen, wringing her hands and weeping, "plausis manibus, plorando," speaks of her misery, her great grief for the death of Jesus Christ, whose mercy in forgiving her for her "grave sins" she holds in memory. The Tours playwright momentarily breaks the unity of the lamenting Magdalen by trying to place her in the twelfth-century setting of the celebration of Easter day. But after the Magdalen thanks Jesus for having been "killed" for her and her audience, "pro nobis occisus est," and praises the greatness of "this day" to be celebrated in "joy," she resumes her lament.[2]

She further mourns the death of Jesus Christ, "God and man," her "hope," and the "living health of the world." She pleads: "Remember Magdalene and your friend Lazarus." She hopes, she says, to see Jesus "living," with the "sceptre of the Empire." And again lamenting, she exclaims: "What shall I do? What shall I say?"

> Deus et homo! Deus et homo! Deus et homo!
> Ihesu Christe, tu spes mea, salus viva seculi,
> Memorare Magdalene tuique amici Lazari.
> Te vivum spero videre cum sceptro imperii.
> Me misera! me misera! me misera!
> Quid agam? Heu! tristis, quid dicam?
> [Ll. 151–56]

The scene dramatized in the *Quem quaeritis* plays follows: the angel at the tomb asks the woman why she weeps, whom she seeks, and tells her and the other Marys that the Christ has arisen. But again the Magdalen laments. She lifts her hands toward heaven and begs her Lord not to abandon her but to appear to her. "Miserere Magdalene," she begs. "Pity Magdalene."[3] And in her grief, she faints. The other Marys come to her, and with Mary Jacobi holding the Magdalen by her right arm and Mary Salome holding her by her left arm, they lift the Magdalen up from the earth and tell her that her grief is "too great."[4]

The Magdalen cries out: "My heart is burning; I long to see my Lord; I search and I do not find where they have placed him."

> Ardens est cor meum; desidero videre
> Dominum meum; quero et non invenio
> ubi posuerunt eum.
> [Ll. 170–71]

The poetic laments and the dramatic action given the Magdalen by the Tours playwright in his drama celebrating Easter day demonstrate both the attempt to isolate the Magdalen as the feminine figure closest to the Christ and the desire to embody in the literary figure of the Magdalen the Bride of the old Song of Songs celebrating the return of Spring to the earth.

A twelfth-century Provençal artist tried to capture the emotional scene of the Tours figure of the Magdalen fainting from her grief for the death of Jesus. The stone carving appears in the Chapel of Modena in Italy.[5] The Magdalen in the sculpture has fainted on the sepulcher itself. Her head lies on Jesus' tomb, her hands caress the tomb. The two other Marys stand on either side of her, looking down on her with pity and trying to comfort her. Mary Salome's hand rests tenderly on the grief-stricken Magdalen. Although the figures are not personalized in this twelfth-century sculpture, the Magdalen's face, exhausted by grief, centers the artist's work and draws attention to her as an individual woman mourning for the man-god whom she, like the Bride of the Song of Songs searching for her Beloved, has sought and not yet found.

The scene treating the appearance of the risen Christ to the Magdalen is lost from the manuscript of the Tours Easter play.[6] But in the extant parts of the play we can see further enlargement of the Magdalen's role. Playing a role similar to that given her in the second-century *Gospel of Mary*, the Magdalen of the Tours play is the woman privileged to explain to the male disciples the "mystery" of the Christ's Resurrection.[7] And coinciding with the expansion of the Magdalen's role in the Tours play is the expansion of the play itself.

Included in the Tours playwright's additions to the *Quem quaeritis* play is a scene in which the three Marys go to buy ointment from a "Mercator" and his young apprentice. The merchant scene places a potentially comic figure in the Easter play and becomes, particularly in later medieval German plays, highly farcical. In, for example, *Das Erlauer Österspiel III*, where we saw Peter's long-lived resentment of the Magdalen dramatized, the merchant, the merchant's wife, and "Rubin" indulge in a lengthy bickering match.

In the Tours play, the three Marys lament the death of Jesus as they go to purchase ointment from the merchant. The Magdalen begins: "Omnipotent Father most high, most sweet head of the angels, what have your sufferings brought? O! how great is our dolor!"

> Omnipotens Pater altissime,
> angelorum rector mitissime,
> quid faciunt iste miserrime?
> Heu! quantus est noster dolor!
> [Ll. 21–24]

The two other Marys lament, with the refrain "Heu! quantus est noster dolor!" And Mary Salome announces in her lament that they are en route to buy ointment to anoint the body of Jesus as a protection against putrefaction and worms.[8]

The merchant, a shrewd businessman, knows the right chord to sound to the bereaved women. He invites them to buy his ointment to anoint "the sacred body of the Lord," because, he tells the Marys, if they use his ointment to anoint the body, it can no more putrefy, nor can the worms infest it. The merchant says:

> Quod, si corpus possetis ungere,
> non amplius posset putrescere,
> neque vermes possent commedere.
> [II. 37–39]

The Marys ask the merchant how much his ointment costs, he asks them how much they want to buy and finally offers them the ointment at a ridiculously high price, which the Marys accept "libenter," willingly.[9] The Marys, still lamenting, go to the tomb and are told by an angel that they do not need the ointment after all, "Non eget ungentum," for Jesus has arisen.[10]

The merchant scene, like the scene of the Magdalen fainting at the tomb of the Christ, appealed to the artist who did the work in the chapel at Modena.[11] In the sculpture, the three grieving Marys stand beside the merchant's counter while the elder bearded merchant weighs the ointment on his scale and his young apprentice, with a hint of a smile on his face, looks on, perhaps pleased with learning the tricks of the trade.

Although the merchant scene is not, in the text of the Tours play, explicitly comic, it could be acted as comedy. The mingling of the potentially comic with the solemn, of contemporary medieval figures with the New Testament figures, reveals the twelfth-century playwright as *homo ludens*. While he dramatizes the event central to the Christian afterlife, he turns his eyes and the eyes of his audience toward life on this earth and toward people living in this world where the comic and the serious mingle, where worms can gnaw even a sacred body buried in the earth. Just as the playwright emphasizes the humanity of the Christ, he places the Magdalen close to the man-god. At the same time, the Tours poet links the lamenting Magdalen with the Bride of the old Song of Songs.

The literary figure begins, in the twelfth-century Easter play from Tours, to fulfill the potential of the mythical figure created during the early centuries of Christianity. By the thirteenth century, the Magdalen attracts the attention of the wandering scholars who write for the "worldly" Magdalen goliardic songs. The Magdalen begins to speak the language of her audience, and yet the ambiguous attributes of an ancient goddess still cling to her. For the Magdalen is, in the thirteenth-century Benedikt- beuern Passion play, a Venus, a dangerous but fascinating goddess of love.[12]

The Magdalen's life of "sin," simply mentioned by Jacobus in his *Golden Legend*, is dramatized, along with the suffering and death of the Christ, in the Passion play from the Benediktbeuern monastery. By dramatizing her life as a prostitute and her subsequent repentance, the playwright pictures the Magdalen as a figure capable of change. Even though the change reflects the old either-or dualism, the vitality of the literary figure is augmented. The play itself is a lively music-drama, and the Magdalen sings to the audience satirical songs, mostly in German, the language of her audience. Although contemporary with her medieval audi- ence, she remains a vessel for a notion tied to woman for countless ages. She embodies the paradoxical feminine, that awesome cohort of Eros.

Carl Orff, apparently sensing both the medieval and the timeless characteristics in the Benediktbeuern Magdalen's music, incorporates into his twentieth-century composition *Carmina Burana* the Magdalen's vernacular *carpe diem* song. Along with the Latin hymns to "Venus generosa" and to the "God of Love," we can hear today in Carl Orff's *Carmina Burana* the rollicking "Chramer, gip die varwe mier," once sung in the Passion play by the "wordly" Magdalen as she adorned herself to seduce the young men and urged the men and women in her audience to seize the day and practice the "ennobling" art of love.[13]

As the bold seducer of the "iungen man," the Magdalen undergoes another metamorphosis. The "pure spiritual Mariham," the Christ's sister-bride, becomes a comic figure. The comic element stems partly from the playwright's mingling the contemporary with the timeless, blending the "courtly love" advocate with the deep-rooted notion of woman as the "dangerous sex." Sex and woman, we do not have to be told, are classical targets for satire. But the entrance into the Christian drama of the comic Magdalen coincides with a rise of antifeminism most blatantly expressed in Jean de Meun's section of that popular poem, *The Romance of the Rose*. Although the Benediktbeuern poet reflects in his playful mockery of the Venus-Magdalen a closer kinship with *homo ludens* than does Jean de Meun in his treatment of woman, he reveals in his picture of the Magdalen's *Weltleben* the old ambivalence toward woman and sex evident in the second-century Gnostic writings which we have seen earlier. The thirteenth-century Magdalen parodies the "mystery of sex," and through exaggerated songs of seduction offers comic relief to the medieval audience.

Although her seduction songs are in the vernacular, her theme song is a Latin lyric, "Mundi delectatio," which she sings three times, twice in rejection of the Good Angel's admonition that she leave her worldly lovers and follow Jesus. The song, with its wordplay and lilting abandon, introduces the Magdalen to her audience as a woman delighting in the world, the sophisticated courtly world, with its pleasing and admirable "conversation" to be enjoyed, its "wantonness" not to be shunned. And the Magdalen makes quite clear that she has a body which is to be enjoyed and adorned. She hymns the joys of the world:

> Mundi delectatio dulcis est et grata;
> Eius conversatio suavis est et ornata.

Mundi sunt delicie, quibus estuare
Volo mundo gaudio vitam terminabo;
Bonus temporalibus ego militabo.
Nil curans de ceteris corpus procurabo,
Variis coloribus illud perornabo.
[Ll. 42–49]

As she vows, "In worldly joy, I shall end my life; I shall serve under the banner of temporal goods; caring nothing for the rest, I shall look after my body; with various hues I shall greatly adorn it," she goes to the merchant.

She sings her desire to buy, "for much money," perfume for her body. Certainly the patron saint of perfume makers deserves nothing but the best. When the merchant sells her his most expensive perfume, the Magdalen sings, in German, her request for rouge for her cheeks. She sings the song revitalized in Carl Orff's *Carmina Burana*. "Shopkeeper," she begins, "give me color which will redden my cheeks so that I may compel the young men to think of wooing me."

Chramer, gip die varwe mier,
    die min wengel roete,
da mit ich di iungen man
    an ir danch der minnenliebe noete.
[Ll. 58–61]

She turns to the young men and sings: "Look on me, young men; allow me to delight you."

Seht mich an
iungen man
    Lat mich eu gevallen.
[Ll. 62–64]

Then addressing her audience with a *carpe diem* song, the Magdalen-Venus urges the "good men" and "lovely ladies" to make love, for "wooing" will, she preaches, ennoble them, let them be "held in high esteem."

Minnet, tugentliche man,
    minnekliche vrawen.
Minne tuot ev hoech gemut
    unde lat evch in hochen eren schauven.
[Ll. 65–68]

Again she tries to entice the young men with her charms as she asks them once more to look on her and to allow her to delight them. She hails the world so rich in joys, "also vreudenriche," and vows to obey the world always.[14]

She goes to sleep, and the Good Angel enters, addresses her by name, and tells her of "Jesus the Nazarene" who forgives sins and is now at Simon's house. The Magdalen, unimpressed with the Angel's news, arises and again sings her hymn to the world's joys, "Mundi delectatio." Amator, her lover, approaches and she happily greets him. Then, assuming the role of Venus as teacher of the courtesan's art, the Magdalen sings to the young girls the wonders of the cosmetic merchant's wares. "They make us beautiful and pleasing," she says.[15] And she escorts her protégées to the merchant where they purchase cosmetics while he echoes the Magdalen's song in praise of his merchandise.[16]

Again the Magdalen sleeps while the Angel repeats his message to her, but she once more arises singing "Mundi delectatio." With the Angel's third message, the Magdalen at last laments her past life, full of evil, "Heu vita preterita, vita plena malis," and the Angel rejoices in her repentance.[17] The Magdalen condemns her worldly ornaments, her dazzling clothes, and puts on a black cloak.[18] The seductive Venus is quickly transformed into the penitent Venus in sackcloth. With the Magdalen's symbolic "resurrection," Amator, and "Diabolus," not mentioned before in the text, depart. "Evil," like winter, is expelled.

The Magdalen goes to the merchant, this time to buy "precious ointment" to anoint Jesus. She goes, weeping and lamenting her sins, to Simon's house. And the anointing scene, with which we are familiar, takes place. But after Jesus forgives her for her sins and sends her away in peace, the Magdalen again sings a lament for her sins, with a refrain, "Oi wei, oi wei, that ever I was born!" ("Awve, auve, [sic] daz ich ie wart geborn!" [l. 144]). The second penitential lament seems to be misplaced in the text.[19] If it belongs, as I think it does, in the scene showing the Magdalen on her visit to the merchant to buy ointment, the contrasting trips to the "Mercator" sharply dramatize the Magdalen's exchange of her cosmetics box for her ointment jar, her eroticism for asceticism, her devotion to Eros for devotion to the Christ.

Although the Magdalen's role takes up about one-third of the Benediktbeuern play, her part in the remaining scenes is negligible.[20] She is not, as was the Magdalen in the Tours play, given extended laments for the Christ. Instead, Mary the mother of Jesus is given by the Benediktbeuern playwright long laments for the Christ in the Crucifixion scene, which concludes the play. The Benediktbeuern playwright concentrates on the *Weltleben* of the seductive Magdalen and stresses the seeming incongruity of her role as a Venus in the medieval Christian Passion play.

The thirteenth-century playwright, in making the "worldly" Magdalen at once a medieval and a timeless figure, sets a precedent for later playwrights. And the Magdalen's *mondanité* is treated with a difference by Jean Michel in his *Mystère de la Passion*.[21] The Magdalen of Jean Michel's fifteenth-century mystery play is again the seductive woman. But unlike any other medieval figure, she anticipates Nikos Kazantzakis's twentieth-century Magdalen featured in his novel *The Last Temptation of Christ*, for she fixes her eye on Jesus himself.

Jean Michel, plainly *homo ludens*, juxtaposes the Magdalen's worldly life with Jesus' transfiguration. The playwright fore-shadows the Magdalen's worldly life with the dramatization of the *mondanité* and repentance of Lazarus. While Lazarus has been addicted to hunting, the Magdalen is, as she was in the Benediktbeuern play, devoted to adorning herself to attract lovers. Jean Michel spices the *mondanité* of the Magdalen by placing her in the company of her two saucy chambermaids, Perusine and Pasiphée. The worldly Magdalen is, as she was in the thirteenth-century play, a comic figure.

The Magdalen, dressed in an elegant gown, first appears on stage with her maids, and she suggests that they sing some "new songs" and live the "joyous life."

> Disons quelques chanchons nouvelles
> Et vivons de joyuesse vie.[22]

The three women sing a "popular song of their own choice."[23]

As they chatter about woman's privilege of making joyous noise to attract lovers, the Magdalen declares that she is spirited and daring, so "Jamais ne me tiengs a ung!" [24] Never, she says, confine me to one. Pasiphée remarks that not being confined to one lover is indeed the common custom. Immediately after this criticism directed toward his audience, Michel has Jesus appear on stage "transfigured." [25]

After Jesus' transfiguration and his return to "human form," the Magdalen calls for her perfume, her jewels, and her mirror to make herself gorgeous for the men. She performs her "toilette" on stage. After she completes her "transfiguration" she asks her maids for approval of her looks, and she is assured that she is altogether "à la mode." [26] The scene switches to Jesus performing miracles amongst a crowd in the street and moves on to Martha and Lazarus expressing concern for their wayward sister. Lazarus says that the Magdalen has acquired a very bad reputation: "Elle acquiert tres [sic] mauvaix renon." [27] And Martha sets out to persuade her sister to save her reputation by changing her way of life.

The Magdalen orders Perusine to bring her finest jewels to her as Martha enters to reproach her sister. "Only for the love of you, my sister," Martha prefaces her pleas. [28] "Only for the love of you, my sister," the Magdalen mocks. After a rapid-fire exchange of well-meant admonishment by Martha and sharp-tongued retorts by her sister, the Magdalen orders Martha out of her castle. [29] And the playwright sets the scene for the Magdalen's first sight of the handsome newcomer, Jesus.

Crowd noises in the street draw the Magdalen to her castle window. She asks Tubal, "Gedeon," and "Abacut," biblical prophets who anachronistically appear on the scene, why such a crowd is gathering. Tubal tells her that the people are coming to hear the "fruitful" sermons of the "very holy prophet." [30] The Magdalen asks what his sermons deal with: "Does he speak at all of joyous things in his sermons?" And Tubal tells her that Jesus' "sweet eloquence" makes all that the prophet says joyous. [31] The Magdalen, whose own "sweet eloquence" was praised by Jacobus in the "life" of the saint, is now less interested in Jesus' eloquence than in his physical appearance. "And is he of a very beautiful appearance to see?" "Abacut" (Habakkuk) answers that he is tall, straight, wise, steadfast, sedate, and grave. But this is not enough to satisfy the Magdalen's curiosity about the man newly come to town. She wants a full description of him.

She inquires: "Is he well formed? What is the shape of his face? How old is he? What kind of a beard and hair does he have? What color? What is his complexion? What are his eyes like? His hands? 'Les autres choses?' His clothes?" She learns from the men that Jesus is the most handsome man in the world, is thirty-two years old, has long hair and a beard slightly curly and a little golden, is of a rosy brown complexion, has eyes "clear as the beautiful moon," and beautiful well-shaped hands, that he is altogether pleasing to look upon.[32]

Asking Perusine and Pasiphée if she is pleasing and pretty enough, and being reassured by her maids that she is quite charming, that her body is well corseted, "derrière et devant," the Magdalen goes to the temple to cast her eyes on the "most handsome man in the world." She stands apart from the crowd, clearly hoping that she will attract the attention of the good-looking preacher and that he will find her irresistible. But at the end of the sermon, it is the Magdalen who finds the words of the handsome "prophet" irresistible. The charmer is charmed.

The Magdalen weeps, laments her sins, and her maids praise Jesus.[33] Still dressed in her finery but placing a "simple kerchief" on her head, the suddenly converted Magdalen goes to Simon's house.[34] She washes Jesus' feet with her tears, dries them with her hair. And the patron saint of the perfume makers anoints the Christ's head with a very special scent, "l'eau de Damas." [35] Simon mutters about "la belle Magdeleine" so full of "sin," and Jesus chides him and forgives the Magdalen her past sins.[36] The Magdalen exits, saying "J'en quicte la mondanité" as she removes her worldly clothes, and goes in a "simple garment" to tell Martha of her conversion.[37] Again, as in the Benediktbeuern play, the seductive Venus undergoes metamorphosis, but in Michel's play the transformation is not brought about by an angel. Instead, the Magdalen's sudden change is brought about by the Christ himself.

Although the Magdalen is not given extended laments for the Christ in Jean Michel's *Mystère de la Passion*, she is, as in the Gospel of John's account of the Resurrection of the Christ, the first to whom the risen Christ appears, and she is sent as an "apostle to the apostles."

It is the picture of the worldly Magdalen which links Jean Michel with the thirteenth-century Benediktbeuern playwright, for the Magdalen in her *mondanité* is again simultaneously a figure contemporary with her audience and a figure outside time. Even as she sings popular songs of her day and dresses in the fashion of the elegant courtesans of fifteenth-century France, she remains a seductive Venus whose mission is to bewitch man. Jean Michel's boldest innovation consists, of course, in his having the Magdalen set out to bewitch Jesus himself. Through this innovation, Michel not only brings out the manness of Jesus but also draws a thin line between spiritual and physical love in his dramatization of the Magdalen's swift transition from erotic attraction to ascetic devotion to the Christ. Like the Benediktbeuern playwright, Jean Michel tries to separate eroticism from asceticism through mockery of Eros and Venus. The Magdalen indeed carries into medieval drama both the "Common" and the "Heavenly" Aphrodite long since set on the world stage through Plato's *Symposium*.

By dramatizing the Magdalen's life as a prostitute and by isolating the Magdalen as the woman closest to the Christ, medieval playwrights expand the literary figure of the Magdalen to incorporate into her the attributes of the paradoxical feminine latent in the mythical figure shaped in Christianity's beginnings. And the expanded figure makes a strong impact on medieval drama. For new scenes, new figures, vernacular songs and speeches, and comedy accompany Saint Mary Magdalene onto the "stage" where the lengthened Easter play is performed. Medieval playwrights, like the writers of second-century apocryphal works, use the Magdalen as a vessel for ideas that reflect an ambivalent view of Eros and of woman.

The Magdalen also serves as an outlet for the medieval playwright's individual creative imagination. She is a source of inspiration for poetry and verse, for solemn and comic action. Metamorphosed into an Erato or a Polymnia, the Magdalen emerges as a Muse for *homo ludens* in medieval Christendom.

With the waning of the Middle Ages the Magdalen waxes into a full-blown heroine. The author of the Digby play *Mary Magdalene* goes beyond other playwrights by dramatizing the *Golden Legend*'s account of the Magdalen's mission to Marseilles, her life a hermit, and her death in the desert. The sprawling Digby spectacle starring the Magdalen reveals a highly eclectic imagination playing in jest and earnest, an imagination inspired by the Muse it celebrates.

9

The Magdalen as a Full-blown Heroine in a Late Medieval Play

Of Jerusalem, ye virgyns clere,
Schew my best love that I was here!
Tell hym, os he may prove,
That I am dedly seke
And all is for his love.
         Mawdleyn in the Digby *Burial of Christ*

Sustain me with raisins,
    refresh me with apples;
    for I am sick with love.
O that his left hand were under my head,
And that his right hand embraced me!
         Song of Songs 2:5–6

Yff Ony thyng Amysse be,
blame connyng, and not me:
I desyr the redars to be my frynd,
yff ther be ony amysse, that to amend.
         Epilogue to the Digby *Mary Magdalene*

THE Magdalen reaches the stature of a heroine in drama just as the era loosely called the Middle Ages fades and begins to merge with the rising Renaissance. In the Digby playwright's England, Wyclif has come and gone, but the seeds of religious reform he planted are fast taking root underground. Above ground the mythical Magdalen opens to full bloom as a literary figure in Christian drama. In the century immediately before the religious figure once again becomes an object of open controversy among theologians, the literary figure moves to center-stage in the Digby *Mary Magdalene*. And the star in the Digby play curiously displays closer kinship with the second-century Magdalen than does the literary figure in any earlier medieval play.

The Digby heroine is, as was the Magdalen in Eastern writings of the early Christian period, a goddess both of wisdom and of fertility, the Bride of the Song of Songs, the Christ's "companion," an Isis, an Athene, and a Venus. The Digby heroine is also used as a vessel for the ancient dualistic split between body and soul, dark and light. But the Digby playwright, unlike the early Gnostic sects or their medieval descendants, does not identify dark with either the material world or woman. He does not therefore use the Magdalen as a vessel for the view of woman as "matter" and consequently "evil." The Digby playwright identifies darkness with human mortality and with ignorance of the Christian doctrine.

The Digby heroine, like the Pistis Sophia, does forsake the "mysteries of the intercourse" for the mystery of union with the divine. Like the soul whose journey through the Aeons the Magdalen describes in the second-century gospel attributed to her, the medieval Magdalen sheds her seven "soul-garments" to become the "pure spiritual Mariham," Jesus' "beloved friend," whom he completes in all the "mysteries of the things of the Height." She is once more the enlightened one who enlightens others.

The Digby playwright follows Jacobus's "life" of Saint Mary Magdalene more closely than do his predecessors, but like the Benediktbeuern playwright and Jean Michel he too goes beyond Jacobus to dramatize the Magdalen's life of "sin." And her life as a prostitute again provides comic relief for the audience. But major differences separate the Digby author from earlier playwrights.

The Digby playwright, whether or not he is in fact Miles Blomefylde, anticipates a reading audience, and he makes his presence known by directly addressing his readers in an epilogue to the play.[1] He wants them to be his friends, and he asks them to blame "connyng," knowledge, and not him for anything they find "amyss" in his most eclectic spectacle. Concerned with finding reasons to explain the Magdalen's becoming a whore, the Digby playwright invents a motivation for his heroine's fall. The playwright, like Jacobus, rejects the popular explanation for the Magdalen's having become a prostitute because of her wrath at Jesus' calling her betrothed John away from her. The Digby playwright pictures his heroine as Syrus's beloved daughter, "ful fayr and ful of femynyte," so weakened by grief for her father's death that she is vulnerable to temptation.[2] More openly didactic than earlier playwrights, the Digby author identifies the Magdalen's sin as pride and emphasizes the Judeo-Christian virtue of humility represented in the penitent Magdalen.

The English playwright also differs from earlier Christian playwrights in juxtaposing scatologically comic scenes with serious scenes and in bringing to life the Magdalen's famous seven demons through the technique of the morality play. Transformed into the "seven deadly sins," but too much like braggart buffoons to seem deadly, they assault the Magdalen's castle and lure her into prostitution immediately after her father Syrus dies.

While the Magdalen and Lazarus and Martha are still in mourning for their father's death, the World, the Flesh and his wife Lechery, the Devil, and their cohorts, Wealth, Sloth, Gluttony, and Sensuality, hold council to plot the seduction of the Magdalen. World brags of his omnipotence over the fate of man but promptly expresses fear of the Magdalen's powers over one area of his domain. He says, "Yf she in vertu may dwelle," she will be able to destroy all hell.[3] Flesh sends his "Lady Lechery" to tempt the Magdalen, and Satan sends "spirits malign" to enter into that "beral of bewte" so that he may win her to his kingdom.[4]

Lady Lechery enters the Magdalen's besieged castle, and using the well-worn trick of flattery, compares the Magdalen's "bemys of bewte" to the sun's rays and declares her most "debonairus" with her angelic delicacy.[5] The trick works like magic. The Magdalen agrees to forget her grief over her father's death by leaving her castle in the custody of Martha and Lazarus and going to Jerusalem to concentrate on "sportes whych best please" her.[6]

Lechery escorts the patron saint of "winegrowers" to a tavern in Jerusalem where the taverner boasts of his prize wines, the best in the world. And all imported from medieval Europe. The Magdalen praises him as a true "groom of blysse," courteous and kind to her.[7] While Lechery and the Magdalen sip their wine, a "good restoratyff," Pride, "called Curiosity," dashes into the tavern. He brags to the taverner of his up-to-the-minute clothes, his beautiful "lady constant," his favorite game of "playing" with his hair against a lady's hair.[8] Lechery tells the Magdalen that the "gallant" is exactly what the Magdalen needs. The Magdalen agrees, she will make "full merry" with Curiosity.[9]

Curiosity loses no time. To the "dear duchesse," his "daisy's eye," he tosses out a flowery love speech and vows his eternal love.[10] The patron saint of reformed prostitutes, overwhelmed with Curiosity's fast work, asks him if he thinks she is a "kelle."[11] Curiosity assures her that he thinks her no "whore" and begs her to return his love, for her "womanly person" has undone him.[12] The Magdalen acquiesces, the lovers dance, share "sops in wine," and finally "take a walk" as the Magdalen vows that she would go to the world's end for her "dere derlyng" and, if need be, die for his sake.[13]

While the lovers take their "walk," the Bad Angel, the World, the Flesh, and the Devil enter the scene rejoicing over their success in winning the prized Magdalen. The Devil "trembles and trots with glee."[14]

Time has gone by and the Magdalen has acquired a number of "dere" darlings when we next see her. She enters an arbor sorely astonished not to find awaiting her one of her "valentynes," a "blossom of blysse" who is wont to "hug and kiss" her. But taking her disappointment in stride, she announces that she will rest among the "bamys precyus of prysse" until one of her "loves so dere" comes. She soliloquizes:

> A! god be with my valentynes,
> My byrd swetyng, my loves so dere!
> for they be bote for a blossom of blysse;
> me mervellyt sore they be nat here,
> bot I woll restyn in this erbyr

A-mons thes bamys precyus of prysse,
Tyll som lover apere,
that me is wont to halse and kysse.

[Ll. 564–71]

She falls asleep. And while the playwright sets the stage for the
anointing scene at Simon's house, the Good Angel enters to
reprove the sleeping Magdalen for her delight in "fleshly lust."
He warns her that her soul will lie "in hell's fire" if she does not
leave her "vain and variable works" and follow him.[15] The Digby
Magdalen, unlike her Benediktbeuern counterpart, does not have
to be coaxed. Her conversion is sudden. She laments her sins,
vows to take "swete bamys" to the prophet and to follow him "in
eche degre." [16]

Once more we see her exchange her "worldly" love for love of
the Christ. Her balms of precious price in her bower of bliss
miraculously turn into "swete bamys" with which she will anoint
the Christ. Although the Digby playwright looks for a reason for
her life of "sin," he wheels out the *deus ex machina* for her sudden
repentance.

In the anointing scene which follows, the playwright at once
recalls Jacobus's explication of one of the meanings of the
Magdalen's name and pays due honor to the patron saint of
hairdressers. He shows Jesus praising his anointer for washing his
feet with her tears of "bitter" weeping and for wiping them with
her hair "fayr and bryght shynning." [17] The Magdalen blesses
Jesus as the "lord of ever-lasting lyfe" and a "repast contemplatyff" and vows to clothe herself in "humility" for she has sinned
in the sin of "pryde." [18] Jesus applauds her as "expert in
contrition." He tells her that her soul has an "inward might" that
has "purchased" light from darkness, and her faith has saved her
and made her "bright." [19] With Jesus' words of praise, the stage
direction tells us, the seven devils leave the Magdalen and enter
"into hell with thondyr." [20]

When the Magdalen, like the Soul whose journey she describes
in her own second-century gospel, sheds her seven "soul
garments," the "kingdom of the flesh" and "desire" come to an
end for her too. The Magdalen thanks Jesus for restoring her soul

to health, and Jesus promises her that if she keeps free of "negligence" she will be "partner" of his "bliss." [21] We see Jesus' partner, his "companion" of the second-century Apocrypha again resurrected in the medieval Magdalen. We also hear an echo of the second-century Magdalen in the Digby heroine's hymn to Christ the Light as she reports her repentance, her transition from the darkness of ignorance to the realm of light, to Martha and Lazarus:

Cryst, that is the lyth and the cler daye,
He hath on-curyd the therknesse of the clowdy nyth.
of lyth the lucens and the lyth veray,
Wos preachyng to vs is a gracyows lyth,

[Ll. 768–71]

The Magdalen praises Christ the true light and the clear day, who has uncovered the darkness of the cloudy night, and whose preaching is to her and her audience a gracious light. And the Digby heroine, like the heroine of the *Pistis Sophia*, is chosen to share the light with the Light of Lights. Like the Pistis Sophia Prunikos herself, the Magdalen receives a "crown" from the Light "veray" at her death when her soul ascends to heaven to unite with the deity.[22]

The Digby playwright foreshadows the death and Resurrection of the Christ with the dramatization of Jesus' raising Lazarus from the dead. And he uses the scene tᴄ convince "all the people and the Jews, Mary and Martha" thaᵗ Jesus is the "Savior." [23]

In his dramatization of the Christ's Ressurection, the playwright expands the recognition scene between the risen Christ and the Magdalen to include a dialogue between the two. The Magdalen, herself an expert in allegorical exegesis in the second-century *Pistis Sophia*, is the woman privileged to hear the Christ's fifteenth-century mystical explication of his role as a "gardener."

At the tomb, the Magdalen laments the "dolor and dyssese" that dwells in her heart. And just as she asks the angel to tell her who has borne away her "Lord," Jesus says to her, "Woman, woman, why do you weep, whom do you seek?" [24] Not recognizing him, she asks him if he has taken away her "specyall lord" whose "lover" she is.[25] "O mari!" Jesus exclaims. Elated, the Magdalen desires to anoint him and to kiss him. "But now I will kiss you," she says.[26] Just as in the Gospel of John account, Jesus forbids her to touch him now and asks her to tell the disciples that he will ascend to his father.

But the Magdalen, reluctant to leave her "specyall lord," prolongs the meeting. She tells him that when she first saw him she thought he was "Symovd" the gardener.[27] Jesus answers, "So I am for-sothe, mary." [28] And he explains that man's heart is his garden, in which he sows seeds of virtue all the year, rends up by root foul weeds and vices, and when the garden is watered with tears, he says, virtues spring up and smell full sweet.[29] The Magdalen delights in this "joyful news" given her by the "worthy emperor," the "high divinity." [30] Jesus says that he will appear to all sinners, as he does to her, if they will seek him with "fervent love" and that if she remains steadfast he will always be with her and with all those who are "meek." [31]

The Digby playwright, like the writers of the *Pistis Sophia* and the *Gospel of Mary*, singles out the Magdalen as the sharer of Jesus' special knowledge, however different the knowledge appears. This particular bit of knowledge which Jesus passes on to the Magdalen comes, as the eclectic Digby playwright clearly knew, from a sermon on the Song of Songs by the twelfth-century Bernard of Clairvaux.[32] The patron saint of gardeners hears the lines "Veni in hortum meum, soror mea sponsa," Come into my garden, sister my bride, explicated by the Christ, whom she mistakes for "Symovd," a particular gardener whom she knows by name. And the Magdalen to whom Jesus explains the lines from the old Song is the same Mawdleyn who, in the Digby *Burial of Christ*, explicitly echoes the words of the Bride of the Song of Songs in her longing for the love of her Beloved. "Deadly sick" with love of the Christ, Mawdleyn begs the "daughters of Jerusalem" to tell her "Best love" that she had sought him and not found him.[33] Through "connyng" *homo ludens* covertly recalls the erotic love celebrated in the Song of Songs while he overtly sermonizes on the virtue of humility.

Homo ludens continues to work on the line between jest and earnest as the Digby playwright sandwiches between the Magdalen's hymn to Jesus "king in heaven" and the Christ's thoughts of the "kyndness" of "mary Maudleyn," Jesus' hymn to the Moon, his mother, the vessel of pure "cleannesse" in whom he rested before he ascended to the Sun.[34] As Jesus concludes his astrological hymn to his mother, whose "joys" no "clerk" can write, he thinks of the Magdalen on earth and sends his angel Raphael down to bid his "beloved frynd" to go alone to convert the land of Marseilles to belief in him.[35]

The playwright has already given us a hint of the work cut out for the Magdalen in a scene picturing the king of Marseilles out-Heroding Herod. He harangues his people, "blabber-lipped bitches," who refuse to bow down to his "lawdabyll" presence when he not only is "King of all Heathendom" but besides has a wife who is "most delicious" and a priceless "beryl of bewte." [36] The playwright has also presented a picture of the "heathen" religion which the Magdalen is sent to wipe out. Through a parody of the Roman Catholic mass and the worship of relics in a service dedicated to the god of Marseilles we discover that, *mirabile dictu*, the deity worshipped by all "Heathendom" is none other than Mohammed, who died in A.D. 632. The founder of Islam, medieval Christianity's sibling rival, against whom the Crusades raged, miraculously gains "true believers" in the West before the Magdalen reaches Marseilles.

Religious reform breaks through the ground beneath the scene in which the Moslem clergymen administer the mock ritual. The Moslem churchmen must have taken lessons from Chaucer's fourteenth-century Pardoner. A "presbyter" and his "clericus" perform the service while they indulge in a bawdy "flitting" match which ends with the boy getting a beating on the "ars" from the outwitted "presbyter." For a few pieces of gold from the king and queen, the churchmen sing a hymn to "Mahomet" before they display the relics of Mahomet himself, the relics including a "neck-bone" and an "eyelid" which, for an additional fee, can work wonders.[37] Wonders perhaps as great as those wrought by the "relics" owned by Chaucer's Pardoner, or, the Digby *homo ludens* may imply, by a strand of the Magdalen's famous long hair or one of her "bitter" tears preserved in sanctuaries.

Even though the Digby playwright follows the *Golden Legend* more closely than his predecessors, he is clearly no slave to Jacobus's "life" of Saint Mary Magdalene. He further deviates from Jacobus not only in having the Magdalen go alone as "an holy apostylesse" to Marseilles but also in setting her out in a sound ship. She boards ship onstage and to the tune of the shipman's "mery song" the patron saint of sailors voyages safely to the land of Marseilles. She disembarks, prays to the Christ for victory over the "fiend's flame," and goes straight to the king's palace. She asks the king for permission to stay in his land and receives nothing but insults from him.[38]

Despite lengthy word battles, the "eloquent" Magdalen fails to convince the King of all Heathendom that her deity's powers are superior to those of his god. But she finally converts the king and his people to belief in her deity through miracles. The "idol" in the temple quakes, and the temple itself is set on fire, but the king needs more proof of the power of the Magdalen's God before he will accept him.[39] He will believe in her God, he says, if the Magdalen can bring about the queen's long-desired but never-realized conception of a child.[40]

The Magdalen, hungry, thirsty, and cold, prays for help, and Jesus agrees to send aid to "mary" his "lover." [41] He sends two angels to accompany the Magdalen to the king's chamber where she will ask the king for some of his "goods" to save her from her misery.[42] Casting a light so bright that the queen fears the room will burn, the Magdalen appears in a "vision" to the royal couple.[43] And with the Magdalen's help, the queen soon conceives a child, right away feels the babe move in her womb, and the "heathen" turn Christian, charitable and humble.[44]

The playwright dramatizes Jacobus's story of the king and his pregnant wife setting sail for Rome, with the Magdalen's blessing.[45] The queen prays to the Magdalen, "blessyd lady," flower of womanhood, to save them from drowning on the voyage.[46] Hardly are the king and queen aboard ship when the queen gives birth to her child, and without woman's help in her "nede," she dies. She calls on "mary Maudleyn" to "lead" her soul and commits herself to God's hands.[47] And it is the "blessyd Maudleyn," the goddess of fertility and the protector of life, who restores the dead queen to life and preserves the life of the infant after the distraught king persuades the shipmen to allow him to place his dead wife and his crying infant son on a "rock" on shore. When the king on his journey back from Rome stops at the "rock" and discovers both his wife and his son alive and in good health, he praises that "pure virgin" the Magdalen and thanks the "mighty Lord" in heaven.[48] The queen hymns the Magdalen, her soul's comfort and her body's sustenance:

> O almyty maydyn, ower soulys confortacyon!
> O demvr Maudlyn, my body's sustenance!
> [Ll. 1902–3]

Again the queen hails the Magdalen as "chosen and chaste of women alone" when the royal family returns to Marseilles to find the Magdalen preaching the Christ's Sermon on the Mount to the people. She exclaims that she has not wit to tell the Magdalen of her "nobleness" in saving the lives of her and her son.[49] The king hails the "blessyd Maudleyn" as "the health of our souls and repast contemplative," just as the Magdalen had hailed Jesus when he forgave her of her sins.[50] But the king adds a special praise for the goddess of life. To the Magdalen he exclaims: "Hail, comfortable succor for man and wife!"[51]

The Magdalen's mission accomplished, she announces that she will "labor forth" to "purchase" more spiritual strength.[52] The queen and king try hard but fail to persuade her, "blessyd Mary," their "sweet succor," not to go, and they sigh and weep when the "lady fre," the "sweet cypresse," leaves them empty of "game and glee." But the Magdalen promises them that she will always be their "bead woman," and the king says that he will forever deny "Mahomet" as he vows to build Christian churches throughout his land.[53]

The Digby Magdalen, simultaneously a goddess of life on land and sea and the feminine counterpart of Christ the Light, finds her "game and glee" in her last thirty years as a hermit. Jesus hears the "sweet" prayers of the "contemplatyff" and praises her as his "wel-belovyd frynd" and has his angels daily lift her to heaven where she is fed "manna." [54] The angels tell the Magdalen that she is to be honored with "joy and reverence," enhanced in heaven "above virgins." [55]

The Digby playwright telescopes her thirty years of hermit life and swiftly dramatizes the Magdalen's death, which leads to her union with the deity in heaven. Jesus promises her a "crown" and a "joyous life" with him in heaven. A priest comes to give her the "bred of lyf," the Magdalen gives her soul to God's "bliss" and asks her Lord to open his "blessed gates." And just before she dies she proclaims: "Thys erth at thys tyme fervently I kysse." [56]

The angels take her soul to heaven amidst "mery song." [57] The priest rejoices and says that the Magdalen's body will be buried "by name, with all reverence and solemnity." And the play closes with the fifteenth-century audience singing a hymn to Saint Mary Magdalene as her soul ascends to the realm of Light.[58]

The Magdalen's final gesture discloses much of the paradox of the mythical Magdalen. For in fervently kissing the earth as she dies, the saint demonstrates the Christian virtue of humility, emphasized by the Digby playwright, while at the same time the goddess of life pays homage to her earth. Embodied in the Digby heroine is the dualistic split between body and soul, between life on earth and the Christian afterlife. As *homo ludens* the Digby playwright preserves in the literary figure of the Magdalen attributes of antique goddesses placed in the figure during the early centuries of Christianity and brought to fulfillment in the popular medieval saint.

Although Donatello's sculpture, contemporary with the Digby heroine, captures none of the Digby Magdalen in his tense, pathetic hermit, the full-blown heroine lives again in Marochetti's marble Juno-Magdalen. Donatello's shrivelled, life-denying penitent reveals, however, a more profound sensitivity to the unresolved paradox embodied in the mythical Magdalen than does either Marochetti's monumental goddess or the Digby playwright's "lover" of the Christ.

The Digby Magdalen who is the Christ's lover to be honored

in heaven beyond virgins reincarnates the second-century "companion" of Jesus who is to be the Pleroma of the Pleromas, the "companion" of the "true prophet" who is Wisdom and the "mother of all." In the Digby heroine's switch from love of her "valentynes" to love of the Christ, the Magdalen once again exchanges her role as the "Common Aphrodite" for her role as the "Heavenly Aphrodite." She thus embodies the mystic view of Eros represented by both Origen and Bernard of Clairvaux in their symbolical interpretations of the Song of Songs.

Yet she also embodies the humanistic view of woman as a generative force in her role as a genius and preserver of life on this earth. She is an Isis, a Diana, the Bride of the Song of Songs. But the frank eroticism celebrated by the Bride and her Beloved in the old Song enters the Digby play either in the profligate, the "kelle" whose "valentynes" are buffoons, or in the "contemplatyff," the mystic whose Beloved is a spiritualized Eros. The fifteenth-century Magdalen perpetuates the paradox of mysticism. For in the spiritual love shared by the Magdalen-Bride and the Christ-Bridegroom lies a memory of the sexual love which was once itself an unashamed "holy mystery."

The love shared by the Magdalen and the Christ, so strongly emphasized by second-century writers and revived again by the Digby playwright, stands trial in Lewis Wager's sixteenth-century play, *The Life and Repentance of Marie Magdalene*. The mythical Magdalen falls into decline as religious reform rises. But with further metamorphoses the paradoxical Magdalen manages to survive through the ages to center the stage of twentieth-century theater. In Maurice Maeterlinck's play devoted to her, for example, the Magdalen suffers the "passion" of the woman taken in adultery.

IO

The Decline of the Mythical Magdalen

The pleasure of youth is a thyng right frayle,
And is yearly lesse, so that at length it doth faile;
The sweet violets and lilies flourish not alway;
The rose soon drieth, and lasteth not a day.
Mary Magdalene

Of many ladies I am certain you have heard,
Which the people as goddesses dyd regard:
Concupiscence

Surely, Mistresse Mary, we will make you a goddesse anone.
Infidelity

The Life and Repentance of Marie Magdalene

Not long after the heroine of the Digby *Mary Magdalene* plays
the role of preacher during her mission to Marseilles and shortly
before Lewis Wager's Infidelity makes his effort to transform the
Magdalen into a "goddesse," the Flemish Master of the Magdalene Legend paints for an altarpiece scenes from the Magdalen's
"life," including *Mary Magdalene Preaching* (fig. *10*). Elegantly
gowned but with her hair modestly covered, the Magdalen stands
in a woodland between two trees and rests her left hand on an
improvised lectern while her upraised right hand touches her
breast as she addresses the group of listeners gathered about her.
With a serious and intent expression on her face, she looks down
on the fashionably dressed women seated in the foreground. The

small audience, which includes two disinterested children, manifests, through facial expressions and gestures, varied reactions to the Magdalen's sermon. One of the two turbaned men, probably Moslem, standing to the left of the Magdalen, points a finger toward heaven and converses with a neighboring figure whose facial expression suggests puzzlement.

As in the medieval illumination from the *Sforza Book of Hours* (fig. 9), scenes representing events yet to take place in Saint Mary Magdalene's "life" are visible in the background. A distant ship nears shore, the grotto awaits as the Magdalen's hermitage, an astonished priest falls on his knees and looks heavenward. The Flemish artist's painting differs, however, from the medieval illumination in centering not on the wonder of the mystic who is lifted to heaven by angels but rather on the preacher who is sent out to convert "infidels" to her recently acquired faith. Nor does the sixteenth-century *Mary Magdalene Preaching* manifest evidence of the mythologized Magdalen's link with a Venus.

The mythologized Magdalen indeed becomes an object of open controversy in Western Christendom when religious reform pushes its way above ground. The attributes of antique goddesses preserved in the highly revered Saint Mary Magdalene flash danger signals to some Christian theologians. The same century which brings about the transformation of Jean Cousin's painting *Eva Prima Pandora* into a representation of the Magdalen stirs up heated argument over the Magdalen's identity. The debate threatens the long-lived mythical figure identified with Luke's anonymous prostitute, with the woman of Bethany who anointed the Christ, with Mary the sister of Martha and Lazarus, and with the Bride of the Song of Songs. We have seen evidence in the twentieth-century newspaper article headlining the Magdalen as a "Victim of Libel" that the controversy is not yet finally resolved. And the justification for the complex figure set forth in *Sainte Marie-Madeleine: Quelle est donc cette femme?* by a twentieth-century Franciscan, Damien Vorreux, gives further evidence of the persistence of the controversy concerning the Magdalen's identity.

While the sixteenth-century controversy over the complex

Magdalen raged among Roman Catholic theologians, Lewis Wager, a "learned clerk," staged his own protest against the worship of Saint Mary Magdalene as a goddess. Wager follows the tradition set by former playwrights in dramatizing the Magdalen's "worldly life." But the heroine of *The Life and Repentance of Marie Magdalene* stands apart from previous playwrights' figures of the Magdalen by being well-schooled in Ovid's *Art of Love*. It is a knowledge she shares with Infidelity, the figure responsible for transforming the Magdalen into a goddess of love.

Wager ignores the *Golden Legend*'s life of Saint Mary Magdalene, but he accepts without question the identification of the Magdalen with Luke's anonymous whore whom Jesus forgives because she "loved much." The Prologue announces to the audience that it is indeed the story told in the Gospel of Luke which is to be presented on stage.[1] Since Wager's interest rests solely in the prostitute's sin and repentance, the playwright ignores the Christ's Resurrection and the Magdalen's important role in the scene.

Wager shares none of the Digby playwright's enthusiasm for dramatizing the love between the Magdalen and the Christ. On the contrary, Wager's declared purpose is to downgrade love and to upgrade faith as a means of Christian salvation. The sixteenth-century playwright tries to dethrone the Magdalen who is revered as a goddess of life and to set up the penitent prostitute as a prime example of the power of Christian faith. To dramatize his message, Wager uses the morality play and places the Magdalen in the midst of personified abstractions. The personifications of "Evil" are, as they were in the Digby *Mary Magdalene*, buffoons. But Wager's buffoons are clearly well-read and cunning

10. *Mary Magdalene Preaching*
by the Flemish Master of the Magdalene Legend.
COURTESY, JOHN G. JOHNSON COLLECTION, PHILADELPHIA

braggarts. "Infidelitie the Vice" is the gang leader of the group consisting of Pride of Life, Cupidity, Carnal Concupiscence, and Malicious Judgment.

The Magdalen delights in the company of the garrulous crew. Her pleasure climaxes in a scene picturing her as a Muse for the Vices. She inspires them to make a song for her. They sing the refrain:

> With a lusty voice syng we, Hey, dery, dery,
> Huffa, mistresse Mary, I pray you be mery.[2]

And they loudly praise her in harmonious melody. She outshines the charming courtesans of the past. In her beauty she excels Lady Thais, and she exceeds the beautiful Helen in all things. Her hair shines like pure gold, her eyes are grey as glass, her lips ruddy as the red rose, her teeth white as whale's bone. She is the fairest, freshest, sweetest young woman in all "Jewry." [3]

The Vices' song to the "fairest flower of Jerusalem" soon brings onto the scene the solemn rescue squad who will eventually save the Magdalen from Infidelity and his followers. Instead of the Angel brought in by both the Benediktbeuern and the Digby playwrights, the "learned clerk" Wager produces The Law, Knowledge of Sin, Faith, Repentance, Justification, Love, and "Christ Jesus" to bring about the Magdalen's metamorphosis from a sinner to a penitent.

Wager introduces the Magdalen to his audience as a vain and petulant young woman, beautiful, educated in the Latin classics, and spoiled by her wealthy parents, a pushover for Infidelity and his crowd. While Infidelity, also well versed in Latin and full of aphorisms from Ovid, boasts of his monopoly on bishops', kings', and all men's hearts, the Magdalen enters the scene "triflyng with her garments." [4] The Magdalen rants against her "bungling" tailor for making her frock so ill-fitting that it conceals her small waist.[5] Infidelity sympathizes with her as she rails against her maids, "ignorant sluts" who know nothing about choosing attire for a gentlewoman like her.[6]

Infidelity works on the Magdalen through the same device used by Lady Lechery in the Digby *Mary Magdalene.* He flatters her.[7] And he urges her to seize the day and "be merry," for she will never be "younger in dede." [8] He offers to find proper company for her.[9] And as she exits to make herself "pleasant to every man's eye," she complies with Infidelity's request for a kiss.[10]

Infidelity plots to place the "devil himself" in the Magdalen's heart.[11] To abet Infidelity's plot, Pride of Life, Carnal Concupiscence, and Cupidity arrive on the scene. Each tries to outboast the other in enumerating the number of "vices" he "contains" before the three agree to bring "hell on earth" through the Magdalen.[12] Avowing that woman is easily duped, the Vices choose false names and put on disguises. Infidelity becomes Prudence; Pride of Life, Honor; Carnal Concupiscence, Pleasure; Cupidity, Utility. And Infidelity announces that he will be like a "friar" and "temper his look, with one eye on a wench and another on a book." [13]

The Magdalen returns and is introduced to the disguised Vices. She distributes kisses and embraces all around and declares that these persons of so "great wit and policy" please her "exceedingly well." [14] For they have convinced her, through quoting Statius and other Latin authorities, that man is his "own god." Carnal Concupiscence tells the Magdalen, the sometime goddess of love and fertility, that he is certain she has heard of many ladies "which the people as goddesses did regard." She too can be a goddess.[15] Lewis Wager uses no subtlety. It is Infidelity who promises that he and his helpers will indeed make the Magdalen a "goddesse anone." [16]

The Magdalen is not, however, quite "lady-like enough yet," the Vices decide. So they must coach her in the delicate art of becoming a goddess.[17] She learns how to roll her eyes with pride, how to dress seductively by always wearing low-cut gowns to display her "white pappes." Men adore especially the sight of a lady's breasts, Pride informs her. "The sight can make men's noses bleed," Carnal Concupiscence adds.[18] She also learns ways of keeping her hair fair and "yellow as gold" as well as the proper coiffure for catching the eyes of men. She must let most of her long hair be "in sight," for this too is a delight to men.[19]

The Magdalen blushes when Infidelity says that her face looks as if she once had the "pox." But the Vices tell her not to fret, for paint can hide her syphilitic scars.[20] Once the Magdalen masters the intricate art of being a seductive goddess, she must always take lovers who are "young and gay" and who can afford to "pay." [21] Matrimony the Venus-Magdalen must at all costs avoid. The Vices quote Juvenal's satires to support their mocking sermons against marriage.[22]

"Ha! Ha! Ha!" the Magdalen laughs. "Now I pray God I die if ever I did see/ Such pleasant companions as you all be." [23] But she thinks of youth's swift decay and recalls verses from Ovid, verses she learned when she was a child in school. She quotes the Latin lines and translates them:

> The pleasure of youth is a thyng right frayle,
> And is yearly lesse, so that at length it doth faile;
> The sweet violets and lilies flourish not alway;
> The rose soon drieth, and lasteth not a day.[24]

Infidelity consoles her. She need not fear, for a harlot can always be a "bawd" in her old age. Pride and Cupidity also offer consolation and advice, and the Magdalen embraces each and all. The Vices join in song to "Mistresse Mary" whose "pretty person" is a "morsell for princes and noble kynges" and whose beauty excels that of Thais and of Helen.[25] The song finished, Cupidity, Pride, and Carnal Concupiscence exit, leaving Infidelity and the Magdalen alone. The two kiss and embrace, and Infidelity invites her to a banquet "in Jerusalem." [26]

As the lovers leave, Simon the Pharisee and Malicious Judgment enter. They condemn the man who goes about performing miracles by the power of "the great devil," the man who detests "Holy Religion" and calls himself the Messiah. They plot to destroy the man under the guise of friendship. Infidelity joins them and laughingly boasts of his easy conquest of the "bold harlot" Mary Magdalene.[27] Malicious Judgment goes to invite Jesus to Simon's house, and soon the Magdalen enters to describe to Infidelity her most recent bedfellow.[28]

The Law walks in, explains his origins, and announces that he is a "mirror" for all sinners.[29] The Magdalen looks at him, feels the "prick of conscience," and properly upset, begins to repent.[30] Infidelity tells her that she is "mad" to believe The Law, for these things "are written only to make folks afraid." Besides, The Law speaks only of men, not of women at all. For "women have no souls." He adds, "This saying is not new." [31] But The Law explains that the term "man" means "all of Adam's seed," so women who sin will be damned just as will men.[32]

Knowledge of Sin enters to "bite" the Magdalen's conscience and cause her to "lament" as he accuses her of "horrible, loathsome, stinking iniquity." [33] Infidelity interrupts to chide: "Lo Mary, have ye not sponne a fayre thread?" [34] The Magdalen, echoing the Benediktbeuern penitent, laments: "Now woe be to the time that ever I was born!" [35] And she begs The Law to show her "some remedy." [36] The Law quotes Moses as his authority, and Knowledge of Sin explains that The Law has no remedy but can only let the sinner know that he has sinned.[37] The Magdalen finds no comfort and sees small "mercy and Justice" in God who entangles men in "such a trade." [38] Infidelity praises her for her "wisdom" and urges her to forget The Law and "make merry in this world" while she may. Why, he says, make two hells out of one? "Be sure of a heaven while you dwell here." [39]

After a long word-battle between the "good" and the "bad" figures, The Law leaves the scene. Infidelity feels the Magdalen's pulse and finds her in good health. But Knowledge of Sin observes that although her body is whole, her conscience is sick, and he stays close by to "gnaw" the Magdalen's conscience.[40] And "Christ Jesus" enters to replace The Law. Infidelity tries to convince the Magdalen to pay no attention to the Messiah but to take her heaven in this world. Jesus tells Mary that he will save her if she can believe in the "Son of God" and repent her former life.[41] Infidelity scorns Jesus' "pride" in calling himself the Son of God, but Jesus banishes him, along with "seven devils," from the Magdalen. Mary falls "flat downe." The devils offstage cry and "roare terribly." [42]

Jesus tells Mary to rise. The Magdalen blesses him, and he asks her if she believes "in God and in his only Son." The Magdalen says that she does but desires her faith to be strengthened.[43] And

11. *The Magdalen* by Correggio.

Lewis Wager, in deadly earnest, plunges into his text as he sends Faith and Repentance on stage to preach. The preachers warn the Magdalen that she must hereafter "scourge her soul," mortify her senses and devote them to the service of God.[44]

The words of Faith and Repentance recall Origen's admonition in his third-century sermons on the Song of Songs, but are here used with quite different intent. For mystic love of God is not the goal. Not Love but Faith, "always joined to Repentance, is "the gyft of the God most excellent." [45] Repentance makes clear to the Magdalen that Jesus has promised forgiveness of her sins "of his own mercy" and not because of any of her "merits." Jesus sends the Magdalen away with Faith and Repentance while Faith promises the penitent Magdalen that the two of them will always be in her heart, "though not in person." [46] Jesus preaches on the text that there is more joy in heaven for one sinner who repents than for many righteous. Meanwhile, Simon and Malicious Judgment set a trap for "Christ Jesus" and Infidelity curses Jesus for stealing the Magdalen from him.[47]

The Magdalen, "sadly apparelled," prepares herself for the anointing scene to take place at Simon's house. In soliloquy she preaches to the audience: "To all the worlde an example I may be." [48] She says that she will now devote all the parts of her body, once "servants of iniquity," to service of the "Lord Jesus," and she tediously enumerates the changes she will make in the use of her hair, her eyes, her lips, and the other "parts" of her "sinful carcass." [49] The anointing scene takes place amidst the insults of Simon and Malicious Judgment, and Jesus forgives the woman because she "loved much." [50] As in the Gospel of Luke, Jesus adds that the woman's "faith" has saved her.[51]

Justification, with the Magdalen beside him as questioner, enters the scene to nail down Wager's point in a discourse explaining Love as a "fruit of Faith." [52] Love appears to further demonstrate that it proceeds from true Faith. Love concludes that when Christ of his mercy forgave the Magdalen's sins, "Love deserved not forgiveness of sins in dede/ But as a fruite thereof did it succeed." [53]

We can hope that the audience managed a chuckle when

Justification observed that he and his fellows could "talk of this matter a long while," but for the sake of the audience they should conclude the discussion. Justification bids the audience take example from Mary and forsake their "synfull lyves." [54] Love sums up the steps in Mary's salvation with a final repetition of Wager's theme: "Thus by Faith only was Marie justified,/ Like as before it is playnly verified." [55] And Lewis Wager strikes his final blow at the mythical Magdalen. For the person playing the role of the Magdalen steps out of character to address the sixteenth-century audience:

> Now God grant that we may go the same way
> That with joy we may ryse at the last day,
> To the salvation of soule and body evermore,
> Through Christ our Lord, to whom be all honor.
>
> [Ll. 2049–52]

Wager's strong reaction against the reverence for the Magdalen manifested in the Digby playwright's heroine, the Christ's "beloved frynd" to be honored in heaven beyond virgins, marks the decline of the mythical figure during the rise of Protestantism. To break the Magdalen's link with a goddess of love, Wager not only debases Eros by placing him in the person of Infidelity but also abolishes the "Heavenly Aphrodite" embodied in the mythical Magdalen. The paradox inherent in the mystical love shared by the Christ and the Magdalen in second-century writings and in the Digby *Mary Magdalene* Lewis Wager tries to eradicate. Through his metamorphosis of his heroine into an example of faith as the prime necessity for attaining Christian immortality, the "learned clerk" attempts to break the mythologized Magdalen's bond with a goddess of life on earth, with the Bride of the Song of Songs. The sixteenth-century playwright

13. *Mary Magdalene*
by Moretto da Brescia.

threatens the very life of the figure so long linked with ancient goddesses. But the Venus-Magdalen survives in paintings of artists from Wager's own century.

She lives on, for example, in Correggio's seductive hermit who cradles her ointment jar and looks out at the viewer (fig. *11*). Correggio's "contemplative" Magdalen also demonstrates attempts made by several sixteenth-century artists to remove the sackcloth from Venus. The Magdalen exposes her breasts above her blue cloak as if she had taken to heart the advice given her by Lewis Wager's *Infidelity*. And her "paps" are hardly those of the harlot described by the third-century Origen in his explication of the Song of Songs. Correggio's Magdalen is indeed a slightly saddened mirror image of his Venus pictured in *School of Love* (fig. *12*). As the Renaissance dulls the line between "spiritual" and "carnal" love, the "Heavenly Aphrodite" merges with the "Common Aphrodite." Only her ointment jar marks Moretto da Brescia's elegantly gowned Magdalen who at once displays her long flowing hair and a wistful profile as the "Heavenly Aphrodite" (fig. *13*).

Wager's play gathers dust while the Magdalen, after a brief decline, survives. In the seventeenth century, a second sculpture of Sainte-Madeleine was made for her church at Vézelay. A self-confident, smiling, gracious figure who carries her ointment jar, the Magdalen stands on a wooden column opposite the choir. Perhaps in an effort to restore the old church to its former glory as a pilgrimage center, the "relics" of the transformed Venus's jewels were put on display in a small window set in the wooden column. The twelfth-century Vézelay sculpture revealing the Magdalen as the Christ's sister-bride carrying a lighted torch gives way to the Counter-Reformation emphasis on the Magdalen as a penitent Venus.

Even though the Magdalen's popularity does wane, she continues to figure in literature and art during the seventeenth century. In both the seventeenth and eighteenth centuries, however, her descendants often replace her in literature as the "whore," honest or wicked, pathetic or comic. But nineteenth-century romanticism brings a revival of interest in the fictionalized Magdalen herself. She figures particularly in German drama, appears in French poetry, and as a "chaste prostitute" attracts the interest of European and American novelists. Maurice Maeterlinck, in *Mary Magdalene*, one of his last plays, written early in the twentieth century and translated into several languages, places the fictionalized Magdalen center-stage. He links the golden-haired courtesan with both Venus and the Bride of the Song of Songs. And Maeterlinck's enigmatic heroine also undergoes yet another metamorphosis.

I I

The Magdalen in the Spotlight on the Twentieth-Century Stage

The scribes and the Pharisees brought a woman who had been caught in adultery, and placing her in the midst they said to him, "Teacher, this woman has been caught in adultery."

Gospel of John 8:3–4

Who is this that looks forth like the dawn, fair as the moon, bright as the sun, terrible as an army with banners?

Song of Songs 6:10

Who are you to criticize her? Who are you to despise her?
Leave her, leave her, let her be now
Leave her, leave her, she's with me now
If your slate is clean—then you can throw stones
If your slate is not clean then leave her alone

Jesus Christ Superstar

THE decline in popularity of the figure of the Magdalen coincides with the impact of scientific discoveries on Western cultural attitudes and values. Yet despite the "new philosophies that put all in doubt," the Magdalen does survive through the ages. And both Maeterlinck's *Mary Magdalene* and Webber's and Rice's *Jesus Christ Superstar* testify to the powerful grip the long-lived figure holds on some twentieth-century writers' imaginations.

The Magdalen undergoes another metamorphosis in Maeterlinck's play. She is specifically identified with an adulteress, and in Webber's and Rice's rock opera the identification is suggested through Jesus' song "Leave her, leave her, she's with me now/ If your slate is clean—then you can throw stones." [1] The Magdalen of these two works absorbs the identity of the anonymous woman mentioned in a story frequently added to the canonical Gospel of John.[2] The woman, accused of adultery and threatened with stones by a mob, is protected by the Christ.

Maeterlinck, through the identification of the Magdalen with the adulteress, foreshadows the Christ's "passion" with the Magdalen's "passion." The Magdalen is persecuted by the same mob which later tortures the Christ. And just as the Christ saves the adulteress from the mob, so the Magdalen miraculously gives strength to the Christ when the crowd attacks him. Since the Christ, consistently called "the Nazarene" in Maeterlinck's play, never appears on stage, it is primarily the Magdalen who makes his presence felt.

Maeterlinck does not identify the Magdalen with Mary the sister of Martha and Lazarus. Although Maeterlinck does not picture the anointing scene on stage, he does retain the old identification of the Magdalen with the prostitute who anointed the Christ. The heroine of Maeterlinck's play also once more embodies the radically dualistic split between erotic and spiritual love. Maeterlinck indeed attempts, through the figure of the Magdalen, to present a sympathetic view of "modern" mysticism.

Early in the play the Magdalen shocks her lover Verus with the cynical announcement that since she has recently learned a "truth" about love, she now sells herself "more skillfully and dearer than before." When Verus tells her that she slanders herself, for she is really "a deeply wounded soul struggling against pain," she retorts: "You are wrong; it is not a soul struggling, but one that is finding itself." [3] It is the Magdalen's internal struggle as her "soul" strives for self-knowledge which Maeterlinck chooses to dramatize. Maeterlinck's twentieth-century heroine therefore reincarnates the soul who reaches *gnosis* through destruction of sexual desire, the soul described by the Magdalen herself in the second-century *Gospel of Mary*.

Maeterlinck explicitly links the Magdalen with the Bride of the Song of Songs and with Venus. Appius, an old friend of the

Magdalen, greets her: "Venus has left Cyprus and soars over Jerusalem!"[4] And another Roman friend addresses her with words from the Song of Songs. Maeterlinck's courtesan retains, however, only the attribute of the seductive goddess. Her tie is not with the life of the earth but with the artificiality of the Roman court.

Maeterlinck's Magdalen in her "worldly life" resembles Lewis Wager's haughty, vain beauty with the long golden hair. But the twentieth-century figure differs from Wager's heroine, for never does she enjoy a laugh with her companions. To her lover Verus, she seems instead to "have recently suffered a great sorrow." The Magdalen's "great sorrow" remains a mystery to us, just as the Magdalen herself remains the "riddle of womankind," intelligent, impulsive, mysterious, in the eyes of her unhappy lover.[5]

Maeterlinck tries to place the Magdalen in historical perspective by surrounding her with Roman noblemen rather than with personified abstractions. He sets the scene in Bethany where the Magdalen has come "to escape the fanaticism of the Jews in Jerusalem" and now lives in a grand Roman villa.[6] Nearby lives her old friend Silanus, who has retired to Bethany with the intention of spending his remaining years studying "the sacred books of the Jews," a study with which the Magdalen has no sympathy.[7] Next door to Silanus lives Simon the Leper, who has been healed of his disease by the Nazarene. The destiny of the Nazarene now lies in the hands of Verus, a Roman soldier sent to help Pontius Pilate keep the peace in the Jewish quarter, a young friend of Silanus, and the Magdalen's devoted lover.

We first see the Magdalen through the eyes of the two Roman gentlemen. Verus speaks of his strong love and desire for her, and Silanus declares that the Magdalen is indeed the "loveliest of all the many women" he has admired during his long life.[8] He praises particularly her glorious hair. "Unloosed," he says, "it would cover the surface of this porphyry vase with an impenetrable veil of gold." Verus objects to Silanus's implication. The Magdalen is "no vulgar courtesan," he contends. And he praises her intelligence and her character as the qualities that "bind love more firmly" than does her beauty.[9]

The sound of a flute interrupts the panegyric to the Magdalen and announces the arrival onto the scene of the "loveliest" of women. We are hardly prepared for the haughty, petty-minded Magdalen who marches solemnly in, "followed by some slaves, whom she dismisses with a harsh and imperious gesture." [10] Silanus greets her with lines from the Song of Songs, lines he has recently learned from his study of "the sacred books of the Jews."

> "Who is this that cometh out of the wilderness like pillars of smoke, perfumed with myrrh and frankincense? Who is she that looketh forth like the dawn, fair as the moon, bright as the sun, terrible as an army with banners," as your sacred books sing at the approach of the Shulamite? [11]

The Magdalen reveals her hatred for her own people. She tells Silanus not to speak to her of those books for she loathes them as she loathes "everything that comes from that deceitful and sordid, greedy and mischievous nation." [12] Verus hails her "in the Roman fashion" as the "youngest and happiest of the Graces." But the Magdalen replies, "Pity me, instead of praising me." And she complains bitterly of having been robbed last night of her Carthaginian rubies, twelve of her finest pearls, the exotic eels from her fish pond, and worst of all, her Babylonian peacock. [13] She has had her slaves "beaten with rods and put to the torture" for "the sacrilege," she boasts. [14] She believes the thieves are to be found among the vagrants who follow the Nazarene, that "sort of unwashed brigand," a "rude kind of sorcerer," who is now in Bethany.

She has one specific complaint against the vagrants. Two days ago, she explains, they insulted her "foully" and threatened her with stones as she was walking in the street. [15] To her, they "are hateful and loathsome!" [16] Verus offers to arrest the leader of the gang, and the Magdalen vows her special gratitude to him if he will do so as soon as possible. [17] Silanus, however, defends the vagrants as "harmless" though "dirty" and says that their leader has "a voice of a peculiar and penetrating sweetness." [18]

That voice spellbinds the vacillating Magdalen as soon as she hears it. From Simon's orchard the sound of a shouting crowd of lame and blind drifts into Silanus's villa, and the Magdalen and the Roman guests, curious about the Nazarene, want to go out, but Silanus advises them not to.[19] Suddenly silence falls on the crowd outside. The Magdalen, with the Romans, hears "a wonderful voice, soft and all-powerful, intoxicated with ardour, light, and love, distant and yet near to every heart and present in every soul," preaching the Sermon on the Mount to the crowd. The Magdalen exclaims, "I want to see!" She moves toward the voice. And "as though irresistibly drawn by the divine voice, goes as if to descend the steps of the terrace and to make for the bottom of the garden." [20] Silanus tries to restrain her, Verus offers to go with her. But she rebuffs them and goes alone into the crowd.[21]

Above the voice urging the crowd to love their enemies, to do good to those who hate them, sound cries and shouts: "It is the Roman woman! The adulteress! Shame! Magdalene! The strumpet! Drive her away! Stone her! Death!" [22] The crowd disperses, and Verus goes to escort the Magdalen up the steps of the terrace. She rejects his aid "with a harsh and fierce gesture, and staring in front of her, alone among the others, who look at her without understanding, slowly climbs the steps of the terrace." [23]

The mercurial character of the Magdalen dominates Maeterlinck's picture of the figure. Woman, changeable as the moon! We next see her run to throw herself into the arms of Verus, whom three days ago she had ordered to stay away from her. She apologizes for her past "vanity" and so dazzles Verus that he does not recognize "the voice that has so often and so harshly repelled" him. "It is not the same voice, it is not the same soul," the Magdalen says.[24] She has changed so that she no longer knows herself, she explains, because she is herself no more.[25] She sobs, afraid of something she cannot name, and begs Verus to protect her, to take her away.[26] Her plea made, she promptly chides Verus for "abandoning" her for three days and blames the Nazarene for abandoning her also.[27] Verus asks her not to speak of that "wretched man" whose "hours are numbered" but to take joy in their new-found love for each other. Again she begs Verus to take her away from this place where she can no longer stand to live.[28] Verus agrees that they must go, but he must first complete his "errand" although it now repels him to arrest the Nazarene. The Magdalen, who only three days earlier so much desired the Nazarene's arrest, is now distraught.[29]

She tells Verus that "a sort of light" overtook her thoughts when her eyes first met the eyes of the Nazarene. She knew that he recognized her without having seen her before and that he wished to see her again. "He seemed to choose me," she concludes, "gravely, absolutely, forever." Verus, not surprisingly, thinks the Nazarene and the Magdalen have made love together. But the Magdalen reassures Verus that the Nazarene "dared nothing." And "bursting into convulsive sobs on Verus's breast," she cries out, "I love you. I know it." [30]

But soon Lazarus, just restored to life by the Nazarene, walks onto the courtesan's terrace and says to the Magdalen, "Come. The Master calls you." [31] The Magdalen, "as though walking in her sleep," starts to go to Lazarus. When Verus blocks her path to ask her where she is going, she answers, "Wherever he wishes." Verus restrains her, and she collapses in his arms.[32] He vows to protect her and to take her away from the "madness" of the place. He orders Lazarus to go and to report to his master that "the woman whom he covets" has found refuge against his "barbarous witchcraft and his childish spells," and furthermore his master's life lies wholly in Verus's hands.[33]

Again, the Magdalen about-faces. As she struggles to free herself from her lover's arms, her hair "becomes loosened and falls over her shoulders." [34] The sight of her flowing long hair convinces Verus that she has given herself to the Nazarene. He accuses her and tells her to leave. The Magdalen sobs, swears she loves Verus, her love for the Nazarene is "a different thing." [35] Verus declares his continuing love for her, since he possesses "more constancy" than does woman. And he announces his determination to destroy the Nazarene in order to save the Magdalen, whom the Nazarene "wished to destroy." [36]

Venus has put on sackcloth when we next see the Magdalen, "beside herself, dishevelled, barefoot, with torn garments," in the midst of the followers of the arrested Nazarene. She accuses the followers, who fear for their own lives, of cowardice and begs them to demonstrate their love for the man who healed so many of them.[37] She refuses to believe Joseph of Arimathea when he explains that they are only doing the "will" of the Nazarene.[38] The Magdalen is determined to save the life of the Nazarene. She places her hope in Verus.

Verus comes in search of the Magdalen. And she immediately launches into a long speech lauding the Nazarene. She finally gets to the point and asks Verus how they can save him. Verus asks the crowd to leave.[39] The stage is set for the final battle between erotic and spiritual love.

Verus places full responsibility for saving the Nazarene's life on the Magdalen. He will spare the Nazarene only if the Magdalen gives herself, soul and body, to Verus. "Say no if you dare," Verus says, "and let his blood be upon her who has brought him to this pass and who is destroying him twice over!" [40] The Magdalen flatly refuses Verus's offer. She tells him that he understands nothing of her love for the Nazarene. She says:

> I know all that he wishes, I know all that he is as completely as though I were within him, or as though he were there, near me, fixing upon my brow his glance in which the angels come down from heaven, as on the evening when I kissed his feet and wiped them with my hair.[41]

Furious and jealous, Verus begs her again, this time for the sake of her "lover" the Nazarene, to give herself to him now. She refuses: "If I bought his life at the price you offer, all that he wished, all that he loved would be dead." [42] She does not know why it is so, she admits. "If I destroy him in myself, I destroy him in us! I know no more, I understand no more." [43]

The "Common Aphrodite," not quite turned into the "Heavenly Aphrodite," asks Verus to leave her alone, to let her "contemplate." For she does not yet love the Nazarene as he would be loved.[44] Then, begging for pity, she falls into Verus's arms, saying, "Do with me what you will!" And when Verus exclaims, "Magdalene, Magdalene, I knew," the Magdalen shrinks from his touch.[45] She implores him not to ask the impossible of her but to save the life of the "God of Gods descended upon earth." [46] She throws herself at his feet, and clinging to his garments, pleads: "I will be your slave, I will live at your feet, serve you on my knees for the rest of my days; but give me his life without destroying in my soul and throughout the earth that which is the very life of our new life!" [47]

Verus, his patience exhausted, goes to announce to the crowd that the Magdalen is the betrayer of their God. She cries out: "Verus! Verus! This is not worthy of you!" And Verus replies that he is worthy of nothing. "Not even of you, harlot!" [48] He calls the crowd in and tells them that he offered to save their master, but the Magdalen refused his offer and therefore she "orders the Nazarene's death." [49]

The followers of the Nazarene surround the Magdalen. They scream: "Strumpet! Harlot! Judas!" and threaten to kill her.[50] Joseph of Arimathea intervenes to speak "as a father" to the Magdalen. He begs her to say "Yes" to Verus. But the Magdalen remains motionless and silent while the Nazarene's followers engulf her with an "explosion of hatred." [51]

Cries of "Crucify him!" draw the crowd to the window.[52] They shout, "He staggers!" But the Magdalen "stands against a column, in the middle of the room, staring before her, without turning towards the window," unheedful of Verus calling her by name.[53] When a man at the window reports that the Nazarene has fallen, Verus again addresses the Magdalen: "Magdalene, I still promise you." But the Magdalen does not move, does not look at Verus, as she says, "without anger, simply, in a voice from another life, full of peace, full of divine clarity and certainty," to her erstwhile lover: "Go!" Immediately comes the report from the crowd at the window, "He rises to his feet! They drag him along!" [54]

The "spiritual" Magdalen has miraculously given the Nazarene strength to rise. And, we are to assume, to meet his impending death. Verus exits slowly, gazing at the motionless Magdalen who remains center-stage, "as though in ecstasy and all illumined by the departing torches." [55]

The departing torches also throw some light on the paradox embodied in Maeterlinck's mystic heroine. The prostitute's eroticism detached from the "soul" rather easily becomes the mystic's eroticism detached from the "body." The old dualistic split between body and soul stands wide open. Maeterlinck's Magdalen sacrifices the possibility of human love offered her by Verus early in the play for the ecstatic union with the divine. Nothing is resolved *within* Maeterlinck's heroine "illumined" in ecstasy when the curtain falls.

Maeterlinck's heroine, unlike any earlier figure of the Magdalen in drama, undergoes a "passion" just as does the Nazarene. Both are outsiders who are persecuted. But the converted Magdalen, even though Maeterlinck probably did not intend that she should, grimly demonstrates the negative element of the irrational inherent in the "true believer" of yesterday, today, tomorrow. For "terrible as an army with banners," she is not only willing to martyr herself for her newly received "TRUTH" but she is equally willing to destroy others for her belief. Is there a great difference between the self-centered courtesan who has her slaves tortured because of the theft of her exotic treasures and the Magdalen who, "in a voice from another life, full of divine clarity and certainty," unmovingly orders out of her life the man who loves and desires her and to whom she has declared her love?

Separating Maeterlinck's enigmatic, vacillating Venus-Mystic from the Magdalen who costars in *Jesus Christ Superstar* lie Hitler and Hiroshima; a multiplicity of unresolved wars; Freud's, Jung's, Marx's, Einstein's "far-out" ideas, assimilated or contradicted or both; Dadaism; Cubism, Surrealism, Op, Pop; Existentialism; journeys to the moon; jazz, rock; liberation movements for students, for blacks, for gays, for women. Yet the Magdalen who costars in *Jesus Christ Superstar* shares with Maeterlinck's heroine the "change" from profligate eroticism to mystic love for the Christ.[56] And like Maeterlinck's pre–World War I heroine, the Magdalen of the rock opera finds her love for Jesus disturbing.

"He scares me so/ I want him so/ I love him so," she sings.[57] But the Magdalen whom Jesus Christ Superstar saves from slander, unlike Maeterlinck's solemn self-centered heroine, finds her switch from prostitution to love of Jesus comic. "Don't you think it's rather funny/ I should be in this position," she sings.

That she, "no lover's fool," the one who has always "been so cool," and "running every show," has come to this! [58]

This Magdalen of rock, unlike any of her predecessors, medieval or modern, wastes no time lamenting her past. No sackcloth for this Venus. Despite her awe of the Superstar, she easily assumes the role of Jesus' comforter. Motherlike, she soothes him with her ointment, calms him with song, lulls him to sleep.

> Try not to get worried, try not to turn on to
> Problems that upset you oh don't you know
> Everything's alright yes everything's fine
> And we want you to sleep well tonight[59]

While Maeterlinck's heroine embodies the dangerously seductive attribute of the antique goddess, the old protective Mother Goddess, in modern dress, returns to life in the Magdalen pictured by Andrew Lloyd Webber and Tim Rice in *Jesus Christ Superstar*. The Magdalen who rocks out songs of consolation in Webber's and Rice's show is the most recent descendant of the mythical figure who made such a great impact on medieval Easter plays. And the "good whore," the "holy prostitute," Jesus' "beloved friend," hardly shows her age. Her ambiguity intact, she has made it through Inquisitions and witch-hunts without a strand of grey in her long flowing hair.

The novelist Nikos Kazantzakis, whose *The Last Temptation of Christ* precedes *Jesus Christ Superstar* by slightly more than a decade, also preserves both the Mother Goddess and the seductive feminine in the figure of the Magdalen. But Kazantzakis's figure more nearly fulfills the potential of the mythical Magdalen shaped during the early centuries of Christianity than does any other recent literary figure. For in Kazantzakis's further metamorphoses of the figure, the implications of the concepts carried by the Magdalen into Western culture become explicit. Not only does the long-lived "holy harlot" stir sexual desire within Jesus himself but she also becomes Absolute Woman.

12

The Magdalen as
WOMAN Born of Man

My principal anguish and the source of all my joys and sorrows
from my youth onward has been the incessant, merciless battle
between the spirit and the flesh.

Nikos Kazantzakis

Beloved wife, I never knew the world was so beautiful or the flesh
so holy. It too is a daughter of God, a graceful sister of the soul. I
never knew that the joys of the body were not sinful.

Jesus

One day my beloved will again pass through this narrow street,
and then I shall fill my arms with pomegranates and place them at
his feet. He will bend over, take one and refresh himself.

Magdalene
The Last Temptation of Christ

W<small>HILE</small> Kazantzakis's *The Last Temptation of Christ*, with its
extreme emphasis on the unconscious and on dreams, reflects the
impact of Freudian and Jungian ideas on modern literature, the
novel, with its concern for the conflict between flesh and spirit,
also demonstrates the· persistence into the twentieth-century
cultural climate of radically dualistic ideas represented in early
Gnostic writings. And Kazantzakis, like the second-century
Gnostics, revises biblical events and figures to fit his particular
"cosmogony." The serpent again becomes a symbol of wisdom
and of immortality, a feminine figure whom Kazantzakis places in

Jesus' dreams as a "temptress." The "God of Israel" again becomes a "tyrant" who, in Kazantzakis's novel, commands the martyrdom of both Jesus and the Magdalen. "Saul," pictured as an ugly "hunchback" so "wretched" and self-hating that he must kill others, appears as the one sent by the "God of Israel" to carry out his commands. Jesus appears as a most reluctant worker for the "kingdom of heaven." A visionary in whom the desires of the "flesh" and those of the "spirit" are in mortal combat, Jesus the ascetic is plagued with erotic dreams of the Magdalen up to his last moment of life.

Kazantzakis takes for granted that the flesh and the spirit are, as he finds them in himself, forever at enmity within man. And the Greek novelist views the longing for reconciliation of the dualistic opposites as a "universal" desire.[1] Kazantzakis uses both the traditionally fictionalized Magdalen and a personally fictionalized figure of Jesus to dramatize the desire for reconciliation between the body and the soul. By strengthening the Magdalen's bond with the Bride of the Song of Songs, the twentieth-century novelist tries to bring flesh and spirit together in a harmonious union. His failure to bring about the union rests not in the Bride of the old Song celebrating sexual love and life on earth but in his own figure of the Magdalen who "issued from man," from heaven-born man.

Kazantzakis tries to display the Magdalen as a Jungian "archetype," a figure of the paradoxical feminine considered by Jungians to be necessarily present in every man's unconscious. His figure of the Magdalen remains, however, a product of the novelist's eclectic, though not syncretic, imagination. Drawing on past traditions, he incorporates into his heroine the multiple contradictions placed in the mythical figure throughout some two thousand years. A Venus-Diana, a holy harlot, an Athene-Sophia, an Isis-Ishtar, the "pure spiritual Mariham," the "sinner" forgiven by Jesus because she "loved much," the anointer of the Christ, the Bride of the Song of Songs as well as the woman taken in adultery, Kazantzakis's Magdalen merges with Mary the sister of Martha and Lazarus in Jesus' final "temptation."

Kazantzakis also adds his contribution to the Magdalen myth

by picturing her as Jesus' cousin. The two of them share memories from early childhood on into their last days. Kazantzakis's Magdalen, like Jean Michel's fifteenth-century Magdalen, tries but fails to seduce Jesus himself. But the twentieth-century Magdalen stirs a deep, long-lasting desire for her in the man Jesus. And she becomes a prostitute not because Jesus prevented John from marrying her, as earlier myth held, but because of her unfulfilled sexual love for Jesus.

Kazantzakis's Jesus accepts the blame for the Magdalen's turning to prostitution. Trying to destroy the desires of his own flesh in a desert hermitage, the young Jesus confesses to an old Rabbi the "temptation" which the Magdalen arouses in him as she continues to haunt his dreams. "It's my fault, mine, that she took the road she did," Jesus cries out. "I drove her to the pleasure of the flesh when I was still a small child—yes, I confess it." And he tells the Rabbi of the "fateful" experience he shared with the four-year-old Magdalen when he was a boy of three. The two of them undressed and lay together with the soles of their feet pressed together in "great joy" and from that "joyful sin," Jesus says, came the Magdalen's insatiable desire for men.[2]

Again, Jesus blames himself and expresses his own desire for the Magdalen when, in one of his frequent visions, he hears the voice of God urging him to work for "the kingdom of heaven." Jesus shouts to the voice: "I don't care about the kingdom of heaven. I like the earth. I want to marry, I tell you; I want Magdalene, even if she's a prostitute. It's my fault she became one, my fault, and I shall save her. Her! Not the earth, not the kingdom of this world—it's Magdalene I want to save. That's enough for me!" [3]

The beautiful whore, this time with long, blue-black hair, remains the source of Jesus' internal struggle between the desires of the flesh and the yearnings of the spirit up to the moment of his death. The erotic Magdalen haunts his dreams even though he obeys the voice commanding him to work for "the kingdom of heaven." She could, his unconscious tells him, bring Paradise on earth for him. For in one of his dreams the serpent appears to him and in a feminine voice urges him to marry the Magdalen and let her open to him the "doors of Paradise." The serpent, supporting her plea with an old allegorical exegesis of the Song of Songs, compares the Magdalen to the Bride who had been symbolically debased into the "whore of Jerusalem." "Look how God married the whore of Jerusalem even though all nations passed over her." [4]

The serpent at last wins Jesus to her side with an appeal to the man's desire for immortality. The immortality offered by the serpent is immortality on earth and is acquired by the begetting of offspring. "God created man and woman to match, like the key and the lock." And, in words recalling the advice given the Babylonian immortality-seeker Gilgamesh, the serpent commands Jesus to "open" the Magdalen, for in her "beautiful, cool, and accomplished body" Jesus' children wait to be born and to "walk in the sun." [5] Jesus will obey. He envisions the Magdalen coming to seek him. And with the Magdalen-Bride and their many children he enjoys a long life, "sweetened" and "more human," with his wife weaving clean garments for him throughout their years "under the sun." [6] But only in dreams does Kazantzakis's Jesus marry his "beloved wife."

Kazantzakis has the Magdalen herself state the case for "woman." He pictures her sitting at the feet of Jesus, "under a budding almond tree," and explaining to her "Rabbi" that woman lives out eternity on earth. The Magdalen says: "Rabbi, why do you talk to me of the future life? We are not men, to have need of another, an eternal life; we are women, and for us one moment with the man we love is everlasting paradise, one moment far from the man we love is everlasting hell." [7]

Erotically drawn to the earthbound Magdalen, Jesus finds the joy of sexual union with her during his "last temptation" when an angel enters his dream and offers him the taste of all the pleasures he ever secretly longed for. Jesus thinks that he has already died and entered heaven until the angel assures him that he is still on earth. Jesus hears the "tinkling of bracelets and necklaces" and turns to see the Magdalen, "crowned with lemon blossoms," standing before him, "bashful and trembling." He takes her in his arms and crying, "Magdalene, beloved Magdalene," tells her that he has many years longed for this moment.[8] "Under a flowering lemon tree," the Bride-Magdalen and the Bridegroom-Christ unite in sexual love. And Jesus says: "Beloved wife, I never knew the world so beautiful or the flesh so holy." Kazantzakis's Jesus learns through his vision that the "joys of the body are not sinful." [9]

Outside the world of dreams, Jesus has learned little from the Magdalen-Siduri-Athene-Isis-Bride. He has, however, in the world of "reality," succeeded in bringing about her transformation from eroticism to ascetic devotion to him. She forsakes her life of prostitution, scourges her flesh until she becomes again a "virgin," laments her sins, anoints Jesus, and spends the rest of her days weaving a cloak for her "Beloved" and dreaming of a marriage which will never take place, even though the young Jesus had once thought life with her would be the "only way of salvation." [10]

Kazantzakis pictures the young tormented Jesus, long before the Magdalen's "transformation," discovering from the prostitute herself the "only way of salvation." One day Jesus finds himself irresistibly drawn to the "perfumed hermitage of his cousin Magdalene" where he joins the line of "worshippers at the shrine" until he is called in by the "holy harlot." [11] Discovering that the visitor is Jesus, the Magdalen furiously reminds him that she is trying to forget him by giving herself to all other men.[12] Jesus begs forgiveness of her. "Forgive me, my sister," he says, and he offers to "save" her. The Magdalen calls him a coward, tells him that it is really her body which he covets. "A woman's soul is her flesh," she blurts out. "You know it, you know it; but you don't have the courage to take this soul in your arms like a man and kiss it—kiss it and save it! I pity you and detest you!" This, Jesus is not ready for. He shouts: "You're possessed with seven devils, whore!" The Magdalen shudders and, weeping, protests that it is not seven devils but seven "wounds" which plague her.[13] The young Jesus now wants to "clasp her in his arms, wipe away her tears, caress her hair, and gladden her heart," to take her away where they can "live like man and wife, have children," and "suffer and rejoice like real human beings," for that is, he thinks, "the woman's way of salvation and the way in which man could be saved with her—the only way." [14] But he does nothing, says nothing.

Man's "only way of salvation" seems to lie in the world of dreams. For with the "beloved wife" of his dreams Jesus learns that woman is a "fountain of immortal water." And he worships his Magdalen-Bride as the maternal goddess. "I bow and worship you, Mother of God," he tells his visionary Magdalen-Bride. And he begs forgiveness of the goddess.[15] He discovers the road by which the "mortal becomes immortal" and admits that he went "astray" seeking a "route outside the flesh," going the "way of clouds, great thoughts, and death." [16] He asks the Magdalen-Bride what they should name the son they're going to have, and when the Magdalen says "Name him what you will," Jesus says: "Let's call him Paraclete, the Comforter." Then, satiated with sexual love, the Jesus of the vision falls asleep.[17] While Jesus sleeps, the Magdalen is attacked by a mob.

Kazantzakis, in his effort to incorporate into the Magdalen all the attributes formerly given the figure and at the same time to portray her as his concept of the "archetypal feminine" dwelling in man's unconscious, blurs "reality" with dream. He pictures the Magdalen as the woman taken in adultery during Jesus' vision-filled dying moments on the cross. As the woman taken in adultery, Kazantzakis's Magdalen, like Maeterlinck's earlier figure, undergoes a "passion." But since Kazantzakis's dying Jesus does not protect the woman from the mob, the Magdalen becomes, not of her own volition, but at the command of God, a martyr, the "First Martyr."

The voice of God addresses the Magdalen: "Great Martyr!" And the voice orders her to prepare for death so that she may become "immortal." [18] The Magdalen-Bride protests. She wants neither death nor immortality. And especially now when, she says, for the first time both her "flesh and soul" were kissed.[19] But God insists: "Magdalene, you have attained the highest joy of your life. You can go no higher. Death is kind. . . . Until we meet again, First Martyr!" [20] And Saul inflames the mob against the "adulteress." [21]

The dying Jesus hears cries and envisions the Magdalen stoned to death. But his unconscious metamorphoses the scene. He sees the stones turn into a loom. And he sees a woman sitting at the loom, weaving, and lamenting in a voice "exceeding sweet." [22] Leaning over, he kisses the earth. He says: "Mother, hold me close, and I shall hold you close. Mother, why can't you be my God?" [23]

The woman at the loom, the Isis-Mother-Goddess, is the same Magdalen who during Jesus' life sat at her loom weaving a winter cloak for Jesus and thinking: "One day my beloved will again pass through this narrow street, and then I shall fill my arms with pomegranates and place them at his feet. He will bend over, take one and refresh himself." [24]

Kazantzakis brings Jesus down that "narrow street" in order to link the Magdalen with Luke's "sinner" whom Jesus forgave because she "loved much." When the Rabbi Jesus appeared, the Magdalen ran out to meet him, fell down at his feet, hugged his knees, with her "blue-black hair, which still smelled of its accursed perfumes," spilling over the earth. Jesus bent over, took her by the hand, lifted her up, and held her "just as an inexperienced bridegroom holds his bride." Although his "body rejoiced from its very roots," it was really, he said, "the soul of man" he had lifted from the earth.[25] On this day Jesus forgave the Magdalen for all her sins, for she had "loved much." She gave the pomegranates to her "beloved." And she watched him refresh himself with the "cool red fruit." [26]

When Jesus asked her why she gazed at him "with troubled eyes" as if she were saying "goodbye," she answered:

> "I must look at you, because woman issued from the body of man and still cannot detach her body from his. But you must look at heaven, because you are a man, and man was created by God. Allow me, therefore, to look at you, my child."

And as she spoke, Kazantzakis tells us, "her breast filled out and stirred as though she were giving suck to her son." [27]

It is the same Magdalen-Bride, the Venus-Aphrodite, the Mother-Earth Goddess who is the First Martyr. The Mother Goddess has no place in the patriarchal cosmos. The angel tells the visionary Jesus that God killed the Magdalen. Jesus shouts to the Almighty: "Even the most boorish woodchopper trembles to cut down a tree in bloom, and the Magdalene had blossomed from her roots right up to her topmost branches." But the angel philosophizes as he attempts to comfort Jesus with a final "temptation." He transforms the Magdalen into WOMAN. The angel declares:

> "Only one woman exists in the world, one woman with countless faces. This one falls; the next rises. Mary Magdalene died. Mary the sister of Lazarus lives and waits for us, waits for you. She is the Magdalene herself, but with another face." [28]

Or, as a street-corner "philosopher" would likely say: "Put a sack over her head, and you'll never know the difference." So Jesus enjoys in his death dream a long happy life with Magdalen-Mary-Woman. But at last Saul, having become the converted Paul, intervenes to complete Jesus' death "for the sake of man" and for fulfillment of the "words of Matthew." [29]

The struggle within Jesus parallels the conflict between the Magdalen and the Christ. Kazantzakis suggests that the battle between woman-flesh and man-spirit is nothing less than the battle between Eros and Death. Kazantzakis explicitly uses the Freudian idea of the eternally waged war between Eros and Death in his picture of the Magdalen carrying a flagon of perfume as she goes to anoint the Christ against his death. The Magdalen has saved the bottle of Arabian perfume given her by a former lover in hope of using it to wash the hair of her Bridegroom Jesus on their wedding day. Weeping, she goes to anoint Jesus. She cradles the flagon of perfume as if it were an infant, for she knows that it is not "Eros" but "death" in her "beloved's body." [30]

14. *La Madeleine à la veilleuse* by Georges de la Tour, formerly in the Louvre, now in the National Gallery of Art, Washington, D.C.
PHOTOGRAPH COURTESY OF CAISSE NATIONALE DES MONUMENTS HISTORIQUES, ARCHIVES PHOTOGRAPHIQUES-PARIS

Kazantzakis makes a desperate effort to reinstate the Magdalen as the life-bringing Bride of the Song of Songs in his twentieth-century cosmogony. But he can no more envision her without the skull, the *memento mori,* and the whip to "scourge the flesh" than could Georges de la Tour in his seventeenth-century painting *La Madeleine à la veilleuse* (fig. *14*). The "contemplative" Magdalen, with her whip beside her, pictured as the keeper not "of the vats the gods gave her" but of the vigil, watches the burning candle while she cradles a skull in her lap.

We assume that Kazantzakis's Magdalen, the goddess of love and life, had the power to resurrect the "beloved corpse" and therefore restore life to the earth. But Kazantzakis pictures no resurrection in *The Last Temptation of Christ.* Eros is simply temptation. And, as in the painting of the Magdalen by Georges de la Tour, Death triumphs over Eros. So the old "incessant, merciless battle between spirit and flesh" rages on. For woman "issued from the body of man and still cannot detach her body from his" while man, "created by God," must "look to heaven." Woman-matter and male-spirit are once more viewed as irreconcilable opposites.

The plunge into twentieth-century neoromanticism carries us full circle back to the second century of the present era. The Gnostic ambivalence toward Eros and toward woman persists in the twentieth-century Magdalen. Kazantzakis's Magdalen becomes WOMAN. Kazantzakis does not say, as some modern men have said, that "woman is matter, man is mind," and woman is no more than "a bundle of animal lusts, merely in the world for the purpose of procreation," while man transcends matter, space, and time through his unique intellectual ability.[31] But Kazantzakis does make of woman a lifeless abstraction.

In his attempt to present the Magdalen as the Jungian "archetypal feminine," a product of the "collective unconscious" and present in every male "psyche," he produces a stereotype. Woman is again either deified as a mother goddess or she is at once feared and desired as a tempting Venus who "cannot detach herself" from man's body. Kazantzakis's "holy harlot" reflects also the dread of death and the desire for continuity not only of life on earth but also of cultural traditions which brought about the fictionalization of the Gospel Mary Magdalene almost two thousand years ago. And Kazantzakis's Magdalen-Woman, willy-nilly, solemnly perpetuates the radically dualistic ideas implanted in the mythical figure of the Magdalen in Gnostic writings during an earlier Age of Anxiety.

13

The Magdalen Monument:
A Caveat and Some Conclusions

Loving you thus
And hating you so,
My heart is torn in two.
Crucified.
> Eldridge Cleaver's "To a White Girl" in *Soul on Ice*

Venus would lie in the dark, the deep of the fathomless ocean
Had not Apelles' art lifted her bright from the foam.
> Ovid's *Art of Love*

The fig tree puts forth its figs,
    and the vines are in blossom;
    they give forth fragrance.
Arise, my love, my fair one,
    and come away.
> Song of Songs 2:13

Both the longevity of the Magdalen and the significance of the fictionalized figure stem from her link with a prostitute, a seductive Venus, and with the life-affirming Bride of the Song of Songs. Although she centers no literary work produced by writers of the stature of Chaucer or Shakespeare, the Magdalen through the centuries exerts an influence on other literary figures of women. Embodying ancient personifications of the "feminine" principle in the cosmos, alongside ambivalent views of the feminine as a force which is simultaneously creative and destructive, the Magdalen becomes in Maeterlinck's play as well as in Kazantzakis's *The Last Temptation of Christ* a stereotyped image of paradoxical woman. The stereotype shows up in works of important twentieth-century writers. Her very name is dropped by such differing writers as Günter Grass, Saul Bellow, and James Joyce to connote some aspect of the old notion of the paradoxical feminine. And in the ancestry of James Joyce's Molly Bloom one could, I suggest, more readily discover the fictionalized Magdalen than Odysseus's Penelope.

The Magdalen's importance reaches beyond the specific representations of the figure in art and in literature, and that importance cannot be overlooked. As a stereotype, the figure of the Magdalen exerts an influence on cultural attitudes and human values. For the stereotyped figure results from, and perpetuates, a simplistic split between the masculine and the feminine, spirit and flesh, mind and body, MAN and WOMAN, light and dark, WHITE and BLACK, with the not always implicit distinctions between absolute "good" and absolute "evil." Eldridge Cleaver's love-hate poem "To a White Girl" boldly illustrates the perpetuation of radically dualistic ideas into the contemporary cultural climate and uncovers a danger hidden in stereotypes. The poem begins: "I love you/ Because you're white," and describes the poet's deep hatred for the white girl. She is the black man's "Moby Dick, White Witch,/ Symbol of the rope and hanging tree,/ Of the burning cross." The poem concludes:

> Loving you thus
> And hating you so,
> My heart is torn in two.
> Crucified.

And Eldridge Cleaver confesses that he becomes a "rapist." [1]

Eldridge Cleaver's poem and his book *Soul on Ice*, from which the poem comes, make manifest some disturbing effects that a persisting stereotype can have on an individual human being who feels that he himself is included in the general stereotype. He retaliates by stereotyping others and therefore perpetuates the radically dualistic attitudes which produced the original dehumanizing stereotype. And finally "absolutes" reverse roles so that "black" is equated with "good," "white" with "evil." Since Cleaver's self-defeating reactions to a persisting stereotype are not unique, they may stand as a caveat, a warning against accepting as "real" a figure who has been masked as the TRUTH and led onto the cultural scene. Behind a masked stereotype lies propaganda. And propaganda bastardizes the "culture-creating force of the pure play element" without which, if we accept as valid an idea set forth by Johan Huizinga, real civilization cannot exist. Real civilization "will always demand fair play," and genuine *homo ludens* plays "fair," for he does not debase humanity or human values.[2] The stereotyped Magdalen who propagandizes the fiction of "paradoxical woman" as "fact" can therefore hardly be a product of genuine *homo ludens*'s "happy inspiration."

We can, I think, safely conclude that had no myth been shaped around the Mary Magdalene sketched in the New Testament canonical Gospels, the Magdalen would not have survived through the centuries to rock out in *Jesus Christ Superstar*, "I've been changed yes really changed." Nor would she have appeared as the enigmatic heroine of Maeterlinck's play *Mary Magdalene* and WOMAN in Kazantzakis's novel *The Last Temptation of Christ*. And I doubt that the Magdalen who figures so prominently in medieval Christendom would have come into being had the prototype for the figure not been created in the East during the turbulent centuries of Christianity's beginnings and had the Eastern traditions not been carried into the West during the Crusades.

For the time being, I hold as a valid hypothesis my assumption that John's picture of the recognition scene between the risen Christ and Mary Magdalene, a scene dramatically foreshadowed by the ancient earth goddess searching for and finding the heaven god, is of vital importance in bringing about the shaping of myths around the Mary Magdalene of the canonical Gospels. Both the scene and the fictionalized Magdalen have, as Titian's *Noli me tangere* well exemplifies, inspired artists through the centuries (fig. *15*).

Titian emphasizes the close relationship between the Magdalen and the Christ who center the foreground of his painting. Resting her left hand on her ointment jar, the Magdalen kneels on the earth as she looks in wonder at the risen Christ standing beside her and with her right hand reaches out to touch him. The Christ, whose Adonis-like body is draped in his winding sheet, rests his weight on a gardener's scythe and looks on the Magdalen as he withdraws from her touch. The Magdalen's golden hair falls over her shoulders and onto her brilliant red cloak. A single tree directly behind the two figures leans against the sky. On a hill in the background stands a large farm-dwelling, and the figures of a man and a dog, barely visible, descend a path leading to a distant valley where sheep graze in a green meadow. The scene is humanistic, and the Christ and the Magdalen who dominate the pastoral background are not removed from the earth.

A fourteenth-century *Noli me tangere,* painted in the style of Orcagna, anticipates not only Titian's conventional pyramidal composition of the figures of the Magdalen and the Christ but also his interpretation of the close bond between the two figures (fig. *16*). The earlier painting differs from Titian's, however, in detaching the central figures from the earth. The Christ and the Magdalen, both royally gowned, diminish the stylized landscape around and beneath them. The Christ bends toward the kneeling Magdalen and meets her eyes with his. The Magdalen's golden hair falls onto her red cloak as she lifts graceful hands toward the risen Christ who, although he forbids her to touch or embrace him, also reaches out toward her. Unlike Titian's figures, both the Magdalen and the Christ in this earlier painting bear the ancient mark of divinity, the halo. The gardener's spade, held in Christ's hand, becomes an icon against the gold backdrop which replaces nature's sky. And the Magdalen, separated from the earth, embodies the "Heavenly Aphrodite."

Although the artist responsible for the fourteenth-century painting pictures the Magdalen as more closely akin to the "pure spiritual Mariham" of the second-century *Pistis Sophia* than does Titian, both artists derive inspiration for their views of the Magdalen not only from the recognition scene uniquely drama-tized in the Gospel of John but also from the mythologized figure. And Moretto da Brescia's early sixteenth-century *Pietà,* based on the description of the Crucifixion presented in the Gospel of

15. *Noli me tangere* by Titian.

John, again reflects the impact of the mythologized figure of the Magdalen on the artist's imagination (fig. *17*). While Mary the mother of Jesus and John, "the disciple whom Jesus loved," gaze mournfully on the face of Jesus, the monumental figure of the long-haired, grieving Magdalen centers the foreground of the painting. With her long hair disheveled, her feet bare, a sleeve of her gown torn, she cradles the feet of the crucified Christ and embraces his legs. Near the empty tomb stands the Magdalen's ointment jar. The elegantly gowned Venus-Magdalen who, in Moretto's painting of the "chaste prostitute" (fig. *13*), displays to the viewer her ointment jar, her long flowing hair, and a wistful profile, is pictured in the *Pietà* as the lamenting "companion" of the Christ.

The Magdalen myth is born, I think, of the illicit union of Judaism with Hellenism. The Magdalen grows out of apocalyptic Judeo-Christianity's efforts to prevent the complete disintegration of a people dominated by Hellenistic traditions and to alleviate suffering and fears of impending death by focusing the people's desires away from life on earth and toward an afterlife in heaven. The "kingdom of heaven" is, of course, the "good news" proclaimed in the Christian Gospels. The fictionalization of the Magdalen manifests, however, the failure of attempts to eradicate altogether the appeal to human imaginations of a fertility goddess so long linked with the continuity of life and still worshipped by some of those who lived in the Hellenistic world. *Homo ludens* therefore begins to shape the Magdalen myth in order to fulfill his desire for a Venus, an Ishtar, an Isis, as a "companion" for the male dying and reviving deity. But the dualism inherent in Christianity and overtly doctrinaire in Gnosticism threatens to divorce the ancient goddess from the earth.

16. *Noli me tangere*, in the style of Orcagna.

A cultural climate permeated with heaven-oriented mysticism and a morbid preoccupation with sex, with radically dualistic concepts resulting from an either-or view of the universe, and with ambivalent attitudes toward both sex and women favors the metamorphoses of the Magdalen who figures so prominently in extant writings from the early Christian era. When the earth is viewed as corrupt matter and linked with the feminine, the goddess, through sexless union with the divine male spirit, becomes the "pure spiritual Mariham" of the *Pistis Sophia*. And when sexual love is no longer viewed as natural and beneficent but is seen as unnatural and degrading, the goddess of love and fertility is either debased into a "Common Aphrodite" or abstracted into a "Heavenly Aphrodite." But the ambiguous Magdalen becomes both a common whore and a spiritual Venus through the erotic asceticism planted in the fictionalized figure by Gnostic writers and through the Neoplatonic identification of her with the allegorized Bride of the Song of Songs. And the paradox lives on in the figure who journeys from the East to the medieval West where the Magdalen rises to fame both as a goddess of life on earth and a common prostitute who, by finally denying all earthly life, is transformed into a heavenly Venus to be honored in heaven "beyond virgins."

Through myths attached to the figure during the early centuries of Christianity, then, the Magdalen becomes a prostitute, the anointer of the Christ, the Christ's sister-bride, a goddess of wisdom and of love and of fertility, a second Eve, a preacher, a contemplative, the Christ's "companion," and the "pure spiritual

17. *Pietà* by Moretto da Brescia.
PHOTOGRAPH COURTESY OF
NATIONAL GALLERY OF ART, WASHINGTON, D.C.,
SAMUEL H. KRESS COLLECTION

Mariham" who shares Jesus' *gnosis*. And through elaboration and localization of early myths attached to the figure, during the Crusades the Magdalen goes as an evangelist to Marseilles, converts the French king and queen from the religion of Islam by bringing about the conception of a child for the royal pair, goes as a hermit to the grotto called Sainte-Baume to live for thirty years without material food, kisses the earth "fervently" as her soul is lifted to heaven amidst "merry song." She becomes a Venus in sackcloth, a vessel for ambivalent views of Eros and of women, honored by medieval gardeners and craftsmen, and by mystics, prisoners, and reformed prostitutes. And she becomes a Muse inspiring artists and writers through the centuries.

Not only does the Magdalen inspire playwrights to compose long poetic laments for her, but the "worldly" Magdalen also carries into medieval Easter plays comedy and songs in the vernacular. Artists too are drawn toward the many faces of the fictionalized figure. The "contemplative" Magdalen, during the fifteenth and sixteenth centuries, holds especial appeal to artists inspired by Renaissance Humanism.

The serious-faced figure pictured by the Flemish Rogier van der Weyden in his fifteenth-century painting of *The Magdalen Reading* (fig. *18*) anticipates the figure represented in *Mary Magdalene Preaching*, painted a century later by the Master of the Magdalene Legend (fig. *10*). Also clothed in a magnificent green frock and with her hair modestly covered, the fifteenth-century Magdalen sits in a well-furnished room as she contemplates the words of an open Bible which she holds in her graceful hands, while her ointment jar, itself an object of simple grace, stands on the floor beside her. The painting, originally picturing the feminine figure in company with two standing male figures, was cut down to center on the composure of the contemplative Magdalen.

Equally composed, though facing the viewer, is the Magdalen painted in the early sixteenth century by the Milanese artist Bernardino Luini (fig. *19*). Fashionably gowned, with her long red hair falling down her back, Luini's Magdalen lifts the lid of her chalicelike ointment jar and smiles out at the viewer. And in the face of Luini's Magdalen, we see mirrored the features of his "contemplative" Venus who sits on a luxurious couch and gazes into the distance (fig. *20*).

Titian's paintings reflect, as do Luini's and Correggio's works, a particular interest in both Venus and the Magdalen. But Titian, in picturing the contemplative Magdalen, at once goes beyond his contemporaries and sets a precedent for later artists. Around 1531, some dozen years after he painted *The Adoration of Venus*, Titian painted two versions of the contemplative Magdalen, both of which are now in the Pitti Palace in Florence.[3] The later version, picturing a seductive figure whose tearful eyes look heavenward, anticipates the Magdalen whose name becomes in seventeenth-century England a synonym for a sentimental weeper. Titian's earlier painting of the Magdalen alone in her hermit retreat, however, reveals no sign of the maudlin in the illuminated face whose eyes also look toward the heavens. And beside the figure stands a small round ointment jar whose rim bears the signature of the artist. Titian transforms iconography into Renaissance art, the Magdalen into his Muse. While Correggio drapes the erotic ascetic in a blue cloak (fig. *11*), Titian indeed removes the sackcloth from his sensual mystic whose long curling reddish gold hair does not conceal her voluptuous body but affirms the beauty of the nude Magdalen-Venus.

Ovid's comment on the immortality given Venus by the artist Apelles may be applied to the artists' and writers' roles in restoring the figure of the Magdalen to life during the very period in which Ovid's *Art of Love* was enjoying popularity in Western Christendom: "Venus would lie in the dark, the deep of the fathomless ocean/ Had not Apelles' art lifted her bright from the foam."[4]

If not taken solemnly as THE TRUE WOMAN or as EVERYWOMAN, the fictionalized Magdalen, to whom so many monuments have been dedicated, stands as a monument to the eclectic imagination of *homo ludens,* who selects figures and concepts from cultural traditions known to him and incorporates into the Magdalen a holy harlot, a goddess of love, a goddess of wisdom, a goddess of fertility.

18. *The Magdalen Reading*
by Rogier van der Weyden.
REPRODUCED BY COURTESY OF THE TRUSTEES,
THE NATIONAL GALLERY, LONDON

The figure of the Magdalen falls into perspective when viewed in the light of myths shaped around the Mary Magdalene of the New Testament canonical Gospels during the period of intensive cross-cultural fertilization which characterized the early centuries of the current era. And the perspective becomes comic when one today catches sight of the metamorphosed Magdalen in the brand new church pictured by Robert Heinlein in his *Stranger in a Strange Land*. The church, established on Earth by the Man from Mars, celebrates the "Mother of All, the unity of the many," with a stereovision drama featuring a "liberated" young American woman who, simply by changing costumes, becomes in turn Cybele, Isis, Ge, Devi, Ishtar, Maryam, Mother Eve, Mater Deum Magna, Loving and Beloved, Life Undying.[5] One can "grok," as the Man from Mars would say, in the Maryam who merges with feminine figures akin to her, the long-lived Magdalen. So Robert Heinlein's Jubal Harshaw observes, echoing an old French adage, "Everything always is—and the more it changes the more it is the same."

We see that the significance of the metamorphosed Magdalen extends far beyond specific roles given her in Western literature. And the full import of the feminine figure not only manifests itself in the varied monuments to the Magdalen but also lies in the use of the fictionalized figure as a vessel to carry simplistic dualism into Western culture. Since simplistic dualism at once solemnly produces and perpetuates stereotypes, it deforms both the figure of the Magdalen and the play element which brought about the early metamorphoses of the figure.

When stripped of her radical dualism and her sackcloth, however, the Magdalen survives as a monument to *HOMO*

ON FOLLOWING PAGE:
20. *Venus* by Bernardino Luini.
PHOTOGRAPH COURTESY OF NATIONAL GALLERY OF ART,
WASHINGTON, D.C., SAMUEL H. KRESS COLLECTION

LUDENS. For *homo ludens,* seeking to affirm simultaneously the continued blossoming of the "vines" from generation to generation and the value of human life by preserving in his cosmogony ancient personifications of love and wisdom, works on the borderline between jest and earnest as he creates, with no malicious intent, the Athene-Venus-Magdalen.

NOTES

SELECTED BIBLIOGRAPHY

INDEX

Notes

CHAPTER 1: *Monuments to the Magdalen*

1. *Gospel of Thomas*, in Jean Doresee, *The Secret Books of the Egyptian Gnostics: An Introduction to the Gnostic Manuscripts Discovered at Chenoboskion, With an English Translation and Critical Evaluation of the Gospel According to Thomas*, trans. Philip Mairet (1958; revised and augmented by the author, New York: Viking Press, 1960), p. 370.
   Nikos Kazantzakis, *Report to Greco*, trans. P. A. Bien (1965; reprint ed., New York: Bantam Books, Inc., 1965), p. 228.
   Andrew Lloyd Webber and Tim Rice, *Jesus Christ Superstar* (1969; reprint ed., London, England: Leeds Music Ltd., 1970), p. 14.

2. William E. Phipps, *Was Jesus Married?* (New York: Harper & Row, 1970), pp. 136–138.

3. Sir Herbert Grierson, *Cross-Currents in Seventeenth-Century English Literature: The World, the Flesh, the Spirit, Their Actions and Reactions* (1929; reprint ed., New York: Harper, 1958), n. 2 on p. 181. Grierson notes that Mario Praz referred to the Magdalen featured in Counter-Reformation English poetry as "Venus in sackcloth," and I use the appellative to suggest the paradox embodied in the mythical figure who rises to fame in the West during the Middle Ages.

4. Louis Réau, *Iconographie de l'Art Chrétien*, 3 vols. (Paris: Presses Universitaires de France, 1955–59), 2:849. Hereafter referred to as Réau.

5. Quoted in the Oxford English Dictionary, 1933 edition, vol. 6, ii, 23.

6. Victor Saxer, *Le Culte de Marie Madeleine en Occident, des Origines à la Fin du Moyen-Âge* (Paris, 1959), p. 247. Hereafter referred to as Saxer, *Le Culte*.

7. Réau, 2:849.

8. Ibid., 1:325.

9. Ibid., 2:857.

10. Ibid., 3:852.

11. Ibid., 2:851.

12. Émile Mâle, *Les Saints Compagnons du Christ* (published posthumously, 1956; reprint ed., Paris, 1958), p. 73. My urgent requests of the superintendent of monuments in Florence for a photograph to be reproduced in *Venus in Sackcloth* were unfortunately not fulfilled. A reproduction of Donatello's sculpture of the Magdalen appears in Mâle's *Les Saints Compagnons du Christ.*

13. Dora and Erwin Panofsky, *Pandora's Box: The Changing Aspects of a Mythical Symbol*, Bollingen Series 52, 2d rev. ed. (1962; reprint ed., New York: Harper & Row, 1965), n. 13 on p. 62.

14. According to the Oxford English Dictionary, 2, ii, 247, the word "maudlin" first appears in print in Middleton's *Michaelmas Term* in 1607.

15. Richard Crashaw, *The Poems of Richard Crashaw*, ed. L. C. Martin (Oxford: Clarendon Press, 1957), "Saint Mary Magdalene or The Weeper," pp. 307–14, "motto" and 11. 1–6.

16. Grierson, *Cross-Currents*, p. 181.

17. Maurice Maeterlinck, *Mary Magdalene: A Play in Three Acts*, trans. Alexander Teixeira de Mattos (New York: Dodd, Mead & Co., 1910).
    Nikos Kazantzakis, *The Last Temptation of Christ*, trans. P. A. Bien (1960; reprint ed., New York: Bantam Books, Inc., 1960).

18. *Mary Magdalene*, in *The Digby Mysteries*, ed. F. J. Furnivall, EETS, ES 70 (1896; reprint ed., London, 1930): 53–136.
    Lewis Wager, *The Life and Repentance of Marie Magdalene: A Morality Play Reprinted From the Original Edition of 1566*, ed. with Introduction, Notes, and Glossarial Index by Frederic Ives Carpenter, Decimal Publications, 2d ser., vol. 1 (Chicago: University of Chicago Press, 1904).

19. *Gospel of Mary*, in *Gnosticism: A Source Book of Heretical Writings From the Early Christian Period*, ed. Robert M. Grant (New York: Harper, 1961), pp. 65–68.

20. *Pistis Sophia*, literally translated from the Coptic by George Horner, with an introduction by F. A. Legge (London: Society for the Promoting of Christian Knowledge, 1924).

21. Edith Deen, *All of the Women of the Bible* (New York: Harper, 1955), pp. 200–205.

22. Theodor H. Gaster, *Thespis: Ritual, Myth, and Drama in the Ancient Near East* (1950; reprint ed., New York: Harper & Row, 1966), p. 24.

23. Denis de Rougemont, *Love in the Western World*, trans. Montgomery Belgion (1939; revised and augmented edition, 1956; reprint ed., Garden City, N.Y.: Doubleday & Co., 1957), p. 8.

24. Johan Huizinga, *Homo Ludens: A Study of the Play Element in Culture* (1944; reprint ed., Boston: Beacon Press, 1955), p. 5.

25. Recent studies dealing with Mary Magdalene include:

June P. Bonfield, "The Penitence of the Medieval Magdalen: A Study in the Meanings of Her Appellation 'Penitent' as Reflected in Vernacular Literature of the British Isles c. 1250– c. 1500" (Ph. D. thesis, University of Texas, 1970).

Sister Mary John of Carmel Chauvin, *The Role of Mary Magdalene in Medieval Drama* (Washington, D.C.: Catholic University of America Press, 1951).

Clifford Davidson, "The Digby *Mary Magdalene* and the Magdalene Cult of the Middle Ages," in *Annuale Mediaevale*, vol. 13 (New York: Duquesne University Press/Humanities Press, Inc., 1972), pp. 70–87.

Wiltrud aus der Fünten, *Maria Magdalene in der Lyrik des Mittelalters* (Düsseldorf: Schwann, 1966).

Helen Meredith Garth, "Saint Mary Magdalene in Medieval Literature," in *Johns Hopkins University Studies in Historical and Political Science* 67 (1950): 347–452.

Friedrich Otto Knoll, *Die Rolle der Maria Magdalena in geistlichen Spiel des Mittelalters* (Berlin and Leipzig, 1934).

Gerhard John Reimer, "Maria Magdalena in Werken von Hebbel, Heyse, Schlaf, und Thoma" (M.A. thesis, Michigan State University 1965).

Each of these studies neglects the important place given the Magdalen in writings from the early Christian period.

CHAPTER 2: *The Magdalen's Origins and Early Metamorphoses*

1. Biblical references in this chapter are to the Oxford Annotated Bible, Revised Standard Version of 1952, ed. Herbert G. May and Bruce M. Metzger (reprint ed., New York: Oxford University Press, 1962).

2. Biblical quotations in the notes are from the Vulgate, Biblia Sacra Juxta Vulgatum Clementinam, printed in Belgium, 1956.

Erant autem ibi mulieres multae a longe, quae secutae erant Jesum a Galilaea, ministrantes ei. Inter quas erat Maria Magdalene, et Maria Jacobi, et Joseph mater, et mater filiorum Zebedaei. [Matt. 27: 55–56]

3. The Vulgate: "Erat autem ibi Maria Magdalene, et altera Maria, sedentes contra sepulchrum" (Matt. 27:61).

4. Ibid., 28:1–10.

5. Mark 15:40–41.
6. Ibid., v. 47.
7. The Vulgate: "Et cum transisset sabbatum, Maria Magdalene, et Maria Jacobi, et Salome emerunt aromata ut venientes ungerent Jesum" (Mark 16:1).
8. Ibid., vv. 2–7.
9. Ibid., v. 8.
10. "The contents of vv. 9–20, set forth in a literary style that differs from the rest of the gospel, appear to have been gleaned from traditions known to us from other gospels and Acts. From early Christian times these verses have traditionally been accepted as part of the canonical Gospel of Mark and therefore as inspired Scripture," May and Metzger state in the notes on Mark 16; Oxford Annotated Bible, p. 1238.
11. The Vulgate: "Surgens autem mane, prima sabbati, apparuit primo Mariae Magdalene, de qua ejecerat septem daemonia" (Mark 16:9).
12. Ibid., vv. 10–11.
13. In the Dibgy Mary Magdalene we shall see that the seven demons have been transformed into personified Deadly Sins.
14. Luke 8:3.
15. Ibid., vv. 1–3.
16. In the Vulgate the "idle tale" is "mad raving":

> Erat autem Maria Magdalene, et Joanna, et Maria Jacobi, et ceterae quae cum eis erant, quae dicebant ad apostolos haec. Et visa sunt ante illos, sicut deliramentum, verba ista; et non crediderunt illis. [Luke 24:10–11]

17. John 19:25.
18. Ibid., vv. 38–41.
19. John 20:1.
20. Ibid., v. 2.
21. Ibid., vv. 4–9.
22. Ibid., v. 10.
23. Ibid., vv. 11–12.
24. Ibid., v. 13.
25. Ibid., vv. 15–17.
26. Acts of the Apostles 19:27–34. Demetrius warns the people of Ephesus of Paul's success in deposing Artemis from her magnificence in many parts of Asia and stirs them to loud shouts of "Great is Artemis of the Ephesians!"
27. Apuleius, *Metamorphoses*, bk. 11, chap. 47.
28. Saint Augustine, *The City of God*, trans. Marcus Dods, D.D. (New York: Random House, 1950), p. 43 et passim.
29. Ezek. 8:14.

30. James George Frazer, *The Golden Bough: A Study in Magic and Religion*, 10 vols. (1906; 3d ed., 1914; reprint ed., New York: St. Martin's Press, Inc., 1963).

31. E. K. Chambers, *The Medieval Stage*, 2 vols. (Oxford: Clarendon Press, 1903), 1: 105.

32. Neil C. Brooks, "The Sepulchre of Christ in Art and Liturgy, with Special Reference to the Liturgic Drama," in *University of Illinois Studies in Language and Literature*, vol. 7, no. 2 (Urbana, May 1921), pp. 7, 13. Brooks notes the first appearance of the Christ in Resurrection scenes in art.

33. Matt. 27:3–5 relates the hanging of Judas. Matt. 27:62–66 narrates the Pharisees' demand of Pilate for guards at the sepulcher. Pilate tells them to use their own guards.

34. Luke 7:38.

35. Ibid., v. 47.

36. Ibid., v. 50.

37. *The Epic of Gilgamesh*, an English version with an Introduction by N. K. Sandars (1960; reprint ed., Baltimore, Md.: Penguin Books, 1967), p. 92.

38. *The Canaanite Poem of Baal*, in Theodor H. Gaster, *Thespis: Ritual, Myth, and Drama in the Ancient Near East* (1950; reprint ed., New York: Harper & Row, 1966), p. 220.

39. Matt. 26:6–13; Mark 14:3–9; John 12:1–8.

40. Mark 14:9.

41. John 11:1–2.

42. Ibid., v. 32–35.

CHAPTER 3: *The Heroine-Hero of the* Gospel of Mary

1. *Gospel of Philip*, in *New Testament Apocrypha*, ed. Edgar Hennecke and Wilhelm Schneemelcher, trans. into English by R. McL Wilson (Philadelphia: Westminster Press, 1963), 1: 227. The Coptic text, dating from the fourth or fifth century, is based on a Greek work from the second century.

2. Jean Doresee, *The Secret Books of the Egyptian Gnostics*, trans. Philip Mairet (New York: Viking Press, 1960), p. 198, n. 5.

3. *The Apocryphal New Testament, Being the Apocryphal Gospels, Acts, Epistles, and Apocalypses With Other Narratives and Fragments Newly Translated by Montague Rhodes James*, ed. Montague Rhodes James (1st ed., 1924; corrected ed., Oxford: Clarendon Press, 1960), p. xiii.

4. Hans Jonas, *The Gnostic Religion: The Message of the Alien God and*

the Beginnings of Christianity (Beacon Hill, Boston: Beacon Hill Press, 1958), p. 48. Although Jonas's application of existentialist terms and concepts to Gnostic doctrines may be somewhat misleading, his work does evoke thought and provide much valuable information on varied Gnostic systems. I therefore borrow material from Jonas's study for this chapter's general discussion of Gnosticism. I also borrow material from Robert M. Grant's fine introductions to his very useful editions of primary works related to Gnosticism.

5. Robert M. Grant, *Gnosticism: A Source Book of Heretical Writings From the Early Christian Period* (New York: Harper, 1961), p. 17.

6. Robert M. Grant and Hans Jonas, among other scholars, have also noted the cultural cross-fertilization particularly prevalent during the beginnings of Christianity. No scholar to date has, however, pointed up the impact of that cultural cross-fertilization on the figure of the Magdalen.

7. Jonas, p. 52.

8. Ibid., p. 42.

9. Ibid., pp. 44–45.

10. Ibid., p. 46.

11. *Ecclesiasticus or the Wisdom of Jesus the Son of Sirach*, in *The Oxford Annotated Apocrypha of the Old Testament*, ed. Bruce M. Metzger (New York: Oxford University Press, 1965), pp. 128–97; Wisdom 25:24–25.

12. *Ecclesiasticus or Wisdom*, 1:7.

13. *Gospel of Mary*, in Robert M. Grant, *Gnosticism: A Source Book of Heretical Writings From the Early Christian Period*, trans. E. R. Hardy, pp. 65–68. The fragment of the *Gospel of Mary*, discovered in 1896 and contained in the Coptic Papyrus Berolinensis 8502, comes from the fifth century, according to Robert M. Grant, editor of *Gnosticism: A Source Book* (p. 63). Another fragment of the gospel, written in Greek in the third century, was published by C. H. Roberts in "The Catalogue of the Greek and Latin Papyri in the John Rylands Library" (Manchester, England, 1938, Vol. 3, no. 463). The Coptic text has been edited by Walter Till in *Die gnostischen Schriften der koptischen Papyrus Berolinensis 8502* (Berlin, 1955), and Till's edition has been, with the use of the Coptic text, revised and translated into English by E. R. Hardy. I refer to Hardy's translation. Since Irenaeus mentions the *Gospel of Mary*, we know that the original cannot date later than the second century of the Christian era.

14. *Gospel of Mary*, in Grant's *Gnosticism: A Source*, p. 65.

15. Ibid., p. 66.

16. Ibid.

17. Ibid.
18. Ibid.
19. Ibid., p. 67.
20. Ibid.
   E. R. Hardy notes that the phrases may be either "arousing" or "jealousy" of death.
21. Ibid.
22. Ibid.
23. Ibid., p. 68.
24. Ibid.
25. *Gospel of Thomas*, in Doresee's *The Secret Books of the Egyptian Gnostics*, p. 370.
26. Robert M. Grant and David Noel Freedman, *The Secret Sayings of Jesus* (Garden City, N.Y.: Doubleday & Co., 1960), p. 82.
27. *Das Erlauer Österspiel III*, in *Das Drama des Mittelalters*, ed. Eduard Hartl (Leipzig, 1937), 2:205–60.
28. Part of the Twentieth Discourse of Cyril of Jerusalem, quoted in James, *The Apocryphal New Testament*, p. 87.
29. James, in *The Apocryphal, New Testament*, p. 166, states that Latin copies of the *Gospel of Bartholomew* date from the ninth and eleventh centuries, and, on p. 186, that Latin translations of Bartholomew's *Book of the Resurrection* date from the twelfth century.
30. James, *The Apocryphal New Testament*, p. 88.
31. *The True Prophet*, partly quoted in *New Testament Apocrypha*, 2:115–17. Hereafter referred to as *NTA*.
32. Ibid., p. 115.
33. Ibid., p. 117.
34. Ibid.

CHAPTER 4: *The "Pure Spiritual Mariham" and Pistis Sophia Prunikos*

1. Translation of excerpt from Irenaeus, in Robert M. Grant's most useful *Gnosticism: A Source Book of Heretical Writings From the Early Christian Period* (New York: Harper, 1961), p. 24.
2. Ibid.
3. Translation of excerpt from *Clementine Homilies*, in Grant, p. 27.
4. *Pistis Sophia* (London, 1924), literally translated from the Coptic by George Horner, with an Introduction by F. A. Legge. Hereafter referred to as *Pistis*.
   Pistis Sophia is contained in *Codex Askewianus*, a parchment manuscript which was, according to Schneemelcher and Hennecke,

bought in a London bookshop by Dr. Anthony Askew, an antiquarian, in 1773 and purchased by the British Museum in 1785 (*NTA*, I; 250). The manuscript, written in a Coptic dialect apparently in the fourth century, contains five texts, the first two of which are entitled the *Books of Pistis Sophia*, as Jean Doresee points out in *The Secret Books of the Egyptian Gnostics* (pp. 65, 67). The original *Pistis Sophia*, written in Greek, dates from the second century. F. A. Legge thinks it may well be taken from the works of the famous Gnostic Valentinus.

5. *Pistis*, p. 3.
6. Ibid., p. 6.
7. Ibid., p. 13.
8. Ibid.
9. Ibid., p. 14.
10. Ibid., p. 17.
11. Ibid., pp. 22–25.
12. Ibid., pp. 25–26.
13. Ibid., p. 27.
14. Ibid., p. 28.
15. Ibid., p. 29.
16. Ibid., p. 31.
17. Ibid., p. 57.
18. Ibid., pp. 58–59.
19. Ibid., pp. 59–60.
20. Ibid., pp. 61–62.
21. *The Castle of Perseverance*, in *Chief Pre-Shakespearean Dramas*, ed. Joseph Quincy Adams (Cambridge, Mass.: Houghton Mifflin Co., 1924), pp. 264–87. For the important role played by the Four Daughters of God in *The Castle*, see 11. 3130–3650.
22. *Pistis*, p. 80.
23. Ibid., p. 81.
24. Ibid., p. 91.
25. Ibid., p. 94.
26. Ibid., pp. 98–99.
27. Ibid., p. 100.
28. Jean Doresee, in *The Secret Books of the Egyptian Gnostics* (New York: Viking Press, 1960 [p. 72]), suggests that the *Books of the Savior* begins with the discussion of the Ineffable. I agree.
29. *Pistis*, p. 109.
30. Ibid., pp. 115–16.
31. Ibid., pp. 120–22.
32. Ibid., pp. 124–25.
33. Ibid., p. 141.

34. Ibid., pp. 147–51.
35. Ibid., pp. 171–79, (Jesus' words, p. 176).
36. Ibid., p. 180.
37. Ibid., p. 182.
38. Ibid., p. 183.
39. Ibid., pp. 183–85.
40. Ibid., pp. 188–89.
41. Ibid., pp. 190–91.
42. Ibid., pp. 193–97.
43. Epiphanius's description is quoted by Joseph Campbell in *The Masks of God: Creative Mythology* (1968; reprint ed., New York: Viking Press, 1970), pp. 159–61.
44. Epiphanius, in Campbell, *Creative Mythology*, p. 160.
45. Ibid., p. 161.
46. *Pistis*, p. 198.
47. Ibid., p. 199.
48. Part of Hippolytus's *Refutation of All Heresies*, quoted in *Gnosticism, an Anthology*, ed. Robert M. Grant (London: Collins, 1961), p. 113.
49. *Gnosticism, an Anthology*, ed. Robert M. Grant, p. 113.
50. Mircea Eliade, *Rites and Symbols of Initiation: The Mysteries of Birth and Rebirth*, trans. Willard R. Trask (1958; reprint ed., New York: Harper & Row, 1965), p. 101.
51. Carl Schmidt, Introduction to his editions of *Pistis Sophia* (Leipzig, 1925), p. xxi ff. Quoted in *NTA*, 1: 251.
52. *Wisdom of Jesus Son of Sirach*, in *The Oxford Annotated Apocrypha of the Old Testament*, Revised Standard Version, ed. Bruce M. Metzger (New York: Oxford University Press, 1965), pp. 128–29. The work was actually written by Joshua ben Sira (Jesus the Son of Sirach) about 180 B.C. and was translated into Greek by Joshua ben Sira's grandson around 132 B.C. The work was called *Ecclesiasticus (The Church Book)* and used by the Latin Church in the third century (Introduction, p. 128). A popular work during the Middle Ages, it was quoted by both secular and religious writers to defend either feminist or antifeminist points of view.
53. *Proverbs and Ecclesiastes*, trans. with introduction and notes by R. B. Y. Scott, *The Anchor Bible*, no. 18 (Garden City, N.Y.: Doubleday & Co., 1965), *Proverbs*, pp. 33–187; 8: 30–31.
54. *The Epic of Gilgamesh, an English Version*, ed. N. K. Sandars (1960; reprint ed., Baltimore, Md.: Penguin Books, 1967), p. 99. Epigraph at head of this chapter, p. 97.
55. Victor Saxer, *Le Culte de Marie Madeleine en Occident* (Paris, 1959), p. 3.

CHAPTER 5: *The Magdalen's Link with an Ancient Goddess of Love*

1. R. P. Damien Vorreux, *Sainte Marie-Madeleine: Quelle est donc cette femme?* (Paris: Editiones Franciscaines, 1963), p. 20.

2. The Vulgate:

   > Surgum, et circuibo civitatem; per vicos et plateas quaeram quem diligit anima mea; quaesivi illum, et non inveni. Invenerent me vigiles qui custodiunt civitatem: Nun quem diligit anima mea vidistis? Paululum cum pertransissem eos, inveni quem diligit anima mea, tenui eum, nec dimittam, donec introducam illum in domum matris meae, et in cubiculum genitricis meae. Adjuro vos, filiae Jerusalem, per capreas coervosque camporum, ne suscitetis neque evigilare faciatis dilectam, donec ipsa velit. [Canticum Canticorum 3:2–5]

3. The Vulgate:

   > Pone me ut signaculum super cor tuum, ut signaculum super brachium tuum, quia fortis est ut mors dilectio, dura sicut infernus aemulatio: lampades ejus lampades ignis atque flammarum. Aquae multae non potuerunt extinguere charitatem, nec flumina obruent illam. Si dederit homo omnem substantiam domus suae pro dilectione, quasi nihil despiciet eam. [Canticum Canticorum 8:6–7]

4. *Origen, the Song of Songs, Commentary and Homilies*, translated and annotated by R. P. Lawson, no. 26 in *Ancient Christian Writers: The Works of the Fathers in Translation*, ed. Johannes Quaster, S.T.D., and Joseph C. Plumpe, Ph.D. (Westminster, Md.: Newman Press, 1957). Rufinus's translation of the Commentary and Jerome's translation of Homilies I and II, as well as the Greek fragments of Origen's original Commentary, are in *Patrologiae Graecae*, ed. J. P. Migne (Paris, 1862), vol. 13, cols. 35–216. Page references in this study are to Lawson's translation.

5. In his introduction, Lawson elaborates on Origen's reasons for applying the tripartite man to the written word, pp. 8–10.

6. *Origen*, p. 219.

7. Ibid., p. 221, Origen's explication of Wisdom 7:21–22. Wisdom of Solomon, in the *Oxford Annotated Apocrypha*, pp. 102–27. The "book was composed in Greek by an unknown Hellenistic Jew probably at Alexandria during the latter part of the first century B.C.," according to the introduction to Wisdom, p. 102. Wisdom, like the Song of Songs, was attributed to Solomon.

8. *Origen*, p. 137.

9. Ibid., p. 139.
10. Ibid., p. 29.
11. Ibid., p. 160.
12. Ibid., pp. 12 and 14.
13. Ibid., p. 114.
14. *Origen*, Lawson's phrase, in his Introduction, p. 13.
15. *Origen*, p. 21.
16. Ibid., p. 23.
17. Ibid.
18. Ibid., p. 24.
19. Ibid., p. 79.
20. Ibid., p. 270.
21. Ibid., pp. 28–30.
22. Ibid., p. 29.
23. Ibid., pp. 198–99.
24. Plato, *The Symposium*, trans. Walter Hamilton (1951; reprint ed., Baltimore, Md.: Penguin Books, 1973), 45–46.
25. *Origen*, p. 284.
26. Ibid., p. 297.
27. The Latin hymn to the Magdalen is printed in *Hymns of the Roman Liturgy*, ed. Rev. Joseph Connelly, M.A. (Westminster, Maryland, 1954), p. 214, no. 125.
28. *Origen*, pp. 30–35.
29. Ibid., p. 162.
30. Ibid., p. 60.
31. Ibid., p. 79.
32. Ibid., p. 73.
33. Ibid., p. 160.
34. Ibid., pp. 160–61.
35. Jacobus a Voragine, *Legenda Aurea: Vulgo Historia Lombardica Dicta, Ad Optimorum Librorum Fidem*, ed. Th. Graesse (1850; 3d ed. 1890, reprint ed., Osnabrück: Otto Zeller, 1965), "De Sancta Maria Magdalena," chap. 96, pp. 407–17, 414.
36. The Vulgate:

> En dilectus meus loquitur mihi:
> Surge, propera, amica mea,
> columba mea, formosa mea, et veni.
> Jam enim hiems transiit;
> imber abiit, et recessit.
> Flores apparuerunt in terra nostra,
> tempus putationis advenit;
> vox turturis audita est in terra nostra;

ficus protulit grossos suos;
vineae florentes dederunt odorem suum.
Surge, amica mea, speciosa mea, et veni:

[Canticum Canticorum 2:10–13]

37. *Origen*, p. 229.
38. Ibid., p. 234.
39. Ibid., p. 236.
40. Ibid., p. 237.
41. Origen's exegesis of the lines, pp. 239–63.
42. *Origen*, p. 270.
43. *Origen*, p. 275.
44. Ibid., p. 276.
45. Ibid., p. 277.
46. Ibid., p. 288.
47. R. P. Raymond-Léopold Bruckberger, *Marie Madeleine: soror mea sponsa* (Paris: La Jeune Parque, 1952).
48. Henry Osborn Taylor, *The Classical Heritage of the Middle Ages* (1901; reprint ed., with Foreword and Bibliography by Kenneth M. Setton, New York: Harper & Row, 1963), p. 102.
49. *Song of Songs: A Symposium by Max Margolis, James A. Montgomery, Walter Woodburn Hyde, Franklin Edgerton, Theophile James Meek, and Wilfred Harvey Schoff*, ed. W. H. Schoff (Philadelphia: Commercial Museum, 1924). Meek points out the existence of Egyptian, Babylonian, and Greek parallels in chap. 5, "The Song of Songs and the Fertility Cult," p. 69, and Edgerton discusses the Hindu parallel in chapt. 4, "The Hindu Song of Songs."
50. Mircea Eliade, *Rites and Symbols of Initiation* (1958; reprint ed., New York: Harper, 1965), p. 25.
51. Theophile James Meek, in *Song of Songs: A Symposium*, pp. 60–62.
52. Ibid., p. 49.
53. Part of the lamentation of Isis from the "Mystery of Osiris at Abydos," trans. E. A. Wallis Budge in his *Osiris* (1911; new ed., New York, 1961), vol. 2, pp. 60–61.
54. Wilfred Harvey Schoff, "The Offering Lists in the Song of Songs, and Their Political Significance," in *Song of Songs: A Symposium*, chap. 6, pp. 106–07.
55. Erich Neumann, *The Great Mother: An Analysis of the Archetype*, trans. from the German by Ralph Manheim, Bollingen Series 47, 2d ed. (New York, 1963), p. 331.
56. Jean Seznec, *The Survival of the Pagan Gods: The Mythological Tradition and Its Place in Renaissance Humanism and Art*, trans. from the French by Barbara F. Sessions, Bollingen Series 38 (1940; revised by the author; New York, 1953).

57. Ibid., p. 11.
58. Ibid., pp. 13–14.
59. Augustine, *The City of God* (New York: Random House, 1950) p. 234.
60. Ibid., p. 615.
61. Ibid.
62. Seznec, pp. 16, 22.
63. Ibid., p. 149.
64. Joseph Campbell, *The Hero With a Thousand Faces* (1949; Bollingen Foundation, Inc.; reprint ed., New York: Meridian Books, 1956), p. 302.

CHAPTER 6: *The Rise of the Magdalen in the Middle Ages*

1. Charles Homer Haskins, *The Renaissance of the Twelfth Century* (1927; reprint ed., Cleveland and New York: World Publishing Company, 1957), p. 16.
   Steven Runciman, *The Medieval Manichee: A Study of Christian Dualist Heresy*, 2d ed. (1947; reprint ed., New York: Viking Press, 1961), p. 125.
2. Ibid., p. 118.
3. Bernard Gui, "The Waldensian Heretics," from *Manuel de l'Inquisiteur*, ed. G. Mollat (Paris: Champion, 1926), in *The Portable Medieval Reader*, ed. and with an Introduction by James Bruce Ross and Mary Martin McLaughlin, trans. by Mary Martin McLaughlin (1949; reprint ed., New York: Viking Press, Inc., 1957), pp. 202–16.
4. Ibid., p. 208.
5. Jeffrey Burton Russell, *Dissent and Reform in the Early Middle Ages*, Publications of the Center for Medieval and Renaissance Studies (Berkeley and Los Angeles: University of California Press, 1965), p. 71.
6. Ibid., p. 85.
7. Ernst Robert Curtius, *European Literature and the Latin Middle Ages*, trans. from the German by Willard R. Trask (1953; reprint ed., New York: Harper & Row, 1963).
8. Ibid., p. 122.
9. Ibid., p. 112.
10. Victor Saxer, "Les Saintes Marie Madeleine et Marie de Béthanie dans la Tradition Liturgique et Homilétique Orientale," in *Révue des Sciences Réligieuses* 32 (Paris, 1958); 1–37.

11. Ibid., p. 4.

12. Ibid., pp. 8, 30, 37.

13. Ibid., p. 9.

14. Ibid.

15. Ibid., p. 11.

16. *Acts of John*, portions quoted in *New Testament Apocrypha*, vol. 2. Eusebius mentions the *Acts of John*, so it may date from the third century (*NTA*, 2: 214). A Latin version was current in the fourth century; Augustine refers to it (*NTA*, 2:201). Although the work was condemned by the Nicene Council of 787 (*NTA*, 2:192), Arabic copies were made as late as 1324 (NTA, 2:193).

17. Ibid., p. 243.

18. Ibid., p. 257.

19. *Mirk's Festial: A Collection of Homilies by John Mirk*, ed. from the Bodleian MS by Theodor Erbe, EETS, ES 96 (London, 1905), Homily no. 49, p. 203.

20. Victor Saxer, *Le Culte de Marie Madeleine* (Paris, 1959), p. 108.

21. Ibid., p. 244.

22. Ibid., p. 245.

23. Anglo-Saxon Charm, in H. R. Ellis Davidson, *Gods and Myths of Northern Europe* (1964; reprint ed., Middlesex, England: Penguin Books, Ltd., 1968), p. 114.

24. Saint Jerome, "Letter to Eustochium," in *The Satirical Letters of St. Jerome*, trans. into English and with an Introduction by Paul Carroll (Chicago: Gateway Editions, Inc., 1956), p. 24.

25. "De Sancta Maria Aegyptiaca," in Jacobus a Voragine, *Legenda Aurea* (1850; 3d ed., 1890; reprint ed., Osnabruck: Otta Zeller, 1965), chapter 56, pp. 247–49.

26. Saxer, *Le Culte*, p. 126.

27. *An Old English Martyrology*, ed. George Herzfeld, EETS 116 (London, 1900), p. 127.

28. Saxer, *Le Culte*, p. 126.

29. Ibid., p. 131.

30. Ibid., p. 126.

31. Ibid., p. 68.

32. Ibid., p. 54.

33. Ibid., pp. 94–95.

34. Bernard of Clairvaux, Sermon 57, in *Patriologiae Latina*, ed. J. P. Migne (Paris, 1854), vol. 183, cols. 1050–55. Hereafter referred to as *MPL*.

35. Ibid., Sermon 28, *MPL*, vol. 182, cols. 921–28.

36. Ibid., Sermon 22, *MPL*, vol. 183, cols. 875–84.

CHAPTER 7: *The "Biography" of*
Saint Mary Magdalene

1. Guillaume de Lorris and Jean de Meun, *The Romance of the Rose*, trans. into English verse by Harry W. Robbins, edited and with an Introduction by Charles W. Dunn (New York: E. P. Dutton & Co., Inc., 1962); epigraph is from Jean de Meun's Conclusion, p. 348: sec. 79, 11. 63–67.
   Chaucer, "The Wife of Bath's Prologue," in *The Poetical Works of Chaucer*, ed. by F. N. Robinson (Cambridge, Mass.: The Unversity Press, 1933), p. 99: 11. 688–95.
2. Jacobus a Voragine, *Legenda Aurea*, ed. Th. Graesse (1850; 3d ed., 1890; reprint ed., Osnabruck: Otta Zeller, 1965).
3. Ibid., p. 407.
4. Ibid.
5. Ibid., p. 408.
6. Ibid.
7. Ibid.
8. Ibid.
9. Ibid., p. 409.
10. Ibid.
11. Ibid., p. 410.
12. Ibid.
13. Ibid., p. 411.
14. Ibid.
15. Ibid.
16. Ibid., p. 412.
17. Ibid., p. 413.
18. Ibid.
19. Ibid.
20. Ibid.
21. Ibid., p. 414.
22. Ibid.
23. Ibid., p. 415.
24. Ibid., p. 416.
25. Ibid., p. 417.

CHAPTER 8: *The Magdalen's Impact*
on Medieval Drama

1. The text of the Tours play is in Karl Young, *The Drama of the Medieval Church* (1933; reprint ed., Oxford: Clarendon Press, 1962), 1:438–47.
2. The Magdalen's lament extends from 11. 135–48.

3. Tours Easter play, 11. 165–66.

4. The rubric: "Deinde veniat Maria Jacobi et sustentet brachium destrum, et Maria Salome per sinistrum et levet de terra Mariam Magdalenam" (Young, 1:444).

5. Émile Mâle, *L'Art Religieux du XIIᵉ Sièle* (Paris, 1922), pp. 136–37. Mâle argues convincingly that the sculpture at Modena was carved by a Provençal artist who was quite familiar with the Tours play itself. Illustration in Mâle, p. 137, fig. 116.

6. Young also notes the loss of the scene from the manuscript, 1:448.

7. Tours Easter play, 11. 183–94.

8. Ibid., 11. 28–31.

9. Ibid., 11. 56–65.

10. Ibid., 1. 78.

11. I agree with Mâle that the same Provençal artist carved both scenes in the chapel at Modena. Illustration, Mâle, p. 136, fig. 115.

12. The text of the Benediktbeuern Passion play is in Karl Young, *The Drama of the Medieval Church*, 1: 518–33.

13. Songs from the Bnediktbeuern manuscript, the *Carmina Burana* used in Carl Orff's composition: "Ave formosissima" (Hail to thee most beautiful), no. 24; "Amor volat undique" (The God of love flies everywhere), no. 15; "Chramer, gip die varwe mier" (Shopkeeper, give me color), no. 8. The Magdalen's song, not credited to her by Carl Orff, concludes with her vernacular hymn to the world, "Wol dir werlt, daz du bist also freudenriche." Songs, with English translations, are in the Libretto for the Angel Record, 35415, recorded under the direction of Wolfgang Sawallisch and under the personal supervision of Carl Orff (New York: Angel Records: Electric and Musical Industries [U. S.] Ltd., 1957), pp. 12, 10, 8.

14. Benediktbeuern play, 11. 71–74.

15. Ibid., 11. 83–88.

16. Ibid., 11. 90–95.

17. Ibid., 11. 98–101.

18. Ibid., 11. 104–7.

19. Karl Young makes this observation (1:535).

20. Young first notes this fact (1:534).

21. Jean Michel, *Le Mystère de la Passion*, in *Le Livre de Conduite du Regisseur et la Compte des Dépenses Pour le Mystère de la Passion Joué à Mons en 1501*, ed. Gustave Cohen (Paris, 1925). Gustave Cohen points out that Jean Michel expanded and changed the Passion play of Arnoul Gréban, and in his edition Cohen interlines Michel's text with borrowings from Gréban. The *mondanité* of the Magdalen, along with that of Lazarus, is the most impressive of Michel's additions.

22. Ibid., p. 177.
23. Ibid.
24. Ibid., p. 178.
25. Ibid.
26. Ibid., pp. 181–83.
27. Ibid. p. 207.
28. Ibid., p. 209.
29. Ibid.
30. Ibid. p. 212.
31. Ibid.
32. Ibid. pp. 213–14.
33. Ibid., p. 215.
34. Ibid., p. 216.
35. Ibid., p. 217.
36. Ibid., p. 218.
37. Ibid.

CHAPTER 9: *The Magdalen as a Full-blown
Heroine in a Late Medieval Play*

1. "For Miles Blomefylde," in a script differing from that of the text of
   the play, appears beside the initials "M.B." at the head of the
   manuscript.
   The Epilogue: ll. 2141–44.
2. Syrus so describes the Magdalen (l. 71) as he divides his property
   among his "children" just before he dies.
3. *Mary Magdalene, The Digby Mysteries*, ed. F. J. Furnivall, EETS,
   ES 70 (1896; reprint ed., London, 1930), ll. 419–20.
4. Ibid., ll. 422–35.
5. Ibid., ll. 440–44.
6. Ibid., ll. 456–59.
7. Ibid., ll. 489–90.
8. Ibid., ll. 491–506.
9. Ibid., ll. 507–10.
10. Ibid., ll. 515–19.
11. Ibid., ll. 520–23.
12. Ibid., ll. 524–26.
13. Ibid., ll. 543–46.
14. Ibid., ll. 555–59.
15. Ibid., ll. 588–601.
16. Ibid., ll. 602–14.
17. Ibid., ll. 666–72.
18. Ibid., ll. 673–82.

19. Ibid., ll. 686–90.
20. Ibid., stage direction, pt. 1, scene 14.
21. Ibid., ll. 703–4.
22. Ibid., ll. 2074–75.
23. Ibid., stage direction, pt. 1, scene 20.
24. Ibid., ll. 1061–62.
25. Ibid., ll. 1063–68.
26. Ibid., ll. 1069–73.
27. Ibid., ll. 1078–79.
28. Ibid., l. 1080.
29. Ibid., ll. 1081–85.
30. Ibid., ll. 1086–88.
31. Ibid., ll. 1092–95.
32. Bernard of Clairvaux, Sermon 40, in *MPL* 184, 207–14.
33. *Christ's Burial and Resurrection, A Mystery in Two Parts*, in *Digby Mysteries*, pp. 169–226; *Burial*, ll. 1463–67.
34. Digby *Magdalene*, Magdalen's hymn: ll. 1336–48; Jesus' Hymn: ll. 1349–65.
35. Digby *Magdalene*, ll. 1366–71.
36. Ibid., ll. 925–43 and 958–62.
37. Ibid., ll. 1133–1248.
38. Ibid., ll. 1446–53.
39. Ibid., ll. 1548–58.
40. Ibid., ll. 1563–70.
41. Ibid., l. 1588.
42. Ibid., ll. 1611–18.
43. Ibid., ll. 1627–34.
44. Ibid., ll. 1659–68.
45. Ibid., ll. 1698–711.
46. Ibid., ll. 1746–49.
47. Ibid., ll. 1754–76.
48. Ibid., ll. 1888–89.
49. Ibid., ll. 1944–47.
50. Ibid., ll. 1941–42.
51. Ibid., l. 1943.
52. Ibid., l. 1960.
53. Ibid., ll. 1962–80.
54. Ibid., ll. 2004–11.
55. Ibid., ll. 2020–27.
56. Ibid., ll. 2113–14.
57. Ibid., l. 2123.
58. Ibid., ll. 2131.

CHAPTER 10: *The Decline of
the Mythical Magdalen*

1. Lewis Wager, *The Life and Repentance of Marie Magdalene*, 11.
   59–65.
2. Ibid., 11. 801–2.
3. Ibid., 11. 785–800.
4. Ibid., stage direction, p. 7.
5. Ibid., 11. 57– 76.
6. Ibid., 11. 81–88.
7. Ibid., 11. 105–16.
8. Ibid., 11. 150–59.
9. Ibid., 11. 197–202.
10. Ibid., 11. 223–26.
11. Ibid., 11. 240–42.
12. Ibid., 11. 270–364.
13. Ibid., 11. 367–416.
14. Ibid., 11. 524–25.
15. Ibid., 11. 500–522.
16. Ibid., 1. 523.
17. Ibid., 11. 528–29.
18. Ibid., 11. 582–99.
19. Ibid., 11. 538–57.
20. Ibid., 11. 560–81.
21. Ibid., 11. 674–78.
22. Ibid., 11. 651–67.
23. Ibid., 11. 694–96.
24. Ibid., 11. 711–14.
   The Magdalen quotes from Ovid, *De Arte Amandi*, bk. 2, Canto 113:

   > Forma bona fragilis est; quantum accedit ad annos,
   > Fit minor, et spacio carpitur illa suo;
   > Nec semper viola, nec semper lilia florent,
   > Et riget amissa spina relicta rosa. [Wager, 11. 707–10]

25. Wager, The Song, 11. 783–803.
26. Ibid., 11. 827–30.
27. Ibid., 11. 842–930.
28. Ibid., 11. 988–1018.
29. Ibid., 11. 1027–62.
30. Ibid., 11. 1063–66.
31. Ibid., 11. 1091–98.
32. Ibid., 11. 1099–1102.
33. Ibid., 11. 1103–10; 1115–19.
34. Ibid., 1. 1111.

35. Ibid., 1. 1119.
36. Ibid., 1. 1123.
37. Ibid., 11. 1127–38.
38. Ibid., 11. 1139–42.
39. Ibid., 11. 1143–54.
40. Ibid., 11. 1203–22.
41. Ibid., 11. 1235–90.
42. Ibid., stage direction, p. 57.
43. Ibid., 11. 1319–26.
44. Ibid., 11. 1335–78.
45. Ibid., 11. 1387–96.
46. Ibid., 11. 1431–50.
47. Ibid., 11. 1455–1588.
48. Ibid., 1. 1683.
49. Ibid., 11. 1684–1742.
50. Ibid., 1. 1837.
51. Ibid., 1. 1855.
52. Ibid., 11. 1963–2002.
53. Ibid., 11. 2020–22.
54. Ibid., 11. 2023–30.
55. Ibid., 11. 2031–48.

CHAPTER 11: *The Magdalen in the Spotlight on the Twentieth-Century Stage*

1. Andrew Lloyd Webber and Tim Rice, *Jesus Christ Superstar*, "Strange Thing Mystifying" (1969; reprint ed., London: Leeds Music, Ltd., 1970), p. 8. Hereafter referred to as *Superstar*.
2. John 7:53–8:11.
3. Maurice Maeterlinck, *Mary Magdalene* (New York: Dodd, Mead & Co., 1910), act 1, sc. 3, pp. 26–27.
4. Ibid., sc. 4, p. 28.
5. Ibid., sc. 1, p. 9.
6. Ibid., p. 12.
7. Ibid., p. 6.
8. Ibid., p. 10.
9. Ibid., p. 14.
10. Ibid., sc. 2, pp. 16–17.
11. Ibid., p. 17; Song of Songs 3:6 and 6:10.
12. Maeterlinck, act 1, sc. 2, pp. 17–18.
13. Ibid., p. 18.
14. Ibid., p. 19.
15. Ibid., p. 22.
16. Ibid., sc. 4, p. 34.

17. Ibid., sc. 2, p. 22.
18. Ibid., p. 24.
19. Ibid., sc. 4, p. 45.
20. Ibid., p. 48.
21. Ibid., pp. 49–50.
22. Ibid., p. 54.
23. Ibid., p. 56.
24. Ibid., act 2, sc. 1, p. 61.
25. Ibid., p. 63.
26. Ibid., p. 64.
27. Ibid., pp. 65–66.
28. Ibid., pp. 67–68.
29. Ibid., p. 70.
30. Ibid., pp. 72–73.
31. Ibid., sc. 3, p. 100.
32. Ibid., p. 101.
33. Ibid., pp. 102–3.
34. Ibid., p. 103.
35. Ibid., p. 104.
36. Ibid., p. 105.
37. Ibid., act 3, sc. 3, pp. 123–30.
38. Ibid., p. 131.
39. Ibid., pp. 135–37.
40. Ibid., sc. 4, p. 150.
41. Ibid., p. 152.
42. Ibid., p. 156.
43. Ibid., p. 158.
44. Ibid., p. 160.
45. Ibid., p. 161.
46. Ibid., p. 162.
47. Ibid., p. 163.
48. Ibid., p. 165.
49. Ibid., sc. 5, pp. 166–67.
50. Ibid., pp. 168–70.
51. Ibid., p. 172.
52. Ibid., pp. 174–75.
53. Ibid., p. 177.
54. Ibid., p. 178.
55. Ibid., p. 179.
56. *Superstar*, "I Don't Know How to Love Him," p. 14.
57. Ibid., p. 15.
58. Ibid.
59. Ibid. "Everything's Alright," p. 8.

CHAPTER 12: *The Magdalen as*
WOMAN Born of Man

1. Nikos Kazantzakis, *The Last Temptation of Christ*, Prologue, p. 1.
2. Ibid., p. 141.
3. Ibid., p. 27.
4. Ibid., p. 250.
5. Ibid., p. 251.
6. Ibid.
7. Ibid., p. 346.
8. Ibid., p. 440.
9. Ibid., p. 442.
10. Ibid., p. 89.
11. Ibid., pp. 79–81.
12. Ibid., p. 87.
13. Ibid., p. 88.
14. Ibid., p. 89.
15. Ibid., p. 442.
16. Ibid.
17. Ibid., p. 443.
18. Ibid.
19. Ibid., p. 444.
20. Ibid.
21. Ibid., p. 445.
22. Ibid., p. 446.
23. Ibid., p. 447.
24. Ibid., p. 321.
25. Ibid., p. 487.
26. Ibid., p. 322.
27. Ibid., p. 322.
28. Ibid., p. 449.
29. Ibid., p. 487.
30. Ibid., p. 408.
31. Eva Figes, *Patriarchal Attitudes* (1970; reprint ed., Greenwich, Conn.: Fawcett Publications, Inc., 1971), pp. 130–31. Miss Figes refers in this passage specifically to Otto Weininger's antifeminism.

CHAPTER 13: *The Magdalen Monument:*
A Caveat and Some Conclusions

1. Eldridge Cleaver, *Soul on Ice* (New York: Dell Publishing Co., Inc., 1968), pp. 13–14.
2. Johan Huizinga, *Homo Ludens* (1927; reprint ed., Cleveland and New York: World Publishing Co., 1957), p. 211.

3. As with the Donatello sculpture, my repeated requests for a photograph of Titian's *La Maddalena* proved disappointingly fruitless.

4. Ovid, *The Art of Love*, trans. by Rolfe Humphries (1957; reprint ed., Bloomington, Ind.: Indiana University Press, 1960), bk. 3, 11. 401–2.
   The Latin:

   > Si Venerem cois numquam pinxisset Apelles
   > Mersa sub aequoreis illa lateret aquis.

5. Robert Heinlein, *Stranger in a Strange Land* (1961; reprint ed., New York: Berkley Publishing Corporation, 1969), p. 326.

Selected Bibliography

ANONYMOUS. *Mary Magdalene: Victim of Libel. The State Journal.* Lansing, Mich. 28 August 1965.

The Apocryphal New Testament, Being the Apocryphal Gospels, Acts, Epistles, and Apocalypses with Other Narratives and Fragments Newly Translated by Montague Rhodes James. Ed. Montague Rhodes James. 1924. Corrected ed., Oxford: Clarendon Press, 1960.

APULEIUS, LUCIUS. *Metamorphoses: The Golden Ass.* Trans. William Adlington, 1566. Ed. Harry C. Schnur. 1962. Reprint. New York: Macmillan Co., 1965.

AUGUSTINE. *The City of God.* Trans. Marcus Dods, D.D. New York: Random House, 1950.

Benediktbeuern Passion Play. In Karl Young, *The Drama of the Medieval Church.* Vol. 1. 1933. Reprint. Oxford: Clarendon Press, 1962.

BERNARD OF CLAIRVAUX. *Sermones in Cantica Canticorum. Patriologiae Latina.* Ed. J. P. Migne. Vols. 182–84. Paris, 1854.

Biblia Sacra, Juxta Vulgatum Clementinam. Printed in Belgium, 1956.

BONFIELD, JUNE P. "The Penitence of the Medieval Magdalen: A Study in the Meanings of Her Appellation 'Penitent' as Reflected in Vernacular Literature of the British Isles c. 1250–c. 1500." Ph.D. thesis. University of Texas, 1970.

BROOKS, NEIL C. "The Sepulchre of Christ in Art and Liturgy, with Special Reference to the Liturgic Drama." *University of Illinois Studies in Language and Literature*, vol. 7, no. 2, May 1921. Urbana, Ill.

BRUCKBERGER, RAYMOND-LÉOPOLD. *Marie Madeleine: soror mea sponsa.* Paris: La Jeune Parque, 1952.

BUDGE, E. A. WALLIS. *Osiris.* 2 vols. 1911. New ed., New York, 1961.

CAMPBELL, JOSEPH. *The Hero with a Thousand Faces.* 1949. Reprint. New York: Meridian Books, 1956.

——. *The Masks of God: Creative Mythology.* 1968. Reprint. New York: Viking Press, 1970.

The Castle of Perseverance. Chief Pre-Shakespearean Dramas. Ed. Joseph

Quincy Adams, Cambridge, Mass.: Houghton Mifflin Co., 1924.

CHAMBERS, E. K. *The Medieval Stage.* 2 vols. Oxford: Clarendon Press, 1903.

CHAUCER, GEOFFREY. *The Poetical Works of Chaucer.* Ed. F. N. Robinson. Cambridge, Mass.: The University Press, 1933.

CHAUVIN, SISTER MARY JOHN OF CARMEL. *The Role of Mary Magdalene in Medieval Drama.* Washington, D. C.: Catholic University of America Press, 1951.

Christ's Burial and Resurrection: A Mystery in Two Parts. Digby Mysteries. Ed. F. J. Furnivall. EETS ES 70. 1896. Reprint. London, 1930.

CLEAVER, ELDRIDGE. *Soul on Ice.* New York: Dell Publishing Co., 1968.

CRASHAW, RICHARD. *The Poems of Richard Crashaw.* Ed. L. C. Martin. Oxford: Clarendon Press, 1957.

CURTIUS, ERNST ROBERT. *European Literature and the Latin Middle Ages.* Trans. Willard R. Trask. 1953. Reprint. New York: Harper, 1963.

DAVIDSON, CLIFFORD. "The Digby *Mary Magdalene* and the Magdalene Cult of the Middle Ages." *Annuale Mediaevale.* Vol. 13. New York: Duquesne University Press/Humanities Press, Inc., 1972).

DAVIDSON, H. R. ELLIS. *Gods and Myths of Northern Europe.* 1964. Reprint. Middlesex, England: Penguin Books, Ltd., 1968.

DEEN, EDITH. *All of the Women of the Bible.* New York: Harper, 1955.

DE ROUGEMONT, DENIS. *Love in the Western World.* Trans. Montgomery Belgion. 2d ed. 1956. Reprint. Garden City, N.Y.: Doubleday & Co., 1957.

DORESEE, JEAN. *The Secret Books of the Egyptian Gnostics: An Introduction to the Gnostic Manuscripts Discovered at Chenoboskion, with an English Translation and Critical Evaluation of the Gospel According to Thomas.* Trans. Philip Mairet. 1958. Revised and augmented by the author. New York: Viking Press, 1960.

ELIADE, MIRCEA. *Rites and Symbols of Initiation: The Mysteries of Birth and Rebirth.* Trans. Willard R. Trask. 1958. Reprint. New York: Harper, 1965.

The Epic of Gilgamesh, an English Version. Ed. N. K. Sandars. 1960. Reprint. Baltimore, Md.: Penguin Books, 1967.

Das Erlauer Österspiel. Das Drama des Mittelalters. Ed. Eduard Hartl. Vol. 2, pp. 205–60. Leipzig, 1937.

FIGES, EVA. *Patriarchal Attitudes.* 1970. Reprint. Greenwich, Conn.: Fawcett Publications, Inc., 1971.

FRAZER, SIR JAMES GEORGE. *The Golden Bough: A Study in Magic and Religion.* 10 vols. 3d ed. 1914. Reprint. New York: St. Martin's Press, Inc., 1963.

FÜNTEN, WILTRUD aus der. *Maria Magdalene in der Lyrik des Mittelalters.* Düsseldorf: Schwann, 1966.

GARTH, HELEN MEREDITH. "Saint Mary Magdalene in Medieval Literature." *Johns Hopkins University Studies in Historical and Political Science* 67 (1950): 347–452.

GASTER, THEODOR H. *Thespis: Ritual, Myth, and Drama in the Ancient Near East.* 1950. Reprint. New York: Harper & Row, 1966.

Gnosticism: An Anthology. Ed. Robert M. Grant. London: Collins, 1961.

Gnosticism: A Source Book of Heretical Writings From the Early Christian Period. Ed. Robert M. Grant. New York: Harper, 1961.

Gospel of Mary. Trans. E. R. Hardy. In *Gnosticism: A Source Book of Heretical Writings From the Early Christian Period.* Ed. Robert M. Grant. New York: Harper, 1961.

Gospel of Philip. New Testament Apocrypha. Ed. Edgar Hennecke and Wilhelm Schneemelcher. Trans. R. McL Wilson. Vol. 1. Philadelphia: Westminster Press, 1963.

GRIERSON, SIR HERBERT. *Cross-Currents in Seventeenth-Century English Literature: The World, the Flesh, the Spirit, Their Actions and Reactions.* 1929. Reprint. New York: Harper, 1958.

GUILLAUME DE LORRIS AND JEAN DE MEUNG. *Le Roman de la Rose.* Trans. Harry W. Robbins. Ed. Charles W. Dunn. New York: E. P. Dutton & Co., Inc., 1962.

HASKINS, CHARLES HOMER. *The Renaissance of the Twelfth Century.* 1927. Reprint. Cleveland and New York: World Publishing Co., 1957.

HEINLEIN, ROBERT A. *Stranger in a Strange Land.* 1961. Reprint. New York: Berkley Publishing Corporation, 1968.

HUIZINGA, JOHAN. *The Waning of the Middle Ages: A Study of the Forms of Life, Thought, and Art in France and the Netherlands in the XIVth and XVth Centuries.* 1924. Reprint. Garden City, N.Y.: Doubleday & Co., Inc., 1954.

———. *Homo Ludens: A Study of the Play Element in Culture.* 1944. Reprint. Boston: Beacon Press, 1965.

Hymns of the Roman Liturgy. Ed. Rev. Joseph Connelly, M.A. Westminster, Md.: Newman Press, 1954.

JACOBUS A. VORAGINE. *Legenda Aurea: Vulgo Historia Lombardica Dicta, ad Optimorum Librorum Fidem.* Ed. Th. Graesse. 1850. 3d ed. 1890. Reprint. Osnabruck: Otto Zeller, 1965.

JEROME. *The Satirical Letters of Saint Jerome.* Trans. Paul Carroll. Chicago: Gateway Editions, Inc., 1956.

JONAS, HANS. *The Gnostic Religion: The Message of the Alien God and the Beginnings of Christianity.* Boston: Beacon Press, 1958.

KAZANTZAKIS, NIKOS. *The Last Temptation of Christ.* Trans. P. A. Bien. 1960. Reprint. New York: Bantam Books, Inc., 1960.

———. *Report to Greco.* Trans. P. A. Bien. 1965. Reprint. New York: Bantam Books, Inc., 1965.

KNOLL, FRIEDRICH OTTO. *Die Rolle der Maria Magdalena in geistlichen Spiel des Mittelalters.* Berlin and Leipzig, 1934.

MAETERLINCK, MAURICE. *Mary Magdalene: A Play in Three Acts.* Trans. Alexander Teixeira de Mattos. New York: Dodd, Mead & Co., 1910.

MÂLE, ÉMILE. *L'Art Religieux du XIIᵉ Siècle.* Paris, 1922.

———. *Les Saints Compagnons du Christ.* 1956. Reprint. Paris, 1958.

Mary Magdalene. The Digby Mysteries. Ed. F. J. Furnivall. EETS ES 70. 1896. Reprint. London, 1930.

MICHEL, JEAN. *Le Mystère de la Passion. Le Livre de Conduite du Regisseur et la Compte des Dépenses pour le Mystère de la Passion Joué à Mons en 1501.* Ed. Gustave Cohen. Paris, 1925.

Mirk's Festial: A Collection of Homilies by John Mirk. Ed. Theodor Erbe. EETS, ES 96. London, 1905.

NEUMANN, ERICH. *The Great Mother: An Analysis of the Archetype.* Trans. Ralph Manheim. Bollingen Series 47. 2d ed. New York, 1963.

New Testament Apocrypha. Ed. Edgar Hennecke and Wilhelm Schneemelcher. Trans. R. McL Wilson. 2 vols. Philadelphia: Westminster Press, 1963.

An Old English Martyrology. Ed. George Herzfield. EETS 116. London, 1900.

ORFF, CARL. *Carmina Burana.* Angel Record 35415. New York: Angel Records: Electric & Musical Industries (U.S.), Ltd., 1957.

ORIGEN. *The Song of Songs, Commentary and Homilies.* Trans. R. P. Lawson. *Ancient Christian Writers: The Works of the Fathers in Translation.* Ed. Johannes Quaster, S.T.D., and Joseph C. Plumpe, Ph.D. Westminster, Md.: Newman Press, 1957. Rufinus's and Jerome's Latin translations. *Patriologiae Graecae.* Ed. J. P. Migne. Vol. 13, cols. 35–216. Paris, 1862.

OVID. *The Art of Love.* Trans Rolfe Humphries. Bloomington, Ind.: Indiana University Press, 1960.

Oxford Annotated Apocrypha of the Old Testament. Ed. Bruce M. Metzger. New York: Oxford University Press, 1965.

Oxford Annotated Bible: Revised Standard Version of 1952. Ed. Herbert G. May and Bruce M. Metzger. New York: Oxford University Press, 1962.

Oxford English Dictionary. 1933 ed. Vol. 6.

PANOFSKY, DORA AND ERWIN. *Pandora's Box: The Changing Aspects of a Mythical Symbol.* 2d ed. 1962. Reprint. New York: Harper & Row, 1965.

PHIPPS, WILLIAM E. *Was Jesus Married?* New York: Harper & Row, 1970.

Pistis Sophia. Trans. George Horner. Introduction by F. A. Legge. London: Society for the Promoting of Christian Knowledge, 1924.

PLATO. *Symposium. Dialogues of Plato.* Jowett Translation. Ed. J. D. Kaplan, pp. 161–234. 1951. Reprint. New York: Washington Square Press, Inc., 1965.

The Portable Medieval Reader. Ed. James Bruce Ross and Mary Martin McLaughlin. 1949. Reprint. New York: Viking Press, Inc., 1957.

Proverbs and Ecclesiastes. Trans. R. B. Y. Scott. *The Anchor Bible*, no. 18. Garden City, N.Y.: Doubleday & Co., 1965.

RÉAU, LOUIS. *Iconographie de l'Art Chrétien.* 3 Vols. Paris: Presses Universitaires de France, 1955–59.

REIMER, GERHARD JOHN. "Maria Magdalena in Werken von Hebbel, Heyse, Schlaf, und Thoma." Master's thesis, Michigan State University, 1965.

RUNCIMAN, STEVEN. *The Medieval Manichee: A Study of Christian Dualist Heresy.* 2d ed. 1947. Reprint. New York: Viking Press, Inc., 1961.

RUSSELL, JEFFREY BURTON. *Dissent and Reform in the Early Middle Ages.* Publications of the Center for Medieval and Renaissance Studies. Berkeley and Los Angeles: University of California Press, 1965.

SAXER, VICTOR. "Les Saintes Marie Madeleine et Marie de Béthanie dans la Tradition Liturgique et Homilétique Orientale." *Révue des Sciences Religieuses* 32 (Paris, 1958): 1–37.

————. *Le Culte de Marie Madeleine en Occident, dès Origines à la Fin du Moyen-Âge.* Paris, 1959.

The Secret Sayings of Jesus. Ed. Robert M. Grant and David Noel Freedman. Garden City, N.Y. Doubleday & Co., Inc., 1960.

SEZNEC, JEAN. *The Survival of the Pagan Gods: The Mythological Tradition and Its Place in Renaissance Humanism and Art.* Trans. Barbara F. Sessions. Bollingen Series 38. 1940. Revised by the author. New York, 1953.

Song of Songs: A Symposium by Max Margolis, James A. Montgomery, Walter Woodburn Hyde, Franklin Edgerton, Theophile James Meek, Wilfred Harvey Schoff. Ed. Wilfred Harvey Schoff. Philadelphia: Commercial Museum, 1924.

TAYLOR, HENRY OSBORN. *The Classical Heritage of the Middle Ages.* 1901. Reprint. New York: Harper & Row, 1963.

Tours Easter Play. In Karl Young, *The Drama of the Medieval Church.* Vol. 1. 1933. Reprint. Oxford: Clarendon Press, 1962.

VORREUX, DAMIEN. *Sainte Marie-Madeleine: Quelle est donc cette femme?* Paris: Editiones Franciscaines, 1963.

WAGER, LEWIS. *The Life and Repentance of Marie Magdalene: A Morality Play Reprinted from the Original Edition of 1566.* Ed. Frederic Ives Carpenter. *The Decimal Publications.* 2d ser. Vol. 1. Chicago: University of Chicago Press, 1904.

WEBBER, ANDREW LLOYD, AND RICE, TIM. *Jesus Christ Superstar: A Rock Opera.* 1969. Reprint. London: Leeds Music, Ltd., 1970.

YOUNG, KARL. *The Drama of the Medieval Church.* 2 vols. 1933. Reprint. Oxford: Clarendon Press, 1962.

Index

Adulteress, Magdalen's link with: in Maeterlinck's play, 141, 145; in *Jesus Christ Superstar*, 142; in *The Last Temptation of Christ*, 156

Anointers: in Babylonian *Epic of Gilgamesh*, 16; of Christ, Magdalen's links to, 26–28, 80, 92, 118, 127, 158; of Christ linked to Bride of Song of Songs, 58, 82

Aphrodite: in Gnostic cosmogony, 50; "Heavenly" and "Common" in Plato's *Symposium*, 57; implied in Origen, 61; uneasy synthesis of in Botticelli's Magdalen, 85; carried into medieval drama by Magdalen as, 125, 137, 147, 170. *See also* Venus

Apocrypha: Magdalen's roles in, 12–13, 30–56

Asceticism: in Donatello's sculpture of Magdalen, 5, 55, 77; extolled by Gnostics, 34; preferred over "sexual orgy," 52

—combined with eroticism: in Origen and in Bruckberger's Magdalen "biography," 65; in Massys's paintings of Magdalen and of Mary of Egypt, 77, 82; in Bernard of Clairvaux, 82; in Botticelli's *Vierge Glorieuse*

and the Holy Trinity, 84; Magdalen as vessel for, 98, 170

Bride of the Song of Songs: Origen's interpretation, 60, 62–64

—Magdalen's links with: 58–59, 65; in Tours Easter play, 103; in Digby *Burial of Christ*, 120; Wager's attempt to break, 136; in Maeterlinck's play, 142–44; in Kazantzakis's novel, 152, 157, 160, 162

Christ: Women at sepulcher of, 16, 24; risen, first appears to Magdalen, 17, 18, 19, 55, 68; Magdalen the anointer of, 28; Digby Magdalen's hymn to, 119

—Magdalen's more intimate relationship with: in Gospel of John, 20–21, 23; in Jacobus, 92; in Tours play, 101; in Digby play, 115; in Kazantzakis, 157 passim. *See also* Jesus

—mystic love of: Magdalen as example of, 2; on trial in Wager's play, 125

Companion of Jesus, Magdalen as, 30–31, 40, 55, 125, 170

Contemplative, Magdalen as: in Jacobus, 94; in Digby play, 123–24; in *Sforza Book of Hours*, 127; in Correggio's painting,

139; in Maeterlinck's play, 147; in Georges de la Tour's painting, 160; in Rogier van der Weyden's painting, 172; in Bernardino Luini's painting, 172; in Titian's painting, 173; mentioned, 12

Cosmogony: Gnostic, 32, 51
—*homo ludens*': Athene-Venus-Magdalen in, 180
—Kazantzakis's: serpent's role in, 151, 153–54; God of Israel in, 152

Counter-Reformation: Magdalen as favorite subject of artists and writers, 9, 139

Crucifixion, Magdalen's roles: in synoptic Gospels, 16, 17, 18; in Gospel of John and in Pietàs, 19; in Moretto da Brescia's Pietà, 169

Cult of the Magdalen: in Ephesus, 74; in Aix and Marseilles, 75; at height in Vézelay, 79, 80

Cultural cross-fertilization: impact on fictionalization of Magdalen, 22, 32, 177; impact on medieval Magdalen, 85; mentioned, 188n6

Deities of antiquity: worship of during early Christian era, 21; Magdalen's links with, 21–23, 39, 54–55, 67–69, 76, 80, 84, 95, 98, 105, 107, 112, 115, 124, 125, 131, 132, 136, 139, 140, 142, 143, 146, 150, 152, 157, 162, 169, 170, 173, 180; Gnostic attempts to reinstate, 42, 51, 53, 54; parallel with Bride of Song of Songs, 66–67; survival of, 68–70. See also Fertility deities

Demons: in Gnostic systems often feminine, causes and punishers of sin, 51–52
—seven cast out of Magdalen:

modern explanation for, 13; mentioned in synoptic Gospels, 17; parallels in Gnosticism, 33, 36; personified in Digby play, in Wager's play, 133, and in Kazantzakis, 155

Dualism. *See* Radical dualism

Easter play of Tours: Magdalen's role expanded in, 101–2

Ephesus: Magdalen as preacher there, 3; Artemis of, 21, 74, 186n26

Eros: in Origen, 60–61; conflicting views of in twelfth century, 73, 85; in Kazantzakis, 159, 160

Euhemerus: his ideas alluded to by Jean Seznec and used by Saint Augustine, 68

Eve: as "the first Pandora" in Jean Cousin's painting, transformed into the Magdalen, 8, 9; apocryphal gospel attributed to, 12; revered by some Gnostic sects, 34; interpreted as "type" of the Magdalen, 57, 58, 60, 170

Ezekiel: sees women weeping for Tammuz, 16, 21–22

Female-matter: dark, evil, in conflict with male-spirit, light, good, 31, 35, 52, 160. *See also* Radical dualism

Fertility deities: linked with Christ's resurrection, 21–22. *See also* Deities of antiquity

Gnosis: goal of radically dualistic Gnostics, 31; Magdalen as receiver and revealer of, 32–35, 36, 45. *See also* Gnosticism

Gnosticism: impact on metamorphoses of the Magdalen, 30–31; radically dualistic doctrines of, 31; cosmogonies of, 32, 51; scorn for Old Testament deity and Mosaic law, 34, 35; ambivalent views of women, persistence of, 36, 37, 38, 39, 161; goddess of wisdom in, 42; contrast with Jewish and Babylonian Wisdom, 53, 54; Origen's affinity with, 60; in Kazantzakis, 151, 154, 161; mentioned, 188n4

Goliardic songs: given the Magdalen in Benediktbeuren Passion play, 105; incorporated into Carl Orff's *Carmina Burana*, 106, 107

Gospel of John: reflects special interest in Magdalen, 19. *See also* Recognition scene between risen Christ and Mary Magdalene

Harlot: the Magdalen rebuked as, 148

—holy, as anointer in Babylonian *Epic of Gilgamesh*: the Magdalen's link with, 26, 27, 29, 80, 98, 150, 152, 155; mentioned, 16

Helen: Magdalen's beauty compared with, 130, 132

—as consort of Simon Magus and a goddess of wisdom: compared with Magdalen and with Pistis Sophia Prunikos, 44, 53; mentioned, 43

Hermit, the Magdalen as: 3, 5, 12, 135; Jacobus's account of, 94–95, 98

—linked with Mary of Egypt as: in iconography, 77; mentioned, 76–77

Homo ludens: his role in transforming Mary Magdalene into a mythical figure, 15, 28, 54, 169, 180; linking the Magdalen with the goddesses of antiquity, 80; treating Magdalen of medieval drama, 96–97, 105, 106, 109, 120, 121, 122, 124; Magdalen

serves as Muse for, 113; fictionalized Magdalen as monument to, 173, 177, 178, 180

Iconographic representations of Magdalen: attributes given figure and varied interpretations exemplified, 4; based on Magdalen in Gospel of John, 19; based on Jacobus "biography," 78–79

Isis: worship of, in second century, 21; lament for Osiris, 66, 67; role in medieval "history," 69; Magdalen compared with, 80

Jesus: married(?), 2; will make the Magdalen "male," 38

—as gardener: in Gospel of John, 20; in Digby *Mary Magdalene*, 120; in paintings by Titian, 164; in school of Orcagna, 165. *See also* Recognition scene between risen Christ and Mary Magdalene

—favors Magdalen: in Gnostic works, 37, 45, 46, 47, 48, 49; in Jacobus, 92; in Digby play, 118, 120, 121, 124; in *Jesus Christ Superstar*, 141; in Maeterlinck, 146; in Kazantzakis, 153, 154, 157

John, the Evangelist: Magdalen's links with, 49, 74, 75

Juno: Marochetti sculpture of Magdalen, viewed as, 5, 8, 55

Lazarus: as brother of Magdalen, 28, 109, 110, 116, 119; in Maeterlinck's play, 146

"Libel" of the Magdalen: explained in newspaper article, 13; in Edith Deen's *All of the Women of the Bible*, 14; viewed as myth, 14, 15; indicative of continued controversy over complex figure of Magdalen, 127

Love: mystic, Magdalen as example of, 2, 12, 136, 149; erotic, in Song of Songs, 58, 59, 63, 66; "carnal" and "spiritual," 61, 62, 64, 137; wound of, 61, 62; conflicting medieval views of, 72, 73; divine lauded, 82; courtly mocked, 107, 109; worldly mocked, 117; erotic celebrated, 120; Ovid's *Art of*, 128, 173; as fruit of faith, 135; Correggio's *School of*, 139; battle between erotic and spiritual, 147; sexual, 153, 155; -hate, 163

Male as spirit-woman as matter: in Gnostic writings, 35, 37, 40; in medieval writings, 38; in Kazantzakis, 160. *See also* Woman

Man: as tripartite, 32, 60; woman must be made man, 33; Magdalen had been made man, 36; mocked by Wife of Bath, 89; -god, Jesus hymned as, 102; his own god, 133; Jesus as most handsome in world, 111; woman issued from body of man created by God, 157; is mind, transcends matter, 160

Mariham: scorned by Peter, 1, 2; *Gospel of Mary* attributed to, 12; one of few privileged to receive *gnosis*, 33; name applied to Mary Magdalene in Apocrypha, 44, 45, 46, 47, 55, 90, 98, 152, 170

Marseilles, Magdalen preacher in: in Jacobus, 92, 93, 94; in *Sforza Book of Hours*, 95, 127; in Digby play, 121, 122; iconographic representation of, 126,

127; summarized, 172; mentioned, 3

Martha: Magdalen interpreted as sister of, 27; as figure of active life, 27, 28; in *Pistis Sophia*, 47; in Jean Michel's play, 110, 111; in Digby play, 116, 119

Mary, mother of Jesus: in canonical gospels, 16, 19; in Apocrypha, 39, 44, 47, 48; Bernard's devotion to, 82; given by Benediktbeuren playwright long lament for Christ, 109

Marys, other: identification of Magdalen with, 39

Matter: as evil and female, 31, 35, 52, 160; Sophia's fall into, 44

Maudlin: word added to language, 9, 173

Memento mori: possible interpretation of Donatello's sculpture, 5; in George de la Tour's painting and in Kazantzakis's Magdalen, 160

Merchant scene: in Tours Easter play, 103–4; includes potentially comic figures, 103, 104; sculpted in chapel of Modena, 104

Metamorphoses of Magdalen: begin in East, 26; continue in medieval religious figure, 74; summarized, 170, 172

Midwife: Magdalen as, 3; and protector of woman and life, 76, 94, 96, 123

Miracles: performed by Simon Magus, 43; secretly taught Magdalen and disciples, 49, 50; attributed to Magdalen, 80, 96; performed by Jesus in Jean Michel's play, 110

Muse, Magdalen as: for *homo ludens*, 113; for Wager's Vices, 130; for Titian, 173

Mysteries: explicated in *Pistis*

Sophia, 44, 45, 49, 50, 51, 52, 53; in Origen, 60, 61; of Diana taken over by medieval Magdalen, 85; of sex, parodied by Magdalen in Benediktbeuren Passion play, 106; of the intercourse, forsaken by Digby heroine and by Pistis Sophia Prunikos, 115

Name: Sophia's loss of, 44; as "mystery," 51; Magdalen's etymologically explained by Jacobus, 90, 91; Magdalen's loss of, 91

Noli me tangere (in Vulgate Gospel of John): basis for paintings and indirect cause of invention of saint, 19; words attributed to risen Christ addressing Magdalen in garden, 20. *See also* Recognition scene between risen Christ and Mary Magdalene

Ointment: used by Bride to anoint her lover, by Mary of Bethany to anoint Christ as explicated by Origen, 62, 63; explained by Jacobus, 92
—jar: iconographic attribute given fictionalized Magdalen, 4

Paganism: Euhemerism weapon against, 68; survival of, in Judeo-Christian traditions, 68–69

Pasiphée: saucy chambermaid in Jean Michel's mystery play, 109, 110, 111

Patron saint: a modern view of Magdalen's role as, 14; medieval Magdalen's roles as, 69, 84, 107, 111, 117, 122

Penitent: Magdalen explicated as archetype of Christian, 2;

Donatello's sculpture of, 5, 8, 55, 77; Magdalen's explication of Pistis Sophia as, 46; Magdalen treated as, in medieval drama, 108, 116, 118, 135; Moretto da Brescia's painting of, 139; seventeenth-century Vézelay sculpture of, 139

Perusine: saucy chambermaid in Jean Michel's mystery play, 109, 110, 111

Peter: in *Gospel of Thomas* says women not worthy of life, 1, 37, 38; will give Magdalen a clout, in Erlauer Österspiel III, 38; fear of, expressed by Magdalen, 48; King of Marseilles visits, 93

Preacher, the Magdalen as: in Ephesus, 3; in Marseilles, 3, 75; represented in iconography, 75, 126, 127; in Digby play, 123

Prostitute: linked with Mary Magdalene in Kazantzakis's *Report to Greco*, 1, 2; enters fictionalized Magdalen, 26, 27, 28, 55; Magdalen as reformed prostitute, 80, 96, 170; Magdalen as chaste prostitute, 140, 142, 169
—Magdalen's life as: dramatized in medieval plays, 105, 112, 115, 116, 117, 118; in *Jesus Christ Superstar*, 150; in Kazantzakis's novel, 155

Quem quaeritis play, 101, 102, 103

Radical dualism: in Gnosticism, 31, 37; in Origen, 64; Magdalen a vessel carrying, 72; in medieval Christendom, 72; in twentieth-century culture, 161, 163

Recognition scene between risen Christ and Mary Magdalene: in Gospel of John, 19, 20; impact on art, 19, 164, 165, 169; parallels with other traditions, 22; importance in fictionalization of Magdalen, 23, 164; dramatized in Easter play of Tours, 25; expanded account in Digby play, 119, 120

Resurrection of Christ: described in synoptic Gospels, 16, 18; described in Gospel of John, 19, 20; parallels with fertility deities, 21, 22; importance of Magdalen's role in John's account, 21, 22, 23; effects of inconsistencies in Gospel accounts on medieval drama and art, 23

Sackcloth: Magdalen becomes Venus in, celebrated in art and literature, 9; put on by fallen Sophia, 44, 46; attempts by artists to remove from Venus-Magdalen, 139

Saint Rabony: invented in medieval France, 4, 19

Seven demons: attributed to Magdalen in synoptic Gospels, 17, 18; similar to seven soul garments of Gnostic Sophia, 33. *See also* Demons

Simon Magus with Helen: worshiped by dualistic sects, 43; similarities to Gnostic Jesus with Pistis Sophia Prunikos and Magdalen "companion," 44

Sister-Bride: Heloise as Abelard's, 72

—in Song of Songs: interpreted as Magdalen, 65, 170; parallel with Isis, 66; linked with contemplative Magdalen by Bernard of Clairvaux, 82

—of Song of Songs linked with Magdalen: in Tours play, 102; in sculpture in Modena, 103;

in Digby *Burial of Christ*, 120; in Maeterlinck's play, 142, 143, 144; in Kazantzakis, 152

Song of Songs: symbolical interpretations by Origen, 58–66; lines from, celebrate Magdalen's feast day, 58, 59, 192nn 2, 3; anachronistically attributed to Solomon, 60; explained by modern scholars, 66, 67; importance in shaping Magdalen myth, 67; exegeses made by Bernard used by Digby playwright, 120

Spirit: as good and male, 31, 35; Magdalen becomes pure, 48

Stereotype: Kazantzakis's Magdalen as, 163; propaganda in, 164

Tammuz: Ezekiel sees women weeping for, 16, 21, 22; compared to Bridegroom in Song of Songs, 67

Transfiguration: the Magdalen's juxtaposed with that of Jesus, 110

Venus: interpreted as teacher of the courtesan's art, 69; attributes of, absorbed by Magdalen, 69; role played by worldly Magdalen in Benediktbeuren Passion play, 105, 108; mockery of, by Jean Michel and Benediktbeuren playwright, 112; Magdalen's link with, in Maeterlinck's play, 142, 143

—in sackcloth: in Botticelli's paintings, 84; mentioned, 183n3

Vézelay: center of medieval cult of Magdalen, 79; Romanesque Church of the Magdalen built in twelfth century, 79; scene of preaching of second Crusade by Bernard of Clairvaux, 80;

seventeenth-century sculpture of Sainte-Madeleine installed in Romanesque Church of the Magdalen, 139

Weeper: Crashaw's poem to the Magdalen, 9. *See also* Women
Wisdom, goddesses of: Ishtar, Siduri, Athene, 42; Helen, 43; Pistis Sophia Prunikos, 44; Siduri, 54
—personified: the Magdalen as, 41, 55, 180; in Proverbs, 42, 53, 54; in biblical book anachronistically attributed to Solomon and alluded to by Origen, 60
Woman: as paradox, 8; weeping, Magdalen in Gospel of John's Resurrection account, 20; must become male, 33; conflicting views of, in Middle Ages, 73, 89; mocked by Jean de Meun,

defended by Wife of Bath, 89; target of satire in medieval antifeminist literature, 106; seductive, the Magdalen as, in Benediktbeuren play and in Jean Michel's mystery play, 109; as riddle, 143; as vacillating, 144, 145, 146; born of man, 157; only one woman exists, 158; as flesh, 158; as matter and animal lusts, 160; as stereotype, 160, 163, 173
Women: not worthy of life, says Peter in *Gospel of Thomas*, 1, 37, 38; at sepulcher of Christ, 16, 17; weeping for Tammuz, in Ezekiel, 16, 21–22; in canonical Gospels, 16, 26
Wound of love: explicated by Origen, 61, 62; applied to Magdalen in sixteenth-century hymn, 62